SIX
YEARS
WITH
GOD

*

SIX
YEARS
WITH
GOD

*

Life Inside Reverend Jim Jones's Peoples Temple

BY JEANNIE MILLS

A&W PUBLISHERS, INC.
NEW YORK

*The names of several former and current members of the
Peoples Temple church have been changed in order to
protect their privacy.*

Copyright © 1979 by MBR/Investments, Inc.

Published by
A & W Publishers, Inc.
95 Madison Avenue
New York, New York 10016

Library of Congress Catalog Card Number: 79-50356

ISBN: 0-89479-046-3

Designed by Helen Barrow

Printed in the United States of America

DEDICATION

This book is dedicated to the memory of Leo Ryan, whose life seemed to me to exemplify true religion—doing what you know to be right without fear of taking necessary risks.

It is also lovingly dedicated to my mother, my father, and my mother-in-law. Although they didn't agree with our belief in Jim Jones, and although all of our lives went through many drastic changes as my husband and I became more involved in Peoples Temple, the loyalty of our parents never wavered.

Through the six long years, my parents lived next door to us and helped care for our ever-changing family. Our friends were their friends, and they loved the scores of children that came into our home as real grandchildren. Although I occasionally scoffed at our parents' religious beliefs, their prayers and love were always with us.

During this time, Al's mother always kept her doors open to us and to anyone we brought into her home and loved them simply because we loved them.

When we left the Temple, there were no "I told you so's," no resentment of the way we had treated our dear parents through the years. They were there to help us put the pieces of our lives back together.

Perhaps this, more than anything else, made it possible to have the courage to leave. They were our contact with reality throughout the unreal world of Six Years with God.

CONTENTS

PART III

Those Who Do Not Remember the Past Are Condemned to Repeat It

page 315

(Illustrations follow pages 86 and 185.)

INTRODUCTION

Every time I tell someone about the six years we spent as members of the Peoples Temple, I am faced with an unanswerable question: "If the church was so bad, why did you and your family stay in for so long?" This book is my attempt to work out an answer.

Peoples Temple and Jim Jones appear in these pages as I saw them throughout my years there with him. I depict his activities exactly as I saw them. At the time, we all gave Jim credit for performing miracles and healings. Only months after we defected from the Temple, did we realize the full extent of the cocoon in which we'd lived. And only then did we understand and deplore the fraud, sadism, and emotional blackmail of the master manipulator. We'd been had by a dangerous maniac. And we set out to warn a world that didn't seem to have the time or the compassion to listen. It took the deaths of 912 persons to spark a series of investigations into the Peoples Temple.

I try to portray the members of the Temple as they really were. Most were good people with the highest intentions who were also duped by lofty concepts, such as "apostolic socialism" and "Christian sharing," ideals that were twisted by Jim Jones to become tools to take away our property, our money, and finally our individual rights. Jones manipulated the principles of racial equality and brotherly love to obtain pledges of allegiance, love, and human life from his members.

We would have been horrified if Jim had told us about an outsider who was breaking up marriages or robbing children of their parents' love and time. We would have attacked a person who was abusing children, sexually abusing men and women, or robbing the elderly. But when we saw our self-appointed hero, our Father, our God, Jim Jones, doing these things, we excused him. We rationalized the punishments and disciplines because we believed that he was God—and could do no wrong.

I have reconstructed scenes and conversations, especially in Part II, from my notes and with the help of Al, my husband, and several of our friends who were with us in Peoples Temple. The events described all took place. They seem harrowing and unreal even as I read through these pages. But I want the public to know what can happen behind locked doors—anywhere and anytime. It has been said that more than 3,000 cults exist in the United States alone. I hope, through this record of what happened in one, that people will understand the danger, the depravity of total obedience to one leader. The horror is limitless.

Through our Human Freedom Center in Berkeley, California, which is a halfway house for people leaving cults, we have made our goal the total independence of every individual. We give food and clothing; we help former cultists find employment and shelter. We let them know that we understand and that we love them. But we send them out on their own.

—Jeannie Mills
Berkeley, California
January 1979

*

October 10, 1976
To Whom It May Concern

This document and supporting papers are prepared in evidence against Pastor James W. Jones (a.k.a. Jim V. Jones), pastor of Peoples Temple Christian Church of the Disciples of Christ Denomination, located first in Indianapolis until sometime between 1965 and 1966, then located in Redwood Valley until 1975, and now headquartered at 1859 Geary Blvd., San Francisco, California.

We, Al. J. Mills and Jeannie Mills, formerly known as Elmer J. Mertle and Deanna M. Mertle, were members of this group from November 2, 1969, until October 16, 1975. Five of our children were also members of the church during that time period: Steve, Linda, Diana, Eddie, and Daphene. Linda Mertle is currently still a member of the church.

Because of many of the documents we were forced to write and sign, under threat of punishment or humiliation, we have had to legally change our names. (See Decree No. 473635-2, filed 2/23/76, Superior Court of California, County of Alameda.) We changed our names because we had signed blank sheets of paper which could be used for any imaginable purpose, signed power of attorney papers, and written and signed many unusual and incriminating statements, all of which were untrue. These statements include statements that we had molested our children; statements that we had asked Pastor Jones to have sexual intercourse with us; statements that we had conspired to do harm to the president; statements that we had participated in the bomb explosion in Roseville; statements that we were communists; parts of imaginary letters to nonexistent friends telling of various things we had done; statements that we had conspired to overthrow the government; statements indicating that we were unfit parents; blank statements; and a host of other statements.

The scope and number of these papers are impossible to imagine. We had to sign different statements whenever Pastor Jones felt it was necessary to "protect himself" by having more incriminating statements against us.

After we left this church, Eugene Chaikin, attorney at law, member of the board of this church, took one of these letters which had been signed "Mert" (nickname for Elmer Mertle) and showed it to a Mr. [Johnson] (not a member of the group), father of [Nichol Johnson] a child who has lived with us for five years and still lives with us. This letter had been written by Elmer Mertle (Al Mills) at the insistence of Jim Jones and stated that "Mert" had molested his children and was an unfit parent. Mr. [Johnson] asked [Nichol] about this letter. She assured him it was untrue and that all members of Peoples Temple had had to write similar letters at the insistence of Jim Jones.

We were also forced to write by hand and sign a statement that Elmer Mertle (Al Mills) and Deanna Mertle (Jeannie Mills) had acted together, without permission from the church or Pastor Jones, in preparing and mailing letters and appeals for money for the church.

It is a common practice in the Peoples Temple Church to have people write things and for them to notarize it afterward without the consent or knowledge of the person who has written the statement. It is also common practice in the Peoples Temple Church to notarize statements that are unsigned and then have someone forge the signature of another person. In evidence of this practice we have included pages which were prepared for us by [the church's] legal secretary, June Crym. [See photos.] These statements were prepared without the knowledge or consent of either Zoanna Mertle (ex-wife of Al Mills, not a member of the church) or Tom Updyke (ex-husband of Jeannie Mills and also not a member of the church). These papers were supposed to be forged by Al Mills and Jeannie Mills. These statements, although they are unsigned, were notarized by June Crym. Neither Zoanna Mertle nor Thomas Updyke would have consented to sign these papers, because they were to be used to take their children out of the country without their consent.

With regard to [a statement we signed] which stated that we acted alone in preparing mailings and appeals to represent Peoples Temple, this was not true. Each letter or appeal for money that went out from the Publishing House was approved by Pastor Jim Jones, attorney Gene Chaikin, [Mark Duffy], Karen Layton, and Latitia [Tish] Leroy. Each of the above-named persons wrote, approved, changed, added to, or took out whatever he or she felt was necessary from each letter or appeal for money. Most of the letters or appeals for money were plagiarisms from other "healers'" mailings or brochures. Often Pastor Jones would send an appeal from another minister to the Publications Office and ask us to "use the idea" for our mailings.

This minister, Pastor Jim Jones, has a strange power over his members. The power is fear, guilt, and extreme fatigue. While we were in it we did many strange things. We each had to admit that we were homosexual or lesbians. We were forced to stop all sexual activities with our marriage partners. Pastor Jim Jones claimed that he was the only person who knew how to love, and frequently had the women and men he had had sexual relations with stand up and testify to what an excellent lover he was. We had to participate in humilating and often painful punishments for various things that Pastor Jones felt were "bad." Some of the punishments were boxing matches (unevenly matched by Pastor Jones), beatings, strappings, humiliating people by making them take off their clothes in front of the members of the church, making young and old alike stand for six to eight hours during a meeting, giving them medications that made them appear to "drop dead" as a lesson to others (to be "resurrected" later by Jim Jones's "metaphysical" power). There were catharsis meetings where one person would be brought "on the floor" for all the people in the church to humiliate and embarrass. These disciplines were for such minor things as forgetting to call Jim Jones "Father" or for talking about the church to an "outsider" or for losing secret church papers, for forgetting to pay a bill, for giving a piece of candy to one child and not to another, and other trivial things. These are only a very few of the thousands of inconsequential things that could cause cruel or sadistic punishments to be meted out by Pastor Jim Jones.

The beatings were intensely brutal. They used large people such as Jack Beam and Ruby Carroll, both of whom weigh about 200 pounds. Many times the beatings would be done on children four and five years old. The board they used was three-quarters of an inch thick and about two and a half feet long. Children were beaten the number of times decided by Pastor Jones, often as many as 150 times. During the beating, Jim Jones would demand that a microphone be held to the child's mouth so that the audience could hear the groans of pain. The microphone was unnecessary as the screams could be heard throughout the entire building. After the beating the child or adult would be held up and forced to say, "Thank you, Father." If they didn't say this, they would be beaten again.] During the punishments and catharsis situations, guards would be stationed around Jim Jones in case he became overcome with anger—to keep him from personally attacking the person. One person, Pauline Groot, was not protected quickly enough, and Jim Jones had to be pulled away from choking her.

Pastor Jones operates through fear and through tiredness. His members are praised for staying awake far into the night. His meetings have been known to last all night and his counsellors' meeting always last all night long. Counsellors are expected to go to work the next day after having no sleep at all. Counselling meeting takes place at least once a week—and sometimes twice a week. He is a professed healer, and most counsellors are expected to act for a fake healing or to testify to something that didn't really happen. Each of us was told that we were doing this "for our pastor" and we were the only ones that did it. He claims to be "God Almighty" and to have power over life and death. He claims that if any person ever leaves the group, and does harm to the group, he will "get him." He has men go to people who have left the church and threaten them with torture or death if they ever dare to do anything to harm the church or Pastor Jones.

While we were in the church, we were so frightened of him and his power that we would have sworn to anything he asked. He (Pastor Jones) uses this fear to protect himself. We would have perjured ourselves in court to swear that he was innocent of whatever charge was brought before him, as would most of the people who are still in the church now. We sincerely believed that he would always take care of us and would never do anything to hurt us, even though we witnessed daily atrocities that should have convinced us otherwise. It is impossible to explain the effect of his brainwashing. We do know that it took about two months after we were out of the church before we were able to think and act as normal, reasonable people.

There is a list of names and addresses of others who have gone out of the church, located in a private safe deposit box belonging to Al Mills.

Since we have left the church, we have truly seen the cruelty and insanity of Jim Jones. Our children have been harassed, threatened, and maligned. Pastor Jones sent some of his counsellors to our house, to threaten that if we ever spoke against the church, his wife, Marceline Jones, would have our rest home license revoked. She is an employee of the State of California as an inspector of nursing homes, and she could possibly do this to us, leaving us without any means to support our family. They threatened to beat us up, and to kill us if we did anything to expose them. They took a vote in the church to cut off Deanna's ear because they felt that she (Jeannie Mills) might expose them. They have sent anonymous threatening letters to our home. These letters were left in the morning in our home (after they broke in through a bathroom window), on our porch, or in or on our mailbox.

Reacting to the threats, harassment, and fear our children were experiencing, Deanna Mertle (Jeannie Mills) sent a handwritten letter to Jim Jones apologizing for having asked for the money the church had taken when they made us turn our properties over to the church (amounting to many thousands of dollars). This letter did stop the constant surveillance we had been experiencing and, at that point, we were willing to do anything just to be left alone.

The church operates a mission field in Jonestown, Guyana (near Georgetown). Members of the church who have gotten in legal difficulties or who are beginning to act hostile against the church are sent there to work. Once there, it is impossible to contact them or for them to contact anyone else, except through carefully censored letters by one of the church secretaries. . . .

Mysteries surround the deaths of some of the previous members of the church, such as Maxine Harp in Redwood Valley, who supposedly committed suicide after an altercation with church members. Emily Leonard, who was trying to recover some of the property the church had taken from her, died the day she was supposed to go to court against Jim Jones. Curtis Buckley, a minor child, while he was away from his parents, died without being taken to a doctor when he was sick. His guardians were told to place Jim Jones's picture on the child rather than find him medical help. Most recently, Robert Houston died under unusual circumstances two weeks ago, while working for Southern Pacific. He had been called "treasonous" by the church. His wife, Joyce, had left the church a few weeks before this time. One of the threatening letters to us, attached hereto, makes reference to the death of Maxine Harp. [See pages 23-24.]

These are some of the reasons that the more than fifty persons who have left the church in the past three years have not come forward to prosecute the church and try to recover the money they have lost. We fear for the lives and well-being of our families and ourselves. Pastor Jim Jones is a wise and shrewd man. He is making powerful political connections. He has aligned himself with the Muslims. He brags about Mafia connections through a doctor in San Francisco. He has aligned himself with Cecil Williams (a man he used to say he hated). He courts politicians, who fear him because all Peoples Temple members vote the way Jim Jones tells them to. He has members of his church work in school districts, police departments, legal offices, government positions, and any place he feels will increase his personal power.

To try to fight Jim Jones in court would be useless. Every person who is still in the church would be forced to swear to anything he asked, even going to their death to protect him. This letter is prepared and kept in evidence only as a defensive measure, in the event that Jim Jones or his members should carry out his threat to "kill every person who has ever left the church." It is also a defensive measure if he should try to accuse us of some wrongdoing based on the letters he forced us to write and sign. We do not want to use it to place our lives, or the lives of our children, in jeopardy, unless it is the only alternative in an altercation started by Pastor Jim Jones and Peoples Temple Church.

We, Al J. Mills and Jeannie Mills, swear that the above statements are true. We swear that we have never molested our children, plotted against the government or the president, conspired to bomb trains, sent out mailings that were not approved by Jim Jones, had sexual intercourse with Jim Jones, or did any of the other things we had to write and sign in Jim Jones's presence. We are not communists. We love the government of the United States and would fight to keep it a free country.

Signed *Al J. Mills*   Date *Oct 18, 1976*
Al J. Mills

formerly *Elmer J. Mertle*
Elmer J. Mertle

Signed *Jeannie P. Mills*   Date *October 18, 1976*
Jeannie P. Mills

formerly *Deanna M. Mertle*   *Page seven of eight pages*
Deanna M. Mertle   *J.P.M. A.J.M.*

Signed in the presence of *Sandra K. Dunmohammad*
2040 E. 30th St #219 Oakland, Ca 94606

Harriet Whitman Thayer

Subscribed and sworn to before
me this *18th* day of October, 1976.

Harriet Whitman Thayer
Notary Public
County of Alameda

PART I

*

Human Freedom

1975 September to December

I was so accustomed to calling the church before making any major decisions that I called Mark Duffy, a top-staff member and former television news reporter, and asked him to give Jim the message that we weren't going to return to the church. "As you and Jim know, Al's mother gave us a rest-home business to run. We don't have time for it and services." Al and I had decided to make this message short and to the point. But I liked Mark a lot and couldn't pass up the opportunity to try to make him understand our reasons. I reminded him of the meeting at which Jim refused to give us money to feed our large family for the first month of our new life in Berkeley; that after we had turned over our savings, twenty-two houses, our life insurance, and our jewelry, he was, in effect, turning us out. Al's mother was helping us. Jim Jones wouldn't. He wanted us to give the business to Peoples Temple, so he could have cash for his mission in Guyana.

"It's crystal clear to us, Mark, that he doesn't want us to be members of the church."

We were later told that Mark had faithfully relayed the message, and Jim was furious. He was insulted. I'd implied that he didn't care for children in need. If my message were to get around to the other church members, they might begin to question what he was doing with their money....

*   *   *

The following day, Al and I drove to Redwood Valley to take our names off the deed to the home that we had been living in from 1970 until 1975. Since my mother's name was on the deed with our names, we decided to give her all interests in it until it could be sold. Because of all the blank statements and the power of attorney paper we'd signed, we knew our property wasn't safe as registered.

At the county recorder's office the clerk wanted to know what was going on at the church. She said that the church had filed many deeds in recent weeks and that they were swamped with work. "Legal transfers, and there's no way that we can do anything about it. But it sure seems peculiar." We thought about the deed we'd signed three years earlier, when Jim and Gene Chaikin had duped us into believing that we were going to Kenya with our children as missionaries.

As the clerk asked a few more questions, I was gratified to know that people were beginning to be suspicious about the property dealings of the church.

*   *   *

After I spoke with Mark Duffy, seventeen-year-old Nichol Johnson called her father to explain that she was living with us and that we'd all left the Temple. He came to visit and, for the first time, spoke at length with us. He seemed antagonistic and wanted to know if we thought there was any possibility that we'd ever return to the church. We assured him that we had no such plans. Next, he queried us about the fund that Nichol's grandmother had given her.

We told him that she'd donated the money to the Peoples Temple.

"Well, she's going to get it back. I want my daughter to go to college, and Jim Jones has no right to take her money."

I told him that he could probably make Jim give the money back; that Jim wouldn't harass him, because Jim didn't have means with which to intimidate Mr. Johnson. He asked if he might speak privately with his daughter, and they went outside together.

When they returned he said, "Nichol has assured me that she would rather live here with you than move back with me. I can understand this since she has been with you for so many years. But I told her that if you folks ever start talking about returning to the Temple, she is to call me immediately and I will take her to my house. I don't ever want her to go back there."

Nichol nodded and assured him, "We'd rather die than go back." Her dad said he was going to write to Jim Jones that evening to demand the return of her trust fund.

The following evening six counsellors, including Meri Crawford, Johnny Brown, Mark Duffy, and Tom Adams—six of Jim Jones's most trusted staff members—appeared at the door of our rest home. They asked me to speak with them about our decision to leave the church. Steve and I were home alone, but we invited them in.

"Father understands that your family is leaving the group, and we want to make some parting agreements with you now," Meri said. She sounded friendly enough, so I agreed. Meri had lived with our family several years before, when she wandered to Ukiah from L. A. I'd liked her a lot then and we'd been confidantes. But, as she'd risen in the Temple hierarchy, she seemed to become a cold and distant person, not the friendly girl I'd once taken care of. And yet I had a compulsion to trust her now, to believe that she really did just want to discuss our parting with me.

Mark asked if I would give him the membership lists that I'd kept for the church as part of my duties.

"Yes," I answered. Everything was upstairs, and I said I was ready to return it.

"Can we set a date to get it all back?" Meri asked in a very businesslike voice.

"It's upstairs," I repeated. "I can get everything right now."

I was amazed that they were being so polite. They ignored my offer to return the things immediately and got down to what I thought was probably the real point of the visit.

Meri spoke. "Father is very sorry about your decision. He knows the time will come when he will provide the only protection in the world. He asked us to tell you that he still cares very much for you and your family. If you should ever decide to return, he wants you to know that you'll be welcome."

"No," I answered politely. "I don't expect to return, but tell him we appreciate his offer."

Mark cleared his throat. "Father is also concerned about the relationship that has existed between Al and Nichol. You know, we have evidence that they had a sexual affair one night under a bus." Jim had mentioned this to Al once before, but the night it supposedly happened, Nichol and Diana had been sleeping under one compartment of a Temple bus, while Al and I were together elsewhere.

"Al and I have a very good marriage. I was with him myself the night he was supposed to have been with Nichol, so I know it's not true. Besides, if she had been molested by Al, I'm sure she wouldn't want to be living with us now. She has a home with her father and can go there if she prefers." It was plenty apparent that I wasn't willing to play their game.

Mark tried to sound sympathetic and assured us that "Father" was simply concerned.

At that moment Al, Nichol, and Diana walked into the room. I decided to show our visitors that there were no secrets in the family. "They're telling Steve and me that you and Nichol had an affair, Al."

Al dared them to tell us more, to give us all the lies at once.

"Well, Jim didn't exactly say you two were having sex," Mark said, backing down. "He was just concerned about some of the things that have happened between the two of you."

Nichol broke in. "Look, ask Jim Jones about all the people he is having sex with if you're so concerned about what's going on."

As if on cue, the six got up to leave. They seemed to have forgotten all about the items they'd inquired about earlier in the conversation.

As we were locking up for the night, Nichol noticed that the back door was standing wide open. We began to look around to see if anything had been taken and were shocked to discover that someone had been upstairs, rifling through our belongings. All the items I'd offered to give them were gone, and, in addition, they'd taken the deed to our property in Redwood Valley, some of Al's camera equipment, and eighty dollars in cash that Diana and Nichol had saved to buy Christmas gifts.

"I wonder if they went through our house, too," Al said. We all piled into the car and drove to our house in Oakland. Sure enough, the representatives of Jim Jones's Peoples Temple had done some pilfering there, too. Our family slides and photographs, our slide projector, a stack of tapes of Jim's sermons, and several boxes of books and records were all missing.

Until this time, our son Steve had been a little uncertain about whether he wanted to quit the church or not. He'd thought Jim might be a benevolent person who'd just done a few bizarre things. After this episode, though, his doubts were canceled.

The following morning, we saw an envelope sitting on our dining table, propped up on a salt shaker. In black, smudgy letters we saw our names.

We read the two-page letter inside. It was signed "Alice" and used religious phrases and double-talk to threaten and frighten us.

*   *   *

DEAR DEANNA,

Having had the closest of friendships with you
since childhood I sincerely hope that you will
listen with an open heart to what I have to say
to you. After 20 years of sharing happiness and
sorrows with you I can honestly say that you are
closer to me than any sister.

I listened closely yesterday to what you were saying
about your desires and fantasies of deriving sexual
pleasure out of the torture of children and (aside
from the lesbian thing that you already mentioned before)
although I have tried to empathetically understand
what you were saying I think that you have a serious
problem and should seek psychiatric help. I am
worried about this especially in light of the fact
that you said also that someone had seen you stealing
money and that stealing also was a compulsion with
you, and I think that thatb business of stealing from
your former employer could have caused you years of
trouble. Please get some help, I am telling you this
not out of any judgementalness but rather out of
concern for you. I know that you are upset about
Elmer's affair with the youngster in the house and
I am sure that the pressure of a husband doing this
not only to you but to a child in your home would
drive you to such reactions. I don t mean to
bring up such a sensitive issue with you but one of
the children wrote me about seeing Elmer in the act and,
although I know that you are being noble and silent
I know that it must be hard on you. By the way the
the neighbors down the street know about your problems
and they are having trouble accepting the whole thing.
Fred and I will do what we can to calm down all of them
but they are not always rational in their behavior
either.

I am also worried about you're saying that the IRS
won't catch up with you, but you and I both know that
they always do, and if you don't straighten that mess
out now, look at the mess you will be in later.

You asked me about trust. Well, I do find it difficult
at times to maintain the trust and confidence that I

page 2

once had for y u especially after hurting Mike and
Chris the way that you did. But all in all I am
touched with the honesty that you have written to
me in all your letters... and I have saved every
precious one of them in remembrance of you. As
for trust, how can you expect me to trust you in all
things when you know that you have lied to me and
everyone else.

Deanne, with the little bit of psychology I have had
and I admit that I am not a college graduate or anything
but I do believe, that for what ever sick reason or
emotional stress that you are headed for trouble.
Deanne, you n ed help desperately, you never know
when you are going to push someone too far. And I'm
saying this not only for you but out of a sense of
guilt and responsibility. I know that if I had had the
strength of character to be honest with my own sister
when she was headed down a similar road that she would
still be alive today. I never want to see you go
through what she did.

The reason that I am giving you such a quick response
to your call yesterday also is that Fred got a promotion
and we are planning a move back east where he is being
transferred to the main office. But I will keep in
touch and send you my new address as soon as we get
settled in. Take care and do get some help. Please
don't learn these things the hard way. Please take
my advice and set things straight and get the help
that you so desperately need.

I know if you make your peace with God and accept conditions
as they are I am sure there will be peace with yourself and
others.

          All my love forever,

              alice

We knew that this was a threat, yet we were also aware that neither the police department nor the FBI would call it a threat. Every sentence had been carefully disguised so that only those who had had experience with Jim Jones would know what it was saying.

Up to this time, I hadn't been afraid, but as we read the letter, fear gripped my heart. I panicked at the idea that they might also have poisoned the food in the refrigerator, so we would be accused of poisoning our old people.

Al doubted that they'd go that far, but to be on the safe side I emptied out everything that was in unsealed containers. As we inspected the building to find out how the letter had been placed inside, we saw that the bathroom window had been pried open and that there were footprints on the lid of the toilet where someone had stepped on it while climbing through the tiny window.

The children were terrified. Eddie and Daphene didn't want to go to school alone, so I started driving them to and from. Each time we went out in our car, another car followed us. We were now living under Jim's reign of terror.

*   *   *

When we had quit the church, I'd kept some photographs and documents that I thought would help prove, in court, that the church sheltered a potentially violent and dangerous nucleus. I hoped the documents would be a form of protection should Jim attempt to discredit us by using the blank statements and incriminating letters we had been coerced into writing.

Shortly after we left the Temple, we placed the documents in the safe deposit vault of a Bank of America branch in Berkeley. One day, when we were at a store near the bank, we heard an explosion. A bomb had exploded in our bank! There was a hole in an outside wall, and some of the windows in the store across the street had been shattered by the blast. We wondered if the Temple might have been involved but decided no, that such a thought was only paranoia getting the best of us. Fortunately, the vaults themselves hadn't been damaged.

The following morning another anonymous letter arrived on our front porch. "We saw you two near the bank last night. We know where you keep your belongings."

Later that day, Nichol's father arrived unannounced—and very angry. He demanded to see his daughter. She came out and realized immediately that he was upset. They went out and sat in his car.

When they came back, her father told us that three members of
the Temple had come to his house the night before. One of them
was an attorney, Eugene Chaikin. They'd shown him a letter that
Al had written to Jim, confessing that he had sexually abused his
own children and was not a fit parent. They also told him that
they had two witnesses who swore they had seen Al and Nichol
having sexual relations together.

Nichol broke in, "I told him about all the crazy things Jim made
us write, Al." She turned back to her father and added, "I had to
write those things, too. They don't really mean anything. Jim
made us do all kinds of weird things to prove that we were
dedicated to the Cause."

"I don't understand how intelligent adults can write something
so terrible about themselves," he said, looking at Al and shaking
his head in disgust.

Al confessed, "I don't understand it either, but I did it. Jim gave
orders and members weren't likely to refuse him. There were
attorneys, college professors, a man who had graduated with
honors from MIT, social workers, nurses, businessmen, and lots of
other professional people on that council."

Nichol added, "If you refused Jim, you would be beaten."

We could see that Mr. Johnson, a psychologist, was overwhelmed by all this information, but he did seem to become more
understanding of our plight. He left, somewhat appeased, but even
more worried about his two sons, who were still living in the
Temple. Perhaps he was thankful that at least one member of his
family was out.

*   *   *

Our living arrangements at this stage were confusing,
uncomfortable—and, basically, unfair to the kids who had
already suffered so much deprivation in their young lives.

The rest home was in Berkeley, and the old house we'd bought
was three miles away, just over the city line, in Oakland. Al and I
stayed in the rest home, but licensing regulations prohibited the
kids from living there, too. While the business was bringing in
enough cash to meet our basic needs, we didn't have enough
money to make the monthly payments on the big house. We
decided to rent the top two floors of the house, and we fixed up
living quarters for the five kids in the basement. It wasn't much,
but it was all we had.

My parents were able to stay in the rest home to help us. They
had a tiny room, so unlike the A-frame cabin they'd had on our

Redwood Valley property. But somehow our love for each other overcame all the inconveniences, and—as a family—we dug in for the siege of pestering and threats that we feared was coming from the San Francisco temple.

*   *   *

We heard that another couple had left the church just about a week before our final visit to services. Marvin and Jackie had been friends of ours while we were members, and we hoped that they would want to be our friends now. When we found out where they were, Al phoned them. Marvin first wanted reassurance that we hadn't returned to the Temple. When Al promised that we hadn't and never would, Marvin asked us to come to Redwood Valley to visit with them.

We left the next day, anxious to be able to talk to people who could understand the hell we were going through. The first thing we noticed was that their two boys, Larry and Don, weren't with them. "Didn't your sons come out too?" Al asked.

Jackie shrugged her shoulders. "Larry decided to stay in the church and Don is in the Promised Land." (The Promised Land was the Temple mission in Guyana.)

"Have you tried to get either of them out?" I asked her.

"No, we're afraid to say anything to them," she answered.

We were surprised to learn that Jackie, who had been on the Planning Commission with us, hadn't told Marvin about any of the unusual things Jim had made us do. "I was afraid to," she answered. "I was never allowed to talk to Marvin about anything like that when we were in the church, and for some reason I didn't want to start now."

I was amazed. Al and I had always talked about things. I realized now that Jim had purposely not allowed Marvin to join the Planning Commission (P.C.) so that he could try to break up their marriage.

"Do you mind if we talk about it now?" I asked Jackie.

"No, I'd really like to get a lot of this stuff out in the open," she answered. "I just didn't know how to begin."

Al told Marvin how many times Jim had instructed Jackie not to have sex with Marvin. Then Jackie began to talk, telling her husband about the punishments and disciplines the P.C. members had been subjected to—much more humiliating than those in the regular church meetings.

As Jackie spoke, Marvin shook his head in disbelief and disgust. "You know, Jackie, I should have realized that Jones was just a phony. I saw something several years ago that I never mentioned to anyone because I didn't want to discredit him."

Marvin then told a story that shocked us. He was working on one of the buses one day, when a telephone repairman came over and asked him to check on a suitcase he had found under Jim's house. Marvin thought it might contain a bomb or something, so he took it out to the middle of a field and cut the top off it. Inside, he saw pieces of meat that looked similar to chicken livers, and they were all wrapped in plastic bags. At the time, he thought Jim was probably saving the cancers that people passed. In retrospect, he was sure that they were phony "cancers" that Jim was planning to use in his healing services. When Marvin asked Jim about it later, Jim just said, "An enemy must have put that suitcase there to discredit me."

Our conversation shifted to the mission in Guyana. Marvin's sister and brother were already there, and his parents were getting ready to go. "We figured we'd let Don stay over there," Marvin said. "Now, I'm sure it's not a good idea."

Al told Marvin about the trip he had made to Jonestown the previous year. "It's not at all what Jim has been telling everyone. It's mostly snakes and mosquitoes! The discipline is just as bad there as it is here, and those people have to work in the fields at least fourteen hours a day. When I talked to Charlie, he told me that it's hard to grow crops there and that the food they get isn't really nutritious. If you can, Marvin, get Don out of there."

Marvin was nodding his head in agreement. "Yeah, and I want to get Larry out of the San Francisco Temple, too, if I can," he said. "I don't know how I'm going to do it, but I'm going to get both my sons back."

Since Larry had been Steve's best friend, we promised them that we would have Steve find an opportunity to talk to Larry and tell him the truth about what was happening. Marvin decided that he was going to phone the church and demand the return of his oldest son, Don. After several hours of visiting, we embraced and promised to get together again. It had been an important experience to talk about the church with people who had been there.

A few days later, at school, Steve spoke seriously to Larry, and within half an hour Larry made his decision to quit the church. It was more difficult with Don, though, because he was isolated in the Jonestown project in the Guyanese jungle. To get Jim to release their son, Marvin and Jackie had to promise to move to the East Coast and never to communicate with us or with any of the members of the church—which included almost all of Marvin's family—again. They moved, and shortly before Thanksgiving Don was returned to them.

Don told them what life was like in Jonestown. He talked about the insects, snakes, and long hours of hard work. He complained about the incessant heat and the lack of good food. Most of all, he stressed the unending discipline. "I'm so thankful to be back home. Now all I want to do is try to make up for the years of my life that Jim Jones stole from me."

*   *   *

Thanksgiving Day was dismal. It was out of the question to be in a festive mood when all we had to eat was leftovers from the old folks' supper. Our children were living in an unheated basement. Al and I shared a tiny room in the rest home. My parents missed their lovely cabin in the mountains. Grandma's garden was only a memory now. Our goats and other animals had all been sold, and our dogs had to live in our van because we didn't have a fenced yard. Our only friends, Marvin and Jackie, had been forced to move 3,000 miles away.

Shortly before the Christmas holidays, Al's mother asked us if we wanted to rent her second rest home and run both. We were delighted. It would provide enough income so that we could begin to save money. And—even more important than that—the second rest home had a large attic apartment with five separate rooms. Finally, the kids could get out of the awful basement and into a house. State licensing laws did not forbid minors to use apartment space.

It still wasn't ideal. But compared to what they were used to, it was wonderful. We bought some used rugs for the floors and the kids moved right in. While they had lived in the basement in Oakland, they were constantly fearful that someone from the Temple would break in. Now—three stories above ground—they felt reasonably safe. Life was taking on rosier tones.

*   *   *

Occasionally, we would see one of the Temple members soliciting money in front of the local grocery store, and we would always give him or her a cheery greeting. We didn't want to do anything to reignite Jim's paranoia. One day, Al, trying to be friendly, asked Mildred, one of the solicitors, "How are you doing? Getting a lot of money?" I whispered to him that this might be misunderstood by Jim, and we left quickly. Sure enough, the next morning another letter was waiting on our front porch.

The note began, "Mildred said that you told the manager of the co-op store the church doesn't need any money. We thought we were going to be friends, but we want an answer as to why you have done this."

For two days we ignored the letter and on the second evening, Diana came running into the living room where Al and I were sitting, saying, "The church's guards are right outside the kitchen window." We rushed into the kitchen and saw eight men standing in the street outside the window, arms crossed menacingly in front of their chests. As soon as we had seen them, they jumped into two cars and drove off.

I called the Berkeley Police Department and within a few minutes policemen were swarming all over our yard trying to find traces of the men—but they were gone. In the police report, Diana said, "Yes, I know the men. They are trying to frighten me." But when the policeman pressed her for names she became quiet.

I answered for her. "We do know these men, but they represent a very powerful group, and we don't want any hassles with them. I'm sorry but we can't give you those names."

The policeman appeared to understand, closed his report book, and left.

I got on the telephone and called Mark Duffy. "What is the matter now?" I demanded. "We have been keeping the peace as you demanded, so why are you sending your guards to try to frighten our daughter, Diana? Jim can stoop pretty low!"

Mark said he didn't know anything about the incident, but he would pass my message along. The next day their response was on our porch. "We didn't receive an answer to our last letter so we assumed that our accusations were correct. We want a meeting."

It was more out of curiosity than anything else that Al and I agreed to meet them in front of the Berkeley Public Library.

"We'll bring our attorney," I said.

"No attorneys, we'll meet as old friends," Jim answered.

"If you promise that you won't bring an attorney, we won't bring one either," I agreed.

The day of the meeting arrived. We asked a private investigator to stand nearby, to observe our meeting, because we weren't sure it wasn't some kind of a trap, and we could be attacked. We remembered talk about the guards once beating up a traitor, and we decided it was better to take some precaution.

As we drove around trying to find a space, we saw Dick Tropp, a counsellor, stationed on the library steps. We began to wonder what Jim had planned for us and became a little frightened. We still couldn't believe that Jim would have us physically harmed in a public place, so we got out of the car and walked toward the library.

I couldn't believe my eyes. Jim wasn't there, and instead we were standing face to face with Tim Stoen, an attorney, and Carolyn Layton. Carolyn thrust a note into my hands that said, "Father is not able to be here today, and we are coming in his place. We do not really want to talk to you, so we will write what we have to say. We believe we can make a mutual agreement that will be satisfactory to all of us."

I was so angry because we had been lied to that I shouted, "Jim promised no attorney. We didn't bring an attorney on the strength of his promise, and yet he sent an attorney. He lied!"

"Tim is not here as an attorney, he is acting in Jim's place," Carolyn hastily scribbled.

"Are you absolutely crazy? Tim Stoen *is* an attorney, no matter who he's representing. He is an attorney!" I was trembling with fury.

"Father does not lie. His character is above reproach," Carolyn wrote.

"Come on, Jeannie, let's go." Al was disgusted. "Jim has lied to us again, and we have nothing to say to these two."

Carolyn was writing as fast as she could. She thrust another note into my hand. It said, "Jim wants us to make a parting agreement with you. He is willing to be completely fair. You know that there are others who have left, and they have all made agreements with us. This is why none of them have had anything bad happen to them. You know Georgia continued to live in the same community with us for several years after she left. Father wants to be fair to you."

We came back and sat down. It was a cold day and I was shivering, but we sat there. Six years of obedience to Jim's orders didn't wear off so quickly. "Jim will give you free and clear title to your Richmond property. In exchange, he would like you to collect rents from some church properties in your area. He wants you to tell him whenever anyone who has left the church contacts you. Does this sound fair enough?"

"The Richmond property!" Al stormed again. "We turned over twenty-one homes to you besides that house; nineteen of them were foreclosed because Jim refused to let anyone take care of them. The other two are still nice homes because Temple members lived in them, but the Richmond property has become the neighborhood dump. You call that a fair agreement? And he expects us to collect rents for him, besides? We have nothing to talk about!" We walked away.

The following morning another letter was left on our porch. It said that Jim was still very anxious to get together with us.

We obediently went to the appointed place, blindly believing that this time Jim would keep his word. His letter sounded sincere. We were to meet with him in the Alameda South Shore parking lot.

Just in case, though, Al had me get out of our car a block away from the lot, so if it was a setup, I could get to a telephone to call the police. Al drove into the parking lot. Two carloads of guards were waiting for him. They motioned for him to drive over to a remote corner of the lot but he refused. He hollered to me, "They're over here," and without thinking, I started to walk toward them. I saw the familiar faces of men I had worked with for six years, but now they were faces contorted with hate. I still couldn't believe that they meant to hurt us. These were the same men we had laughed and joked with only a few weeks before. I knew that some of them were also hostile about the disciplines in the church, so I approached them.

Chris Lewis had evidently been hiding in the shadows, waiting. Jim had always used Chris to frighten people. Chris would do anything for Jim, and we knew that he could be very mean. He started to shove and push Al, while Jim McElvane and Johnny Brown began pushing me around. In a stroke of genius Al said, "You guys go ahead and do whatever you want to, you're being watched." They backed off. Chris snarled, "You guys think you're smart, but I hope you know that we're the ones that put a bomb in your bank. We know where your stuff is hid, and one of these days we'll get it."

I turned to these men who had been our friends. "How can you do this? Don't you realize that one day you might be on the other side of this type of confrontation and someone else will be doing this same thing to you?" My words fell on deaf ears.

Al and I got into our car and drove off as quickly as possible. It had taken much too much already to convince us that the church was actually a violent group, but after this encounter we vowed we wouldn't be caught off guard again.

The next morning, Gene Chaikin called. We were still in shock from the day before, and we taped the conversation—on the advice of our attorney—to protect ourselves from the violence that we were sure was impending.

*　　*　　*

*

December 5, 1975

Conversation between Attorney Gene Chaikin, Jim Jones, and Jeannie Mills

Gene Chaikin: Jeannie Mills? Hey, I've got a message for you, to show you our good character. No matter what develops we will not record the deed to the Richmond property, now or in the future so long as you show integrity. We're calling by telephone and that also shows our [good] character. We cannot talk to you about anything else until two important persons get back. We expect it two weeks from tonight. The man we have close association with, Reid [Dr. Ptolemy Reid, Deputy Prime Minister of Guyana], had a stroke. You can verify this by spending a few dollars on the phone yourself. That won't affect our long-range plans, but we had to put in writing what he said verbally about part of our lease. This means talking to him personally, and that when his doctors say we can, providing he doesn't have a further complication, which means *one* of us, [the one] who cares most, may have to go there to talk to his temporary or his permanent successor, and you can verify that. It's not a matter of trusting anyone's word for it. All you have to do is make a telephone call and spend the money and you will find out what the situation is there. Don't break the peace because *one* of us has a basic concern for you at heart or I wouldn't be calling now in the first place. *One* of us would still like to see you help children in the manner we discussed. Those who oppose the forces of good are so great that it minimizes any differences between people of the same goals. For weeks we have been told lots of things you were going to try to do to us, and what you were saying about us. *One* of us has been willing to give you the benefit of the doubt. Not one word was said about you until we had to defend ourselves over that ridiculous lie about our starving your children. None of us worry at all what anyone might try to do to us, and that's a fact. It ought to be obvious we're not worried about the threat you made. [I had threatened to report overcrowded, illegal living conditions inside the San Francisco temple building.] We are sure you do not understand your own position in that matter or you would not have made any threat to begin with.

Jeannie Mills: My threat was a counter to your threat.

Gene: In any event we intend to keep the peace and we hope that you will. We want you to understand that the thing you threatened would be counterproductive to your own best condition. The very thing you accused us of, you did and admitted in writing. As a matter of fact you admitted the same thing to me. [They were aware that we had housed our children in our rest home for a few weeks.] I don't want a response to that, you understand, you don't need to respond.

Jeannie: My only response is that it was a defensive threat rather than an offensive threat.

Gene: Okay, then we understand that, as long as everybody keeps the peace, there's no need to be receiving or delivering threats of any kind, and we'll get back to you as soon as the situation clarifies. I'll be back in exactly two weeks tonight, unless the situation deteriorates there with the man [Reid].

Jim Jones: I like your attitude, I'm on the line now.

Jeannie: Thank you.

Jim Jones: I will do all my power to see that [Joanne Johnson] follows through with giving you support and that she doesn't interfere [about her daughter, Nichol]....

Jeannie: Okay, I just have a couple of other things. We don't want to start a new life with [the] hatred and hostility that we've seen in our children, and this is the reason that we're going to try to have a peaceful beginning.

Jim: We need to stop this nonsense, and I thought you were a person that had some sense. It's this: I have unfortunately reacted to some things I had heard, which came pretty conclusively. Then I began to believe that you were breaking the peace, so I had to defend myself in the usual, typical way that I would have to defend myself, in saying that, uh—I have to defend myself about charges that we are—that I am not loving or that I would starve people and that kind of stuff.

Jeannie: Well, the statement was made. When we needed food, we had to go outside of the group instead of getting it from the commune.

Jim: Well, you see, I understood you to say you didn't need any more money. I wasn't trying in any way to interfere with your economic well-being, and this business of...it was just a matter of...I thought you were going over there [to the rest home] and were going to get that thing going, and [then] going to [Guyana] to be doing this work with children. I had no knowledge of this at all. I don't know what you're talking about, so you should have told me.

Jeannie: Well, both times when it was brought up in counselling, you said you didn't want to hear any further on the subject.

Jim: Well, now, I don't recall that, dear, at all. Now, you said to me your children were starving, and I said I didn't want to respond to that?

Jeannie: I said I didn't have any money at all, and you said we'll take the children, I don't want to hear any more on the subject.

Jim: Take the children?

Jeannie: You remember, I had sent that message.

Jim: No, I don't, I don't. You can see the sincerity of this. I thought I'd been taken, and when I heard certain things that you had [said], I thought you people had betrayed me.

Jeannie: There was no betrayal. It's just that it was purely defensive because we know what you have.

Jim: Well, I didn't know why you said stuff...

Jeannie: The same reason you did.

Jim: No, no, no. But I never personalized that, I don't personalize that.

Jeannie: You've got some pretty personal letters....

Jim: But I don't personalize. We all make our protection for voluntary reasons, for the enhancement of the total group, but it wasn't personalized. Can you think of anybody that hasn't confessed their faults, from Marceline on down? Can you think of anybody?

Jeannie: I'm not sure how that follows with what...

Jim: Well, it does. That's what's terribly disappointing; that you felt for years you weren't trusted.

Jeannie: It hasn't been years—it's only been about the last three months.

Jim: Well, I heard you said for years you hadn't been trusted.

Jeannie: Well, I did say that. I said that...in financial matters.

Jim: That's not true. I trusted you openhanded. More than I would have—oh, God—a host of people. Too bad communications break down like this. I think the forces of totalitarianism have an advantage on us, friend. I think it really does. I think it really does. I just don't know how we can have this kind of break in communications. I was reading a letter you sent to me. One that [said] you'd never leave me, that you saw my character. I was sitting here just before you phoned, and said, "What the hell transpired between that point and this?"

Jeannie: Well, I meant that most sincerely when I...

Jim: I know you meant that most sincerely. I wasn't questioning that, dear.

Jeannie: We went out purely, purely on an economic basis that the commune...

Jim: But that wasn't necessary. I thought we were protecting you, if we had to do that. Who made any big issue about that place being a commune?

Jeannie: You did.

Jim: No, but let's just retract for a moment. Why? Because if we had to deal with it and you went to [Guyana] to establish a children's home, and—I thought there was some prior discussion that we could do things in terms of business—you've got a keen mind of how to...I believed with all my heart that you would go into the mission and do the work that we need badly with children, and also help with your uncanny mind to develop some ways of making funds. I thought that we couldn't operate a damn thing [referring to the rest home] that we didn't have any control over. Now, did I ever come to you after that point, after the mere one mention, did you ever get hounded?

Jeannie: No, just about putting it in legal [terms].

Jim: I just mentioned—well, yeah, but why? Jeannie, you were too paranoid. I don't give a damn for the thing, I don't want any more of it anyway. We've got so much now, you know—unfinished properties—we don't know what the hell we're doing.

Jeannie: We didn't have any money. We presented the need and there was absolute refusal to give us any and we had to go to [Al's mother]...

Jim: Well, that's too bad. Now there's not an absolute refusal.

Jeannie: Then our feeling was if, you know, when we really needed it, in the time of absolute dire need, instead of giving it, you said "We'll take the children rather than giving the money."

Jim: That was only a loving act, too. I couldn't see coughing up...

Jeannie: It didn't seem loving. I loved those children.

Jim:Well, I—it would—it may be lacking in empathy, but it was a loving act. I thought that being close to me, and I do a fair job I think, Jeannie, of trying to provide everything that someone needs. I thought that at least if I can't cough up the money— money's a big problem right now, the liquid kind, you know. We've got property, but money and getting this thing [Guyana] off the ground, getting it off the ground is just the big thing. If I have made any oversights, it's that kind of oversight. When you came with the sweet tone that you had to Gene, then my attitude changed. When people deal with me fairly and squarely, I'll behave fairly, and I'll deal with a most proper approach to it, because I've got an indulgence and love for all my children. So why in the hell wouldn't I be a reasonable person? I think you underestimate the effect of an all-night affair and business meetings on me, and the tiredness that it affects me with, and the pressure it puts my body under. So if I miss a phrase you've got to go over it four or five times. You know that.

Jeannie: Well, I felt that I did.

Jim: I don't always hear...if you don't make your signals clear to me, you're not going to get through. You know that. If I have a weakness, it's that. I'm so damn tired that I try to do the best I can. I just try to do the best I can. But I wouldn't see any of you hungry for nothing. Even in the midst of all this shit, I haven't. I refused to believe that a person that thought as much as you did one night there, and analyzed yourself as well as you did...you can note that I'm not wanting any details of that analysis. I want you to feel my good faith so damn much. I thought, anybody who could look at themselves that well, I just did not believe could be a person doing all the shit that I was supposed to be threatened with, that you were saying about me. Making me out a person that would starve your babies.

Jeannie: Well, I've told you, and I told the group that came over to distract us while the thing was going on—I told them—I told every person exactly the same thing: The reason was that the commune we had given so much to refused to give us any money when we needed it. Therefore we felt that that commune— somehow we did not fit into it. That was our entire reason for leaving.

Jim: Well, if you'd have kept it on that basis; but, naturally, when you said the leader starves...

Jeannie: I never said that. What I said was exactly what I just said. That's what I told the children.

Jim: It put the children in an area of bad faith towards the leader, which is traumatic, and I certainly don't want to repeat that trauma. I've made no efforts and will not make any efforts to get [Nichol], who is [Joanne Johnson's] legal [child]. I wouldn't cause that trauma of a child. But don't traumatize her by giving her a bunch of bull which she obviously had to talk so hostile towards me.

Jeannie: I think the comment that "Well, that wasn't very much" after she had turned in [her grandmother's trust fund]...

Jim: Well, you see, now that's out of context, honey. That's out of context. I don't think Steve has any malice, no more than he did when he told that you were drinking out in a bar, but you know what that did to me? That unsettled me that you didn't have any more sense than that.

Jeannie: Well, you know, we drank in the church—I didn't feel there was anything different. We drank wine in the church and we drank wine—it wasn't in a bar, it was a pizza parlor.

Jim: I heard that you were drunk and he had to drive you home. I'm not trying to get any—you don't have to analyze it.

Jeannie: That's about right.

Jim: You get what I'm saying, though, sweetheart? I didn't see what the hell you were doing—these children you're using—now look what you're doing right now, you see what you're doing? Your rationale? You say we took some wine in the church, so you got drunk. Now later, down the way... who looks up to you more than [Nichol]? No more does she look up to anyone. You and Al are her means of relating to the Cause. I always knew that and it didn't bother me at all. I thought you would delegate it properly. But what I'm worried about, and I say this from a loving father's heart, when you do indulge with children, they later turn around and use it against you for their own indulgence, which may—they may not have the intelligence and insight from experience to keep out of lots of pain. That's all I want you to hear—is be careful, because children—the trust of children is a difficult thing.

Jeannie: Well, okay, but then I'd like to know... you know, I know that the messages that were brought were from you, because I know how strategy works. Why were Steve and I told that you had legal documentation that [Nichol] and Al had had a sexual relationship, if you're not trying to break down lines of communication?

Jim: What's that now?

Jeannie: I said, why were Steve and I told before [Nichol] and Al came in that you had legal documentation about a sexual relationship?

Jim: Well, I don't know anything about telling Steve anything. They should not tell that kind of stuff to Steve. There shouldn't be any of that done.

Jeannie: Well, it was done by your six most trusted people who were over here, and you know, that isn't all that was done.

Jim: I agree one hundred percent. If that was done, it wasn't proper.

Jeannie: Well, it was done, I'm sure you've got the tapes because...

Jim: I haven't got nothing. I haven't been listening to nothing. I am involved in so much. Did you hear what was said to you, that Dr. Reid had had a stroke? He is still in a conscious state but he is unable to speak very well, and one eye will not shut. Well, most of our relationship has been through him, and we've got to have verification of where we stand. A lot rests on that. We need verification from him. If not, I'm going to have to go myself, and I don't like to negotiate anything. I may have to leave tomorrow evening, and I've got a flight scheduled tomorrow. It takes me to New York. Now I'm really trusting you, for God's sake. If it has to be. That's how. Still, it's in abeyance. I want to talk to other officials because I want our leasehold. We have a lease fixed for four thousand some acres, but I want a permanent leasehold in written form. I believe in getting everything down in writing.... Now, in talking to Steve, did you want Steve there? Did you ask for Steve to be there in this meeting?

Jeannie: Yes.

Jim: Well, that was a mistake on your part and a mistake on their part.

Jeannie: Well, if Steve hadn't been in, he may have seen what was going on in the rest of the house, so I'm sure that's why they wanted him in there.

Jim: I don't know. I don't know what you're talking about there, you're a little off base there. Now this thing. We don't want to get back into these games, you know. Back into this kind of situation back and forth. I don't know what you're saying, but there was nothing going on in your house while anyone was there. Nothing going on in your house. I can say that as a matter of fact. Now what about the—ah, this charge that Lillie [Victor] took eighty dollars? She denied that. This just something you're saying?

Jeannie: No, it's the truth. The girls had a steel box and had their money saved up, and had eighty dollars in it. It was there before she left and it was gone after she left. And that's the honest truth.

Jim: All right, I'll check it. I just wanted to be...I get these things secondhand and I wanted to...well, what the hell, people start playing various games and—you say it was locked?

Jeannie: No. She took the steel box. It's one of those little steel cash boxes.

Jim: I'll just check into that. If she stole anything, you'll get it back.

Jeannie: It happened that night while everything else was going on. We do have witnesses who have agreed to tell exactly who...

Jim: I'm not worried about that, I'm not worried about that at all. Let's not get back into that vein.

Jeannie: Well, I want to say one more thing on that vein. That you figured correctly, or whoever figured this figured correctly, because we do care for Lillie and we will not prosecute.

Jim: That's sweet. Now that is sweet. That makes me feel better. Got no problems, Jeannie, got none. We'll work out something. I like your straightforwardness. My opinion about you wasn't wrong. So you've made these children feel good, and tonight I'll make them [children formerly living with Jeannie] feel good about you. Don't misuse it to break up my ranks and I'll make a statement of good faith.

Jeannie: Thank you.

Jim: And then two weeks. You don't need to worry about time. I can understand you're paranoid. Time is on our side....Naturally we looked into our defense and into your situation. You look into it. That's why I said that I wasn't concerned, but I much more appreciate what you just said, that means a lot more to me than what the law has to say about people who are trying to arbitrate their civil disputes. That means a lot more to me that you come right out of your gut and say I care about children. Well, I do too, damn it, and if you're in need I'll help you.

Jeannie: Well, we're fine now, well taken care of.

Jim: But I don't want you to lose sight of that character, that you said you never would leave. The character is there and it will never leave. I'm awfully paranoid about people, and you must admit I've had some reason in the past, so if I put some of you in the mold temporarily, you can understand why. I've been disappointed by some people I've given a lot to—an awful lot to. You know, don't you?

Jeannie: Yes.

Jim: So—and for the sake of all, time will throw us back together again. I'm sure it will. With all the oppositions. And we're trying to build alliances of a good nature. We had some very good things happen in the last week when the mayor candidate came—ought to be the next mayor, hopefully...[referring to George Moscone] and we got those same alliances that will benefit you. Fact of the matter, all you have to do is just talk to us in a loving tone. Not demands of this, that, and the other. Just talk to me in love. I will be there. I will be there to meet your need. My God, that's much more meaningful than this piece of property. I gave my word. When I give my word I don't take back my word.

Jeannie: I think that a lot of the hostility in the last exchange with Jim McElvane and Johnny Brown was because they came on like two macho tough guys.

Jim: Well, if they did, they did not do so with any kind of instructions. I must admit that I went along with some suggestions that I didn't think were warranted because I didn't know what the hell was taking place. I really didn't know what the hell was taking place, but my idea would always be to deal with you on a very frontal level. I thought anybody that can analyze like you did can't be this mischievous, and I hope you remember that, and remember the times I've analyzed myself. Hell, I've laid my life out like a book for you, tried to show my thoughts, my feelings. But when it comes to threats and shit, I don't give a damn what people do to me, no more than you give a damn. Life's a bore for us both.

Jeannie: That's right.

Jim: So why don't we take our frustrations out on some enemies instead of friends? And you haven't got anything to worry about from us.

Jeannie: Okay, thank you. And the same over here.

Jim: I got sucked in. I thought I had to be defensive, and had to defend myself because of all this bull. You ought to very frankly talk to Steve because he helped cause some of this alarm. I considered him as a quiet sort of Gibraltar, and I didn't think much of some things that Lillie said, because I know kids want to get their own corner, and people will use me, just like those kids will use you to get what the hell they want out of life. Anarchy suits everybody best. They don't realize that anarchy—in the short range it looks appealing—in the long range causes a lot of pain. But Steve said some stuff that blew my damn mind.

Jeannie: Well, Steve had not really intended [to quit the church] until what happened here.

Jim: Well, I won't forget that, it is emblazened in my mind. You can affect all that just as I will affect their [the children I had cared for while I was a member] attitudes towards you. And I'll show my good faith—if they visit you, don't take advantage by breaking down the organization that can protect them, because I'll put it in such a way that they'll feel warmly towards you. That means they may call you, that they may see you in the street and be affectionate. Just don't use it to do anything but build up. I saw you tearing down their center. I don't care, I wish I wasn't their center, but I have to be. Forces of history and circumstances have placed me where I'm at. If you tear up the heart of a person's life and meaning, I'll ride herd on the people if they put any castigation, any aspersion about you or Al in the presence of Steve. Children don't get over that kind of shit. I had enough faith to call you without wanting to record, and I hope you've got that kind of faith in me, but I don't give a damn if you do. I don't give a damn what you tape, it don't make a difference to me. What I've got to say I'm saying with my heart. I will hasten to try to breach the gaps of what has been done.

Jeannie: Thank you.

Jim: And I hope you will do the same. Will you do that for the sake of the Cause? If you never come inside this door, which I hope you will . . . I hope you come back where you belong, we need each other, but I'm not going to battle that thing with you. Time and circumstances will show this. The future is going to shake that damned thing up. I was just reading a statement from a president of a bank about advising business people to make proper arrangements of their investments because of the impending dictatorship that will confiscate—what is it, Gene? What is the exact quote: [Jim paused while Gene Chaikin gave him the quote.] Because of the likelihood that your money will be confiscated by a totalitarian state.

You don't need to worry about anything being done in reference to [Nichol]. I know you love her, I know you care for her, that she's your daughter. We're not going to break that. I don't want to break the image of the children. It's a terribly painful ordeal for them to go through, and I never do—only when I feel like someone has abandoned all sense and broken the most supreme image of the benevolent Father who has always cared for all of you, and totally as much as within human limitations. I am extremely sorry that it had deteriorated to this state, and I'm so glad that it was my inclination to call rather than let it be in a stalemate.

Jeannie: Well, I am too, I feel a lot better now.

Jim: When people allow things to continue, you get paranoid and not interested in living. We can make very stupid decisions.

And we have to live, it seems. That is not necessarily so; it seems that way. Maybe forces of change will take care of that. I hope so. As beautiful as I saw our mission field—and tell this to Al, he ought to see it again. Even if he did it privately, he ought to see it again. . . . When I was first there I was contented, you know. I wanted to make my stand here and go down, but when I saw it the last time, radio station up in the middle of the damned jungle, telephones, school, boarding facilities built all around, I didn't even recognize where I'd been. And the change of housing, and then the health program, standardized national health program, and schools standardized, and the buses that had been brought in . . . I was overwhelmed. So life in an agrarian area for our children would be the most wholesome thing. They can't get into so much trouble, and there you don't have to have the strong lines of control and authority that we have here. People can do their own thing because you don't have to worry about them going out and conniving with some fascist element, you know. Here we have had to maintain some structure, and that's the only reason I've tried to build you people up some assets. . . . My love goes to you, and one day I hope you realize it in it's fullest.

Jeannie: Thank you very much. Good-bye.

Jim: Good-bye.

*   *   *

Christmas 1975, finally, came and went. We sat around the big living room with our patients and children and exchanged gifts. The sadness and fear in the kids' eyes made it impossible to feel very happy. Our Linda was still a prisoner in the church, but we were prisoners, too, in a way—prisoners of fear and depression. The church family we'd clung to for so many years now loathed us. This year we were virtually clinging to life—and grasping for some understanding of our new-found freedom.

*   *   *

1976

Although Al was determined to stay in the Bay Area, I was terrified. The anonymous letters kept coming. They threatened that Jim had connections with the Muslims, the Mafia, and the Black Panthers, as well as with many politicians; that Marceline could get our rest home license revoked because of her job with the California Department of Health. They would taunt us about the incriminating notes we had been coerced into writing. "We have kept every precious one of them," one letter warned.

Early one January morning, Diana and Nichol ran into our bedroom. "Mom, Dad," they were screaming. "Christine Lucientis and Debbie Blakey were watching us. They're in a car right across the street from our house. They tried to duck down in their seats when we went past on our way to school."

Al and I were furious. Why do this to children? Al asked Diana to point the way to the car, and then he told the girls to continue on their way to school. We walked directly to the parked car.

Once again Christine and Debbie ducked down in their seats. Al walked over to the passenger side and demanded to know why they were spying on our children.

They both denied that they'd been spying, denied even knowing that we lived here. Debbie added, "I know this sounds strange, but you know I never lied to you. We really are here on another mission that has nothing to do with you."

My instincts told me to believe Debbie, and we left.

* * *

A few weeks later, an article appeared in the San Francisco *Chronicle*, talking about "the unusual leader of an unusually active church." It was written by Julie Smith, a reporter who lived just a few doors away from us. Jim's inflated estimate of his membership was 20,000, she reported. It was a sympathetic article, featuring the tremendous donations the church was giving to charity.

"How can a man who is so evil continue to con people?" Al said sadly. It didn't seem that we would ever be able to convince anyone of our side of the story.

My mother clipped an article from the *Oakland Tribune*. Al and I went through it, noting all the propaganda that people were swallowing. The paper printed a membership figure of 20,000, when *we* knew it was never more than 3,000. After all, I had been in charge of the membership files. The paper said the church had trained eighty members to be registered nurses, instead of the real number—three! The clinic in the San Francisco Temple that "promises to give free checkups" really only handled first aid for members. It said that the man who was finishing medical school was a former heroin addict, when in truth he had only used hallucinogens. We knew Larry Schacht, the doctor. He had lived in our house first. The article bragged that the church had helped in the education of twelve lawyers, when we knew that only two of the young people were in law school. It said that less than 2 percent of the members were on welfare, but I had seen the checks, and the percentage was closer to 20.

It bragged about the 1973 "vacation" trip where 660 people had piled into thirteen buses. Actually, Jim had only eleven buses, and 630 of these people had piled into ten of them. This made an average of sixty-three people on a bus that was built for forty-four passengers.

We were amazed that Jones was getting away with his lies, and we were committed to bare the facts about Peoples Temple—but not while Linda was still in the Temple commune and dependent on Jones.

A few mornings later, we found a newspaper, called *Peoples Forum*, on our porch. We looked across the street and saw the little paper on each porch up and down the row of houses. It was the Peoples Temple "Community News Service," and it boasted a circulation of 600,000.

Al and I read it through, and, for the most part, it sounded like Jim's sermons—filled with paranoia and fear, and much name-dropping of prominent people who supported him.

"Jim Jones Hosts TV Show" was one of the items, bragging that he had hosted a television program featuring District Attorney Joseph Freitas, Sheriff Richard Hongisto, and Assemblyman Willie Brown. "The guests discussed the positive programs and good work that Jim Jones and Peoples Temple are doing in the community." We sadly realized that the political leaders of San Francisco were being used to help Jim gain power, just as the Redwood Valley politicians had been used.

The *Peoples Forum* was delivered to us every month. Each time, more political leaders were lending their powerful support to Jim Jones, apparently without even questioning what kind of an organization it was. Mayor Moscone, Police Chief Gain, and Governor Jerry Brown all smiled as the Temple photographer asked them to pose beside Jim Jones, the great humanitarian. We were sure that Jim was becoming a powerful person, just by association. Again and again, I would try to figure out why all this was happening. Had the world gone completely mad?

*   *   *

Then, during the summer, one of our patients said she had a house she would sell to us cheap. It wasn't big, but she knew that our children needed a place where they could feel at home. She offered to let us have it for only a hundred-dollar down payment. We drove to Spruce Street in Berkeley and looked at the tiny house. It was small and old. Not the home of our dreams by a long shot, but at least a place where our family could sit together and the kids could entertain friends—if they should ever acquire any. (They were shy about forming any friendships in school. In fact, they hadn't yet learned how to make new friends.)

The *Peoples Forum* continued coming to our home. Each issue was filled with stories about Nazi atrocities and horrors. In September, when the church marched in Fresno in defense of the newsmen who were jailed because they refused to reveal their sources, the church put out two papers in one month. A news flash on the second page talked about a testimonial for Jim Jones where the guests were going to be Hon. Mervyn Dymally, Lt. Governor; Hon. George Moscone, Mayor, San Francisco; Hon. Philip and John Burton, United States Congressmen; Hon. Willie Brown, Assemblyman, California; Hon. Teresa Hughes, Assemblywoman, California; Dr. Carlton Goodlett, of the *Sun Reporter*; Joseph Freitas, District Attorney, San Francisco; and the Reverend Cecil Williams, of the Glide Memorial Church in San Francisco.

A footnote said that the governor of California was trying to set aside the date so he could also attend. As it happened, we were later told, Governor Brown sent his regrets. It appeared to me that Jim Jones's tie with the Muslims was strengthening when I read in a brief note that said he was to be the keynote speaker at the invitation of the Honerable Wallace D. Muhammad, Supreme Minister of the Nation of Islam. It didn't elaborate. It didn't have to.

As if this news weren't depressing enough, on October 19, 1976, we read in the *Chronicle* that Jim Jones had been appointed by Mayor George Moscone to the San Francisco Housing Authority.

*   *   *

Occasionally, we would wonder if anyone was leaving the church, but since we didn't have any way of finding out, we assumed that no one was. We often thought of Linda but were never able to see her. She was almost eighteen, and we were afraid that Jim would send her to Guyana.

One day, when we got to work, we found a message written on a piece of paper near the telephone. "Roz called and asked you to call her back. She said that she and Joyce and Grace have all left the church."

Roz had been a good friend; she'd lived with us and helped to make our family a happy one. I returned her call immediately. Her first question was a strange one: She wanted to know about my ear!

"What about my ear?" I asked.

"I'll explain when I see you," she answered.

Later that evening she came to visit, and the first thing she did was examine both my ears. She said, "After you left, Jim kept saying you were causing the church a lot of trouble, so all of us in P.C. voted that you should have your ear cut off as a threat to other traitors."

I felt my ears and gave thanks to the heavens. "No one ever said anything about it to me, and, as you can see, they didn't do it."

"When that happened, I decided to get myself out of there. I'm so glad it didn't really happen. And it showed me what a wild scene we were involved in."

We talked until the wee hours about all the things that had happened up until the time that Roz left. She told me that Jim was up to even more bizarre things, and that the disciplines had escalated. We told her about the rift Jim had tried to make in the friendship with Marvin and Jackie.

Roz gave us the names and phone numbers of some of the other

P.C. members who had quit during the year: Grace Stoen, Joyce Shaw, and the entire Purifoy family. After all the depressing news in the papers, it was fantastic to hear that so many of Jim's good workers had found the courage to leave. We decided that we would have a party for all the "traitors," to celebrate our freedom.

A couple of days later, we saw an article in the paper that Bob Houston had been killed in an unusual railroad accident. This was dreadful news. Bob and I had been good friends through his work with me at the church's Publications Office. He had been a talented photographer and dark-room technician. He had always been a skeptic. This got him into trouble with Jim much of the time, but it also helped many of us to hang on—just a bit—to reality.

Roz and Bob's ex-wife, Joyce, went to the funeral. After it was over, they came to visit us.

The accident had indeed been strange. Joyce had talked to Bob the very morning of his death, and he had expressed some doubts about his church commitment. When Joyce asked him to go to the church to pick up her clothes, he agreed.

Later that evening, when news of his death had leaked out, someone told us that Jim had announced: "Bob planned to quit the church today, but, fortunately, he was killed before he had the opportunity to see what it was like outside this group." The announcement caused most of us to question whether Bob's death was an accident or murder.

They also told a gruesome story about our friend Peter Wotherspoon. Jim, knowing Peter's weakness for small boys, had assigned Peter to be "big brother" to a group of young boys between nine and twelve years old, and Peter had been seen and reported doing something compromising to a little boy we knew and loved. Jim—in a rage—had commanded that Peter be beaten. While the boy, Searcy, was forced to watch, Peter was stripped naked and beaten with a board all over his body. His penis was banged until it drained blood. The nurse had to catheterize him, and a stream of blood and urine poured out. When the beating ended, all the P.C. members had to walk past Peter, one by one, to see his bruised and bleeding body.

The thought of Searcy having to witness this atrocity filled me with pain. No doubt he had been reaching out to find the love that he needed, and this was the result. And Peter, sweet gentle Peter. Jim was sadistic to put Peter in a position of authority over young boys. But we were as helpless to do anything about it now as we had been when we stood by and watched the children being tortured. Anger flooded my heart as I thought of the important politicians and leaders who seemed to be giving their support to this madman without asking why he was surrounded by guards or why his church doors had locked bars in front of them.

Roz was making contacts with people as she had promised, and a celebration was scheduled in Fresno at J. R. Purifoy's house. Then we were surprised and delighted to hear from Grace Stoen.

She had been the Head of Council in the church and one of the few people in a position of power that the church members felt they could trust. Grace always tried to be fair and kind to Temple people. She called to tell us that she was going to be at J.R.'s get-together and asked if she could ride down with us. Nothing could have pleased us more!

Grace came by our house about an hour before we had to leave for Fresno. She confessed that she was still terrified. "Jim publicly and privately pledged that he personally would kill me. He hates me so much," she said. "You know, they wouldn't let me take my son with me when I left."

"I know, that's what Roz explained," I answered. "We had to leave little Candy there, too, even though we had legal guardianship of her. I knew you couldn't take a child out without taking on the whole church."

She confessed that she had been hiding in a little city hundreds of miles away from San Francisco and that she was still afraid. She told us about talking to Jack Arnold and Cindy shortly after she quit the church. "Jack Arnold told me that he and Cindy were happier than they had ever been while they were members. I was so brainwashed that I thought they were lying. I thought they had turned their backs on the truths that Jim had taught them, and I was sure that none of us who had left the group would ever again be happy."

As we gathered in Fresno, Al and I realized we'd been out of the church for more than a year. It was hard to believe that these were the same people who had once sat, crammed together, in P.C. meetings screaming at one another. The atmosphere here was warm and friendly. There was a sense of camaraderie and trust that we had never been able to feel in the church. Jim had come between all of us.

We recounted our experiences for several hours. I told them about Searcy, who had begged to be allowed to stay with us, and how he had been forced to watch the brutal beating of Peter Wotherspoon in the church. We discussed the things we had lost. Money and property that had been taken from us, family heirlooms and jewelry that had been coerced into the offering buckets. Grandpa Purifoy told us that he had left the church in such a hurry, "I forgot to grab my false teeth!" Most of them had escaped with only the few things they could grab.

"It was worth it just to get out" was the consensus.

The talk wandered to those we knew who were unhappy in the group but who hadn't found their way of escape yet. The beatings and cruel punishments were mentioned, but it was too painful to dwell on these memories.

So many memories and questions, but no answers. It was painful to review the years of terror, but it seemed cleansing to be able to talk about it with people who also knew and understood.

Roz said, "No one will believe me when I try to tell them about it, so I just don't mention the church to any of my friends." The stories were so weird, so bizarre. Even those of us who had lived through it had a hard time believing it had actually happened. How could we expect strangers to believe that this highly praised and respected man actually laughed while chldren were beaten? No, it was better left unsaid.

*   *   *

The November issue of *Peoples Forum* read like a "Who's Who" of California politics. On the front page were Governor Jerry Brown, Supervisor Bob Mendelsohn, and Sheriff Richard Hongisto "conferring" with Rev. Jim Jones. Beside it was a photo of Jim Jones, who had accompanied Mayor George Moscone to speak with vice-presidential candidate Walter Mondale. Inside the paper was a picture of Jack Anderson extending his appreciation to Jim Jones for his efforts on behalf of the Fresno Four. As I looked on the back page, I was appalled as I saw attorney Bob Wallach introducing Jim Jones to Ralph Nader.

I had admired and respected Ralph Nader for years. Since the photograph said he was just meeting Jim Jones, I hoped that he would still be open to hearing the truth about this "man of God" who seemed to be doing so much good.

I wrote an extremely guarded letter to him, telling of the cruel and inhuman things that Jones was doing. I enclosed several of Lester Kinsolving's articles and some of the articles from an Indianapolis newspaper from several years before when Jones had been encouraged to leave the area. I ended my letter saying, "I have always respected you, and I know that you cannot be bought off. I am telling you these things as my last resort. I live in daily fear for my life. In fact, I am so afraid that I do not dare tell you my name. If you believe this letter, and would be willing to hear more, please put a classified advertisement in the personal section of the

San Francisco *Chronicle* to Angela, and I will get in contact with you. You are the last hope I have that justice will prevail."

Two weeks later, in the middle of the night, Mark Duffy called: "We know all about the letter from Angela, and we know you sent it. Don't you know that Ralph has pledged his undying support to our group? If you ever..."

I was stunned! I had to assume that Nader, whom I had admired for so many years, had betrayed my confidence and even risked my life by turning my letter over to Jim instead of being concerned enough to respond to it. I felt totally defeated. I was certain now that there was not one person in the world who had the courage to stand up against Jim Jones in his rise to tyrannical power.

There were hundreds of people who knew about Jim's cruelty and sadism, but not one of them would speak out publicly. Each person had, in some way, been silenced by his threats or by his money. Jim would use whatever he felt a person would fear the most; either his armed guards, his political power, connections with terrorist groups, his "divine" gift, witchcraft, the great number of his members, or whatever he thought would keep the person quiet.

*   *   *

Al's oldest daughter, Lorie, who had never joined the church, was about to get married. As she planned her wedding she asked Al if she could invite Linda.

"Of course, and we'll just hope she will be allowed to come," he answered. Lorie sent the invitation, and, to our surprise, Linda accepted.

"But I'll have to bring Robin, a church escort, with me," she added.

When we heard the news we were ecstatic. We hadn't been permitted to see or communicate with Linda for more than a year. We didn't have any idea how she would treat us, but we hoped that at least she would be willing to speak to us.

The wedding was held in a park, and the beautiful redwood trees formed a graceful canopy over the clearing where the bride and groom were to stand. As we drove up I caught a glimpse of Linda. I was shocked. She had always been so careful of her appearance, and yet today she looked tacky. Her hair looked as if it hadn't been cut or cared for in the year since we had last seen her. The cap on her front tooth had fallen off and had not been replaced.

Al was first to approach her. He walked over and hugged her. "Hello, daughter," he said, and to his surprise she returned his hug. They talked about the wedding for a moment, and then Robin beckoned her away.

The wedding was about to begin, and I hadn't had an opportunity to speak to Linda. I noticed that Robin, who was dressed in jeans and an old jacket, was sitting off near the edge of the benches, but Linda was sitting in the front row. I decided to sit beside her. I reasoned that she wouldn't be able to get up and move away until after the ceremony.

As I sat down I got a glimmer of a smile from her. "Linda, I'm so happy to see you. We've missed you more than you can imagine," I said. The wedding was beginning, and since Linda didn't show any signs of wanting to move, Al came over and sat beside us. We whispered to Linda, "Is there anything you need?"

Linda whispered back, "No, not now, but thank you for offering."

When the ceremony ended, Robin was at her side again. Linda and Robin rode over to the reception with Diana, Steve, and Nichol in the back seat of Steve's car.

During the reception Robin didn't leave Linda's side, but we both noticed that Linda took the champagne that was offered to her. She did so several times, in fact, and we realized that Linda wasn't following church rules.

When Robin announced their departure, Al and I went to Linda. We embraced her and kissed her on her cheeks and assured her that we welcomed a time when we could see her again.

The following week Linda called Al's ex-wife, her mother, Zoe. "Momma, can I come home and live with you? Can you come get me now?"

Zoe left immediately. She phoned Al from a pay phone and said "I don't know if Linda's going to quit the church or just wants to live with me and keep going to church, and I don't even care. I'll take her back on any terms. Maybe after she gets home we can talk her into quitting."

As it turned out, Linda had become thoroughly disillusioned with the church, and neither Zoe nor Al had to do any persuading. She told us a few tales of the increased disciplines and the boxing and wrestling matches that Jim was forcing the members to participate in. "I really think he's gone crazy," she said.

Every meal until Thanksgiving was cause for celebration. It was as if Linda had returned from another country or from a long term in prison.

After Thanksgiving dinner, Linda felt better able to talk about her experiences. She told us what her last year in the Temple had been like, and everything she said confirmed the reports we had heard from Roz and Grace. Naturally Jim had treated her well at first, because he was afraid that she too would leave the church to come live with us.

"They knew I was smoking and drinking, but nobody ever said anything because Jim told them to leave me alone."

Al asked her the question we both had on our minds: "Did Jim ever ask you to have sex with him? We were really afraid since your parents weren't there that he might make you be one of his lovers."

"You didn't need to worry about that," Linda said with a smile. "I never would have wanted to have sex with him—he was too fat and mean."

She had weathered her year well. Linda had taken full advantage of Jim's fear that she would leave, and she had had a relatively easy time of it. She had some bruises where she had been hit during the boxing matches but she proudly boasted, "I was never the one in trouble—I was one of Jim's boxers for the Cause. I was the one he used to beat up the smaller kids."

As she spoke, Linda realized the ugliness of her words. "You know, he really was evil, wasn't he? He knew I could knock hell out of the little kids, so he made me do it. It really makes me ill that I did that for him."

Diana chimed in, "We were all brainwashed in there, Linda. The one thing we have learned is not to blame ourselves for the things Jim made us do."

Nichol added, "Look at all the money we gave him. All the times we turned people in and they got beatings because of something we told Jim."

"Yes, Linda," I said. "As you begin to think clearly you begin to realize that none of this was normal. Jim was using us to do his dirty work. He is sick enough to enjoy watching little children getting the 'hell' beaten out of them. And we were so brainwashed that we would do it for him. No, we can't blame ourselves."

Al walked over to Linda and put his hands on her shoulders. "How do you think I feel knowing that I stood by while you were being hit with that board and I didn't do anything to stop it?"

"That's right, Daddy," she said. "But at the time I thought I deserved it, and I wasn't mad at you at all. Now, though, it really makes me mad at Jim. All I did was hug someone. Nothing is evil enough to earn a person seventy-five whacks with that board."

We knew now that Linda would be all right. As soon as a person started remembering the events of the church life and putting them into perspective, then it was only a matter of time before she could begin to think clearly enough to forgive herself.

Linda's education had really been botched at the Opportunity II High School. (The head of this school was a Jones supporter and so he sent the Temple children there.) We discovered this when we tried to transfer her records to Berkeley High. She hadn't been given adequate courses to allow her to graduate in June, even though she was going to be eighteen in a few more days. Opportunity II refused to release her transcript, and we couldn't enroll her without the records. After the third call to the principal at the school, someone finally agreed to bring her transcript to us—at our home. This seemed peculiar. However, her transcript never arrived. Instead the next day we found another anonymous note on our porch saying "We know where you are planning to send Linda to school."

Linda decided to wait until after the holidays before she tried again to get into school. Our children were getting tired of being cooped up in their small quarters, and Diana was the first to broach the idea of moving. She told me that Zoe had an extra bedroom and that she wanted to go to live with her and Linda in Richmond.

She tried so hard to make it easy on us, and Al was taking it pretty well, but I thought my heart would break. Diana—our sweet, sensitive Diana. She knew that I was suffering and in her teenage way tried to make it easier for me, but everything she said only made it more painful. It was a growing-up experience for me. I had always known that the time would come when our children would begin to leave, but it still hurt when it happened.

Next Steve struck out on his own. He and a friend decided to move into "bachelor quarters," and since I had survived Diana's move, I was better equipped to handle his.

Christmas was approaching, and our family was all free. Occasionally our thoughts would drift over to the San Francisco Temple where children we loved were still being held prisoners. Lillie, who had never had the opportunity for a happy childhood, was now a young woman imprisoned behind the bars of the doors of the Temple. Searcy, whom we loved as if he were our own son, was still waiting to be old enough to come out and live with us. And what of little Candy and Najah, our other little guests, we wondered? Many times I would think back to the last hot-fudge sundae Candy and I had eaten together. I knew she wasn't getting any ice-cream sundaes now. Her last words, "Mommy, I want to come home with you," rang in my ears over and over. I would wonder what I could have done—could do—that I hadn't.

Nichol moved into a room in the rest home where she could have private living quarters and at the same time make money by being our night guard.

By the end of '76, Al and I shared our little home with only two children, Eddie and Daphene.

*

───────────────

1977

On January 14, we read in the *Chronicle* that there was going to be a ceremony honoring Martin Luther King, Jr., at the Peoples Temple in San Francisco, sponsored by the Council of Churches. Among the guests slated to attend were Governor Jerry Brown, Mayor George Moscone, and Senator Milton Marks. On January 17, we read in the same paper that another Martin Luther King celebration was going to be held at the Glide Memorial Church, where Rev. Cecil Williams would hand out awards. The recipients of the Fourth Annual Martin Luther King, Jr., Humanitarian Awards were none other than Rev. Jim Jones, Dr. Goodlett, the United Farm Workers Union, and Public Advocates, Inc.

Our feelings of isolation and fear increased now in proportion to the apparent increase in public support that Jim Jones was receiving. We actually feared that he would soon be able to position himself in a way that he would carry out his prediction of taking control of the government.

In desperation we tried again to tell people—anyone who might be willing to listen. After all, Jones professed to be a communist, and we thought that politicians wouldn't want to be connected with him if they knew. We'd tried before, but usually we found that either people didn't believe the incredible stories or they thought we had been crazy for subjecting ourselves and our children to such insanity.

One person listened. His name was Dave Conn. After he heard our story, he expressed genuine concern for our welfare. He told us that he would put us in contact with a friend who was an investigative reporter; a friend to whom we could tell our story and who could document the events we'd described. Dave felt that if something happened to any of us, at least there would be verification that we were really being threatened. We were deeply appreciative of his offer to try to help, and, since Dave was the very first person who had been willing to listen to the whole story, we decided to trust his judgment. A few days later he brought the reporter, George, over to our house. Grace Stoen was also visiting us that day, so together we told him as much as we could about the beatings, Jim's sadism, his politics, and the threats and fear we lived under. Dave took copious notes which he promised no one would ever see. George promised that he wouldn't use his notes either, unless we gave him our express permission or unless something were to happen to one of us and the information was needed to back up our testimony.

At last something positive was happening. At least we knew that if one of us were killed, maybe someone would suspect and investigate the Temple. Little did we know then how hard it was going to be over the next year and a half to persuade the public to believe the truth about Jim Jones.

George was truly concerned about our safety, and he introduced us to James, an agent from the Treasury Department of the United States government, with whom he had been working on another story. James swore us to absolute secrecy about the fact that we were working in cooperation with a government agency. I must admit that we were a little skeptical at first about talking to an "agent." I remembered the letter that I had sent to Ralph Nader, which had somehow made its way into the hands of Peoples Temple. We weren't at all sure that James wouldn't feed the information we gave him right back to Jim Jones, but he was our only hope, so we decided to trust him.

We told James the same bizarre stories we had told Dave a few days before. We also told him about the weapons we knew Jim was shipping to Jonestown, in the bottoms of crates marked "agriculture supplies." We explained how the counsellors wore money belts around their waists and under their clothes to smuggle in illegal cash. We told him about the supplies we knew were going in there without proper customs papers and about the people who were using phony passports because they hadn't been able to produce a birth certificate. Jim had bragged about these things in church as he scoffed about his contempt for government

rules. James took notes of everything we were saying, and as he
left he gave us his telephone number. "Please call me any time,
day or night, if you need to. We're really going to dig into
everything you've told me tonight."

On March 25, we glanced through the San Francisco *Chronicle*
and read a little article headlined "San Francisco Housing Chief
Collapses." The night before, Jim Jones had been chairing the
Housing Commission meeting, when suddenly he collapsed and
fell to the floor. The article went on to say that half a dozen
bodyguards, including his son, lifted him to his feet and seated
him in a nearby chair. We wondered if anyone influential would
think to question why a minister has to travel to a housing
meeting with six bodyguards!

We had no sooner finished reading the article than we got
a cryptic call from Dave. "Something terrible has happened. I'm
coming right over to talk to you about it."

Before he arrived Grace called us. "I just got the weirdest
anonymous note—it was left on my porch last night." She went on
to read the note to us.

> *Dear Cousin: I think I should inform you that your
> latest course of action is the unwisest of all. I know
> everything Dave Conn boasts of having. Don't you
> know what kind of fool he is making out of you? The
> public will never forgive people who are like unthinking
> robots when in fact they are devious liars. Imagine not
> giving you credit for holding any political beliefs. You
> should know that one hundred will be staying back.
> This man can do nothing without your assistance and
> litigation will begin. I am not talking about just the
> potential of litigation. I am talking about a decision to
> litigate all of the way for sure. So notify all your friends.
> You know the legal dangers of lying to the Treasury
> officials and the police, don't you? You know I would
> think that if you thought how badly things have gone
> for Georgia and her children, then you'd consider what
> are you doing to your child? These lies have lasting
> effects on the child, wherever you choose to have him
> live.*

As Grace read the last line she said, "What in the world has
Dave done to us?"

I promised to call her as soon as I found out from Dave what
was happening. I walked out to our porch and found a letter lying

on the doorstep. It was almost the same letter, but it didn't include the reference to Georgia. Al and I began to suspect that Dave had probably turned against us. "I wonder if the church paid him off," Al said flatly.

As soon as Dave stepped in the door, we could see that he was frightened. He was pale and practically trembling. He had a hard time trying to tell us what had happened, but managed to say that he'd probably made the biggest mistake of his life. Someone was ringing our doorbell and Dave paused as Al let Grace in. Her eyes were flashing fire as she looked at Dave.

Slowly his story came out. "I knew that Dennis Banks of the American Indian Movement had been a supporter of Jim Jones, and my best friend said he knew Dennis Banks personally, and that he would set up an appointment for me to talk with him. I just wanted to let Dennis know the truth about Jim Jones so he'd stop supporting him. I figured I could set him straight on what was really happening in Peoples Temple."

As Grace listened to him she tried to control her anger. "Dave, why didn't you ask me? I could have told you that Dennis wouldn't ever believe you."

"I know that now," Dave said. We fell silent, waiting for him to tell us how he had betrayed our confidences. "I realized last night that I had been set up," he began. "My girlfriend got a call in the middle of the night from a strange person saying they were going to burn her house down. I've already moved into another apartment because I'm afraid they're going to try to kill me."

Grace prodded him: "Well, go on and tell us exactly what you've told them."

"I told Dennis that he shouldn't continue to support Jim Jones. I told him that his case would be seriously discredited after Jones is exposed for the madman that he really is," Dave said, beginning his explanation with an apology.

But our lives were at stake here—we didn't want to hear Dave's excuses. We wanted to know exactly how much Jones knew and how much jeopardy Dave had placed us in. It was almost a tragicomedy that he now shared our terror—by his own foolhardiness. Al said, "Dave, just tell us what you've done."

"Well, my friend set up a meeting where we would meet with Dennis and some of his friends. One of the friends was a tall, dark-haired girl. I think now that it was one of Jones's members. I told them everything—everything. They just kept asking me questions and I just kept talking."

"Oh, God," Grace sighed. "Did you even tell them about the Treasury agent?"

"Yes," Dave answered simply. "I told them everything I knew. I really thought I was helping Dennis."

Grace had regained her composure and she was becoming her logical self again. "Do you think you were being taped?" she asked.

Dave reflected for a few moments before he answered. "I could have been, yes, I imagine I was. Now that I think about it, every half-hour or so the girl would get up and go outside, and then she would return again. Yes, she was probably taping me."

We looked at each other in resignation. Jones knew everything we were doing. He knew the agent that was working with us—Dave had even told them his name in his eagerness to make them believe him. Dennis had seemed so interested that Dave had just kept on talking. "I really thought he believed me, he seemed to want to hear everything," Dave said, shaking his head in disbelief.

Undaunted, though, we called James, the Treasury agent, and told him about the note we had received early that morning. He

---

Dear Cousin,

I think I should inform you that your latest
course of action is the unwisest of all. I
know everything that D. Conn boasts of ahving.
Don't you know what kind of fool he is making
out of you? The public will never forgive
people who are like unthinking robots when
they are in fact devious liars. Imagine not
giving you credit for holding any political
beliefs. You should know that one hundred
willbe staying back. This man can do nothing
without your assistance and litigation will
begin. I am not talking about just the potential of litigation. I am talkingabout a
decision to litigate all the way for sure. So
notify all your friends. You know the legal
dangers of lying to the Treasury officials and
the police don't you?

                    K

You know, if any of your lies ever surface, it's
going to be kind of refreshing. You make false
accusations of brutality. How would you like to
hear all about yourself? The brutal acts you have
done. What went on in your home, Liz under
hypnosis etc. Dont you know you were never
trusted? When the whole story comes out it will
be shown in your own words and through photographs, just who were really the violent and
sick sadists, along with other bizarre, sick
behavior. I am looking forward to it, it will
be quite invigorating. The first time I am
bothered the whole country will know of your
lies and behavior. I expected something like
this you see, so I am ready for it. You've
just gone too far. Don't count on my friend not
being well. He is as well as can be. Don't
believe that all workers are going somewhere else.
Some are, and always will be, pledged to stand for
justice right here in the Bay Area as long as they
have breath.

Better let me know between 3 and 5 p.m. Saturday,
March 26th, if you are through with any and all
involvements. I want the same commitment from the
rest, Liz, Grace etc. All involvments, including
those outside your little circle of friends.
Otherwise, after that hour, the wheels of defense
will be set in motion. I expect a committment
from all, so contact your friends and make it plain.
If any one of your friends refuses to drop his or
her campaign of defamation, then you call person
to person for that person. If all agree to pursue
the wisest course, then you call person to person
for James Beasley. If I receive no call, then the
lawyers say the liability will be yours.

                                                    CHRIS

promised to come by and pick it up the following morning, to have
it checked for fingerprints. Before he had the opportunity to pick
the first letter up, though, two more letters were delivered to our
porch in the middle of the night. The last one was the most
threatening.

"Better let me know between 3 and 5 P.M. Saturday, March
26th, if you are through with any and all involvements." It was
signed Chris.

*   *   *

At the same time, unbeknownst to any of us, Marshall Kilduff
and Phil Tracy were preparing an article about Jim Jones for *New
West* magazine. Although Marshall's intention was only to
present Jones as a political powerbroker, Jones in his paranoia
thought that they were working with Dave Conn and James, and

Dear Neighbors,

  I know that your relatives, and Grace and others have
been up to bad things with a man by the name of Conn.
He's making fools out of all of you. He boasts about a
treasury agent. Do you think you are dealing withthefaofeolotoo?
Why don't you just go to the Treasury. It would give me
quite a laugh. I wish you would.
  That Mr. Conn has quite a past. I think you ought to
know that his former wife has provided a lot of helpful
information about his character, as well as Wilson and lots
of others who know about him. Tapes of his interviews were
provided, as recently as this week. He thought two men
believed his lies, but one excused himself to go out with
the dog and handed the tapes over.
  You, Grace, and your friends have reached such a low
level that I don't want you calling or writing, or sending
any messages by Phillip or anyone else. Cindy says she
doesn't want your child bothering her either. I feel this
way because of the lies you told on my friends. Tell all
 of your cohorts, including Conn, that they could get
in trouble with the law, for what they're saying that
was , and is, a matter of record. Eleven witnesses heard
them also, so they had better stop trying to do others
harm in such an un Christian way. I hope this is very
clear.

that Kilduff and Tracy knew everything about the inner workings
of his church. Jones was in a state of panic. Someone later told us
that when he heard about the Dennis Banks conversations, he
was certain his entire operation was about to be exposed. He
received the Banks information the night before the Housing
Commission meeting, and it is said that this caused him to
collapse during the meeting.

Six days later the San Francisco *Bay Guardian* ran a
center-spread article praising the work of Peoples Temple. The
headline read: "Peoples Temple: Where Activist Politics Meets
Old-fashioned Charity. The biggest religion story in the Bay Area
these days is ... the phenomenon of Peoples Temple, a church that
has been in San Francisco less than five years but has already
become the largest single Protestant congregation in the state,
more than 20,000 members."

When Al's ex-wife, Zoe, read the article in the *Bay Guardian*,
she was so angry that she impulsively wrote a scathing letter to
the editor, telling them how the church had treated her children,
and especially what they had done to Linda.

She waited for a week to see if the letter would be printed, but
instead she received a telephone call in the middle of the night
from Gene Chaikin saying, "We know about the letter you sent to

the *Bay Guardian.* Don't ever do anything like that again. If you ever do this again, we'll see you in court." Even Zoe was finding out that there was no place to turn for help in exposing the church and its fear tactics.

* * *

Jones, who was always paranoid, now went into a complete state of panic. Hundreds of letters written by his members and political supporters were sent to the *New West* headquarters in San Francisco, and hundreds more were sent to New York to the owner of the magazine. Phil Tracy was later to say at a news conference, "We seldom get one letter commenting on an article we are preparing, but when we got 300 letters, many from politicians and prominent people, we really knew we were on to something."

In the meantime, though, all we knew was that Dave Conn had told everything to Dennis Banks and that Jim Jones might have the entire conversation on tape.

Someone called to tell me that her sister was still in the church and said that Jones was going to return to San Francisco from a visit to Guyana. "He'll be at the meeting tomorrow night," she said. I thanked her for the information and promptly called James, the agent. He politely thanked me for the information.

Again, we drove past the church and saw two large flatbed trucks packed with crates headed for Guyana. I called James to report it, and once again he thanked me politely.

Next, I called to tell him that several counsellors were making a trip to Guyana, and once again he expressed thanks. Again and again I would be disappointed, because somehow government investigative agencies were unable to find the trucks or the church members who were coming and going, or to check the supplies that were constantly being shipped to Guyana. As time went on and nothing was happening, we again began to get discouraged. No one really believed us, not even the government—or else someone was smothering the investigations.

Then someone told me about a board of directors meeting for the Downtown Association in San Francisco (an association of top business leaders), at which the city supervisor, John Barbagelata, had spoken about voting fraud and about the power of the Peoples Temple church, and said that the businessmen at the meeting had been thoroughly shocked by the supervisor's allegations. I asked if I could get a copy of the comments that had been made, and after swearing me to secrecy about the source, the person sent me the minutes of the meeting. As I read what Barbagelata said and the remarks of the participants at the meeting, my hopes soared.

* * *

On June 11, we got our first hint about the contents of the *New West* article. Another article in the San Francisco *Examiner* stated: "Yet-to-be printed story builds a storm." It told about the hundreds of protest letters they were receiving about an article that no one had even seen. The editor of the magazine was quoted as saying: "I feel threatened."

Al and I had a hundred copies of the *Examiner* article made. We sent the article to every person we knew who had defected from the church, hoping that a few of them would respond by sending information to the magazine to help them find out the truth about the church.

We got only one response, but it gave us real encouragement. A former member of Jim's staff sent us copies of Jim's "revelations" notes, the information he used to convince people that he had a divine gift. There were more than a hundred of these notes, some of them several pages long.

As we looked through them, we were shocked at some of the names of members, such as Gene Chaikin, who thought they were trusted, and yet here were lists of things that had been smuggled out of their garbage cans or from their houses.

There was a note about Gene and his wife, Phyllis. The information had been gathered from an IV (indirect visit) to their home made by Linda Amos on February 14, 1973. In their garbage can, Linda had found such varied items as:

- box Hostess Old Fashioned Donuts .59 (has sugar, shortening with fat preservative added)
- envelope addressed to Phyllis from Ms. (female lib. magazine)
- envelope addressed to Phyllis from the Gray Panthers
- envelope addressed to Phyllis from Planned Parenthood
- news article clipped out, titled "Papers Trial Judge Gives U.S. sanction.
- ad in newspaper clipped out for Sheratin [sic] Hotels and Motor Inns

As we read the list of things that Linda had found, we could easily see how Jim was able to give such an "amazing" revelation such as, "Phyllis, I know that you at one time considered making a reservation at the Sheraton Hotel, and that you have had communications with Planned Parenthood, and that you have been eating donuts."

It was suddenly very clear to us how people were so easily

convinced that Jones had some extraordinary gift. His revelations were coming from garbage cans!

The next note we found that interested us was about Dale Parks
and his wife, again made by an indirect visit by Linda Amos, this
time in December 1972. There were several other church members
living in the Parkses' home, and Linda had gone into their house
while everyone was out. She gathered information on some of
their houseguests, as well as on Dale and his wife.

Linda's own daughter, Liane, was then living with the Parkses,
and Linda wrote that Liane had a bottle of medicine called Atarax
that she was using three times a day. She noted an appointment
card for Liane with Dr. "X", saying that "it was on the right side of
a top level of a white jewelry box on top of a brown dresser in
Dale's bedroom."

The note also said that another guest in the Parkses' home had
received letters from a friend of hers in Philadelphia. One letter
said that "Miss Willing and Miss Best died within one week of
each other."

Then Al and I recalled the time when Jim was trying to woo
members of Father Divine's Peace Mission into coming over to the
Peoples Temple. We remembered his announcement "by revelation" of Miss Willing and Miss Best's dying within one week of
each other.

*   *   *

I decided to call *New West* and speak to Phil Tracy. But I was too
frightened to let him know my real name. "I can't tell you my real
name, so just call me Mrs. Miller," I began. "I read that you are
planning to publish an article about Peoples Temple, and I just
want to ask you to please stay with the story and try to get to the
truth. I'll give you any information I have and answer all of your
questions, but if the church finds out that I'm talking to you, I'm
afraid they would try to kill me or someone in my family."

Phil was wonderful. He listened to everything I said and didn't
tell me that I sounded crazy. I told him about the beatings and
how the church had stolen things from our house when we first
left. I told him how they had threatened and harassed us since we
left, and about the constant fear we lived with. He asked relevant
questions and expressed concern. It felt so good to be telling
someone who might be able to help. So I kept talking. After about
half an hour, I told him that I wanted to hang up. I was afraid he
was trying to trace my call, but he asked me to promise to call him
again in case he had more questions.

The next day the June issue of *Peoples Forum* was on our porch.
In addition to the usual reporting of Nazi atrocities, there was an

article at the bottom of the back page. It said, in part, "Bona fide proof is now in our possession of a reporter's attempts to destroy Peoples Temple through the media.... To this individual who thinks he can continue his schemes without our notice, we say 'we're on to you.'" We knew this was a message to Phil Tracy.

The June 18 edition of the San Francisco *Chronicle* reported "Strange San Francisco Break-in at Magazine." The article stated that the *New West* office had reported a break-in, and that the file on a story about Peoples Temple had been tampered with.

As soon as I read the article, I called Phil again. "That's typical strategy," I warned him. "Jones did the same thing to Lester Kinsolving in 1972. In fact, Jones had shown us, when we were P.C. members, a letter that he had stolen from Kinsolving's briefcase when he had staff workers break into Kinsolving's house. Do you think they found out about my conversation with you?"

Phil put my mind at ease as he said, "The only thing they found was Marshall's first draft. All it tells is about Jim Jones's political clout in this state. All the notes I took from our conversation are in a notebook that never leaves my pocket. If he believes that Marshall's article is the story we're going to print, he should be very happy." Phil asked me several more questions and I could tell that he had been doing a lot of research into Jim Jones's background. At the end of our conversation, though, he said something that set my mind reeling. "Mrs. Miller, or whoever you are, you tell me that your children are safe, and that you and your husband are safe, and that's good. I'm really glad to hear it. But I want you to think about the fact that there are hundreds and hundreds of people in that church who are still being beaten, who are having their property taken from them, and who are still living in fear. Until someone has the courage to come out publicly, until one person is willing to have their name and face made public, the atrocities will continue. I know that you still love and care for the members who are still in there. You might be the only person who is willing to take that risk."

I promised to call him the next day and give him my decision. Al and I talked for a long time. As always, we knew that whatever I decided, or whatever he decided, we would do it together. The fact that children who had lived with us—Candy, Searcy, Najah, Ollie, Joey—and so many other children we loved were still living in the church, still facing punishments and deprivations, meant a great deal to us. We believed that if we spoke out publicly, we'd probably be killed. By now our own children weren't little anymore. It was not an easy decision—the decision to be willing to die—to expose Jim Jones; but after a lot of soul searching, we made it. Together we invited Phil Tracy and Marshall Kilduff to come to our home, where we would let them take our pictures and use our story.

Since Grace had been through so much with us, we decided to ask her to join us. Of course, she was frightened. Her husband and son were still in the church, and she didn't know how Jim might decide to punish them, but she said that she, too, would be willing to talk to Tracy and Kilduff.

More came forward, and soon there were ten people willing to let their names and faces be used for an explosive article to be published July 17.

In our conversation with Phil, I reminded him he could be killed for taking on this church. "They have powerful connections."

His answer gave us all the more courage. "I've lived a good life, and if I die trying to expose this kind of corruption, at least I will have died for something worthwhile."

In the meantime, the July *Peoples Forum* bragged: "NO BURGLARY. The investigation ordered by Police Chief Gain revealed that there was no evidence of a break-in, and that the only fingerprints found on the outside of the window were those of a *New West* employee."

But another article in the same issue contained a point-by-point rebuttal of the Marshall Kilduff article! Marshall had shown us his first draft; we could see that each paragraph in the church's article challenged a statement from his story. The same paper also had a full column of 101 names of prominent people who, it said, were giving their full support to Jim Jones.

On July 17, *New West* hit the stands, complete with our pictures and testimonies about the frightening things we had all experienced in Peoples Temple. Jim Jones had mysteriously disappeared into the jungles of Jonestown, and so made himself unavailable for comment.

We believed that either we would be murdered or this article would herald the end of the Peoples Temple. We thought surely that all the frightened members of the church would take this opportunity to leave. We knew that Jim Jones couldn't tolerate criticism, so we assumed he would take a few of his P.C. members and just hide in the jungles of Jonestown or some other place of safety. We had drastically underestimated the strength of the Peoples Temple. Instead of his taking a few of his faithful, the entire church membership began preparations to join him in Guyana.

Amazingly, instead of our being killed for our part in the exposé, the threats, harassment, and intimidations ceased entirely. A friend of ours put it succinctly when she said, "They're more afraid of you than you are of them. The only power Jim

Jones had over you was fear." A new era was about to begin for us.

I realized that I could die one death or a thousand, depending upon my fear or my courage. Although Al had never really been caught up in the fear, he was relieved to have the continual harassment stop. We felt we were now on the road to helping to free the people we loved. We didn't know, then, how long it was going to take, or the tremendous price many of the people would finally pay, but we knew that we wouldn't stop until the horror story of Jim Jones ended.

Although Jim Jones was hiding in Guyana, his public relations staff was still active in San Francisco. On July 22, a left-wing Berkeley paper published an article trying to make it sound as if the accusations in *New West* were merely a political weapon.

And as local reporters were searching around for a new angle on the Temple story, one person asked George Moscone if he would inquire into the charges against the person he had appointed to be the Housing Commissioner. His response made the July 27 headlines: "Mayor George Moscone said yesterday his office will not conduct any investigation into allegations that have been made about the Rev. Jim Jones...."

In the *Chronicle* Herb Caen informed the public that Jim Jones had retained "Attorneys Charles Garry and Fred Furth, two of the fiercest, to look into libel angles."

By the end of July, a local San Francisco paper called the *Progress* was the first to observe that there was "An Exodus of Children. Peoples Temple's Communes Look Empty."

Next, the San Francisco District Attorney's office began a full-scale investigation into the activities of the Peoples Temple Church. Al and I got on the telephone, talking to former members who had moved out of the area, explaining that at last Jim Jones was going to be exposed. One by one these families offered to come forward and tell their story to the investigators.

On August 3 the San Francisco *Progress* exposed the Opportunity II High School that was "used as an educational base for Temple affiliated young people during the 1976–1977 school year. Although the alternative high school has a long waiting list, more than 130 Temple teenagers were enrolled at one time last September."

The very next day Jim Jones submitted his resignation from the Housing Authority. The San Francisco reporters took this resignation as his admission of guilt, and during the rest of August newspapers from Ukiah to Santa Rosa and through the entire Bay Area blasted the church daily.

The day after Al and I testified in the closed interrogation room of the San Francisco District Attorney's office, a private

investigator by the name of Joseph Mazor called me, saying that
he'd heard our testimony in the D.A.'s office, and that he wanted
to help us get the two children, Candy and Carl, for us.

A warning bell should have rung in my head. How would Joe
Mazor know what had gone on behind the locked door in that
office? But when he mentioned Carl and Candy—children that we
loved—I was anxious to talk with him. We assumed that they had
been shipped to Guyana, and if there was any possibility to get
them out, I was willing to try it.

Joe asked us to come up to his Pacific Avenue suite to sign the
contract. "I'm only charging you a dollar to take on this case," he
said.

I asked him why, and he told us that getting children back to
their rightful guardians was his specialty. He also told us that he
wanted this case for the publicity. We left his office with mixed
feelings, but he promised to get the two children out of Jonestown,
and we were willing to let him try.

On August 11, the San Francisco *Progress* reported: "Temple
Faces Abduction Inquiry: At least two children reportedly have
been shipped off to the Temple's remote Guyana mission
illegally." As we read on we found that one of these children was
Karen Carr, a little girl who had been hit a hundred times with
the board the last time that Al had been to a meeting.

The District Attorney's office, when asked if they were making
any progress on the investigation, reported, "Six families have
talked ... but we have found no grounds for a criminal complaint
yet."

On August 12, Joe Mazor called again, telling us to be at his
office at two o'clock that afternoon. He said that Candy and Carl
would be there. We had to admit that he was fast.

I put on my best dress, curled my hair quickly, and put on fancy
earrings. Candy had always liked me to dress up "fancy." It's
hard to describe my emotions as I waited to see the child that had
been "our baby," the child whose picture I carried everywhere
with me and whose last words to me had been "I want to go home
with you tonight." It had been two long years since that night.

We had moved into a larger house now, three bedrooms and two
bathrooms, so we did have enough room for both Candy and Carl
if their mother, Ann, wanted us to keep them. We didn't even know
whether she was still a member of the church or not, but Joe had
assured us that she was very willing for us to take the kids.

We sat there waiting and, finally, Ann walked in. She looked
much older than her twenty-four years. She was still beautiful but
tired and drawn-looking. As I hugged her, I broke down crying. We
had always been close friends. The church hadn't only kept us

away from Candy and Carl, but from Ann too. Then little Candy walked in. Her hair was done up in tight little braids and she was no longer the baby I remembered, but she was still ravishing. She ran toward me, threw up her arms, and cried "Mommy," and my tears just wouldn't stop. I hugged her, held her, kissed her, and still couldn't stop crying. I hadn't thought I would ever be able to touch her again, and she still remembered me and loved me.

Then Carl walked in—a little man now. Carl seemed far older than his seven years!

As I held Candy in my arms, Ann and I talked. The children had been living in the San Francisco Temple because she wasn't able to keep them and work, too. She wasn't attending the church services anymore, though. As soon as Joe Mazor had started making inquiries about the children, one of the church counsellors took them back to Ann's apartment with instructions for her to keep them at home.

Her apartment was small, and she had to work, so when we told her about our home, and that we would give the children our love, she agreed to let them live with us. She assured us that she'd wanted us to have the children and that that was why she'd given us the guardianship of them in the first place.

That night, as we tucked Carl into bed he asked, "Why can't my mommy Ann keep us?" I didn't know how to answer him.

*   *   *

On August 15, *Newsweek* carried a full-page article about the beatings and bizarre practices of Jim Jones. We were elated. We had been assured that once the news got into the national press that it would get the coverage needed to stop Jim Jones and the church. *Newsweek* linked the names of several politicians with Jim Jones. We hoped that these politicians would now make a public statement denouncing the Peoples Temple and remove their support from Jones. But it didn't happen.

On August 17, the San Francisco *Progress* warned that "Government Checks Follow Temple Members to Guyana." On the same day the Santa Rosa *Press Democrat* stated: "Temple Members Deny 'Exodus' to Guyana."

On August 18, Herb Caen pointed out that "whereas Peoples Temple is 80% black, 90% of those making the wild charges are white." We knew that the church was trying to fight back.

The State Department began an investigation when charges of property swindles began to surface, and our hopes soared again. An unnamed witness gave a story to the *Chronicle* that was printed August 20 telling about some of the punishments being used by Jim Jones in Jonestown. On the 28th, the magazine section of the *Chronicle* carried a syndicated article exposing the church. Once again the news was carried across the United States, and we naively hoped that Jones's supporters would begin to denounce him.

To try to give courage to the defectors, Al and I instituted a lawsuit against the church, asking for a million dollars in damages for the property fraudulently taken from us. The news of this lawsuit hit the papers August 31.

In September, Herb Caen still seemed firmly in Jim Jones's camp. His article on the first of the month said that "Jim Jones first tried to resign in June, but Mayor Moscone talked him into staying. He wrote another letter of resignation July 13, disclosing that Gov. Brown had offered him a spot on the State Board of Corrections."

On the second of September the Santa Rosa *Press Democrat* carried an amazing article that made us think that perhaps Marcie had turned against Jim Jones. "She quoted Jim as saying 'Marcie, I've got to destroy this paper idol,' as he slammed down the Bible he held in his hand. She also confirmed that corporal punishment had sometimes been meted out for disciplinary purposes, such as when Mike Prokes was paddled. This was done, Mrs. Jones said, because Jones was outraged by an expenditure. Another case of corporal punishment involved 'a fine young man but who had this compulsion to molest children.'" She was quoted, "You couldn't leave him with children or he would molest them." Mrs. Jones said this man had been given the choice of submitting to punishment or leaving the Temple. "He was beaten and since then does not molest children."

Al and I puzzled over this article. It certainly wasn't flattering to Jim Jones. Marcie had even boasted that her husband was a "Marxist." Of course, we knew the child molester she was referring to. We had been there when Peter Wotherspoon had been so brutally beaten. But we couldn't figure out why in the world she would want to tell a newspaper.

*   *   *

We had our hands full with Candy and Carl. At the temple they had been left to their own devices, and now they were totally uncontrollable. We knew they had been beaten many times by church disciplinarians, and we determined that we would try to teach them such rudimentary things as eating with utensils and how to go to a store without shoplifting. We did not wish to use physical disciplines. It was incredible to watch these two demolish a room within a few minutes.

I would prepare a meal for them and after a few bites they would run outside saying they were finished. Within half an hour they would both return, pockets and mouths full of gum and candy. I dreaded asking where they had gotten them. Carl's stories were inventive, imaginative, and totally unbelievable. Friends up the street had handed him the gum, or a storekeeper had felt sorry for him and given him a piece of candy. Or he would say, "Somebody dropped a quarter on the sidewalk just in front of me," or "So-and-so down the street, he let me have anything in his house that I wanted." Candy would stand beside him with her eyes opened wide saying, "That's true, Mommy, I was right there when that happened."

On September 8, the San Francisco *Examiner* printed a searing story, exposing Jim's lie to Mayor Moscone. "Jones' letter of resignation to Moscone on July 13th had said 'I have received an appointment to the California State Board of Corrections which I am accepting because I feel I'm better suited to this area of public service,' but Governor Brown's press secretary said yesterday that Jones was not offered a post on the Board of Corrections. She said his name was suggested to Brown and the governor wanted to interview him before 'the process became anything more than a consideration.'"

Now we were certain that Mayor Moscone would soon denounce Jones.

On September 9, Charles Garry announced to the press that Jim Jones had been shot at in Jonestown and that he had told Jim not to answer any questions until he found out who was behind the incident. At the press conference Charles Garry had introduced Dennis Banks's statement about the time Dave Conn had told him "he was working with the U.S. Treasury department, with an IRS agent and other government officials."

On the same day we read in Herb Caen's column, "District Attorney Joe Freitas will announce shortly that his investigation into the sometimes bizarre affairs of Rev. Jim Jones and Peoples Temple has uncovered 'no evidence of criminal activity' and that the matter is now 'inactive.'"

So that was it—Caen, who usually got a scoop on everyone, was telling that there would be a clean bill of health for Peoples Temple and Jim Jones. We were dazed. What about the testimony of more than seventy people—about beatings, fraud, kidnapping, threats, and harassment.... "No evidence of criminal activity." We asked why, and an assistant at the D.A.'s office answered us with ambiguities. One of them said that, since the parents didn't complain, Jones could beat as many children as he wanted to; that if old people were foolish enough to turn over their life savings to him, it was legitimate.

We were so busy with Candy and Carl that we didn't have energy to wallow in our disappointment. I was becoming exhausted—physically, mentally, and emotionally. One day, Diana came over and offered to take the children to Zoe's for the afternoon, and I gratefully sent them with her. A few hours later she returned. "I'm sorry, Mom, but they are too much for us to handle. Carl drew pictures on Zoe's refrigerator with indelible ink and then started a fire in her front yard." I was overwhelmed. Al and I were becoming exhausted trying to undo the negative programming that Candy and Carl had received at the hands of the Temple.

We got through the month before school started, but I'm not sure how. Every night one or the other child would cry as I put them into bed, "Why can't Mommy Ann keep us? I love Mommy Ann. Why'd she give us away again?" After I tucked them into bed, I would go into my room exhausted. Sometimes I'd cry, too. What had happened to the delightful dream of my lovely baby Candy? How could the church have hurt these children so deeply?

With constant supervision, tons of hugs and kisses, and lots of presents, we did survive. The children couldn't eat a full meal, but they wanted to eat constantly. They would grab anything out of the refrigerator and run outside with it. One time they were sucking on raw bacon on our back steps! In an effort to force them to eat enough at one meal to tide them over till the next meal, I had to padlock the refrigerator and put all the other food on a shelf out of their reach.

This only temporarily stopped them. Carl learned to climb to the shelf, and they both learned which neighbors had good food in their refrigerators. One of my neighbors came over sympathetically saying, "Look, I know you are trying to help these children, but I can't allow them in my house anymore. I told Carl not to come in, but he did anyway and went to my refrigerator and took out a piece of chicken, then went upstairs to watch our TV. I told him to leave and he simply refused."

My next-door neighbor came over saying, "Carl was playing with my son yesterday, and when he left he took a toy." We went into the room that Carl was sharing with Eddie and found the toy. I also found a pack of cigarettes in his toybox and several packs of matches.

When school was about to start, I was in for another shock: Carl was old enough for the third grade, but he didn't know colors, numbers, or the alphabet. He had learned to scrawl his first name, but that was all. I remembered all the Temple's brochures advertising their "classrooms for children" and wondered how many of the other church children were illiterate. No one would ever know. Now, in addition to trying to teach him the rudimentary rules of society, I was faced with an hour a day tutoring him.

*   *   *

On September 26, *New West* revealed that the day before Jim Jones submitted his July 13 resignation to Mayor Moscone, he had been confronted with the allegations of brutality and other accusations of former Temple members.

The October *Peoples Forum* was left on our front step. The headline said: "Conspiracy!" It had a full-page statement by Dennis Banks, which featured his side of the Dave Conn issue. There was also an interesting letter to the editor from Jerry Gardner. He wrote: "It is unfortunate that such an exemplary man and organization must be subjected to this sort of yellow journalism" (referring to the *New West* article and the local newspaper stories).

On October 7, Grace Stoen made a public statement about her efforts to get her little boy out of Jonestown. Her husband, Tim Stoen, had left the Temple by now, and he was joining her in a custody battle against Jim.

I was talking with Phil Tracy one day, explaining the problems we were facing with Carl and Candy, and he suggested that I write an article about it. "This is living proof that the Temple's children aren't getting all that fantastic education and training they keep bragging about," he said.

I got out a tape recorder and began asking them questions that I could use in an article. By the time they were finished talking, though, I knew I couldn't write about it. Once again, the truth would have been too grotesque for belief.

Candy told me about the "Blue-Eyed Monster," which we figured was really electric shock treatment. She began, "I got in trouble in the church because I lied, and Father said I'd have to go to the Blue-Eyed Monster. Then they took me into this dark room, and the monsters were all over the room. They said, 'I am the Blue-Eyed Monster and I'm going to get you.' Then a monster grabbed my shirt and tore it open. You remember, Mommy, that shirt I had in my suitcase when I came here, with the big tear in front? That's the shirt the Blue-Eyed Monster tore open."

I did remember the shirt. My eyes were filling with tears as she continued. "Then all of a sudden all the monsters started to say, 'I'm going to get you again,' and then one hit me right here," she said pointing to her chest. "Then it felt like a knife was going right down to my back, and my body started to shake back and forth like this." As she spoke she shook her body so I could understand what she was explaining to me. "Then my teeth were tied together so I couldn't open them." She looked at me seriously and said, "I couldn't believe it, it hurted so bad."

I had heard from Roz about the "Blue-Eyed Monster" that Jim was using for "behavior modification" for the small children. I held Candy tight, wanting to make these memories vanish and give her back the happy childhood she deserved.

Next Carl took the hand microphone, and I asked him what he had gotten in trouble for in the church. "Oh, I guess most was for stealing. After those long meetings we were so hungry, and they had all those food stands downstairs where people could buy food. We didn't have money, so we couldn't buy any of the food, so me and a bunch of guys learned that we could get under the seats and open the ladies' purses and take out quarters and dollars to buy food with."

"What about your allowances?" I asked him, already knowing the answer.

"Well," Carl answered, "every time they would give out allowances, someone else would come by with an offering basket and Father would tell us that we should give our money. But sometimes I really learned how to do it. I'd put the money up my sleeve and then pretend like I was dropping it in. They didn't catch me very often."

"What happened if they caught you?" I asked.

"Well, then you got beat, but they didn't always catch me."

"Was it worth it to steal the money if you got beatings?"

"Oh, yes, because then you could get some food and candy."

Even though I had thought about writing the story, I knew that people would just scoff at me for being so gullible as to believe these things told by such young children. But I did believe them—and I could understand why they stole and why they lied. These were their survival tactics—made necessary by a man who said he cared about children.

School continued to be difficult for Carl. His teacher loved him, but she had twenty-nine other children to work with. She tried bringing in an additional teacher to work with Carl two days a week, but the new woman couldn't understand that Carl was the victim of a brutal group, and she tried using the same tactics that Jim Jones had used—threats and embarrassment. Finally his first teacher, in a very loving gesture, said that she would keep Carl in her class during the morning hours, but I would have to come and take him home before their first recess. I was grateful that she was willing to keep him even for the short time. I knew that Carl required most of my time, and I could understand that she couldn't take care of an entire class with him in the room.

Candy was doing better in her classroom. She immediately assumed the position of ringleader in the toughest gang of girls in the kindergarten class of fifty-four students. She was generally accepted as the decision maker for most of the other children. If a girl wanted a carton of milk, Candy would decide if she should choose chocolate or white. Candy would stop by the neighborhood store on her way to school, pick up gum or candy without the courtesy of paying the grocer, and use these goodies to buy the respect and love of her classmates.

Candy's teacher, too, understood her background. Because of the continuous articles that had come out during the summer exposing the Peoples Temple, I had many sympathetic listeners now. People realized that Al and I had a difficult job of trying to help these children readjust. We found that people were amazingly helpful once they understood the problem.

Then one day Andre came back into our lives. He'd been our foster child while we were living with the Temple up in Redwood Valley. Jim had ordered him to leave us and had forbidden us to tell why. At first, I didn't recognize the handsome six-foot-two man as he walked toward me. He was calm and self-assured and just wanted to see his "mom and dad" again. We were so happy that he'd found us after so many years that we asked him to stay around for a while.

It was hard to explain to Andre why we had sent him away so abruptly many years before. We told him about Jim Jones's statement that Andre would grow up to be a pathological killer, and how Jim had demanded that we return him immediately to the welfare department. Apologies are so trite. How do you say "I'm sorry" to a young man whom you pushed out of your life just because your leader told you to? I remembered Andre's social worker calling, begging us to reconsider. "Andre feels that you are his parents. He doesn't understand what he did wrong. If you could just tell him, I'm sure he would change. At least he deserves the courtesy of an explanation."

Al and I had tried to explain the situation to the twelve-year-old boy without incriminating Jim Jones, but our story had been weak. Andre had had to go to an institution because he was too old to find a family as a foster child.

We knew we couldn't right the wrong, but at least we could offer him a home now. He graciously accepted our offer, and once again became our son. But this time he was a full-grown man. He helped with Candy and Carl. We were glad to have a black person in our house to help them identify with both of the races they represented.

He took Carl to ball games and made him feel important—

probably for the first time in his life. Whenever Carl was accompanied by Andre, his peers had to respect him. Andre's size alone was enough to make an eight-year-old gaze in awe and respect.

*   *   *

On November 10, Charles Garry told the press, "I went to Jonestown. I have been to Paradise." On the 13th, Bob Houston's parents spoke out against the church for the first time. An impressive story told about the sadness and pain that they had endured through the years and their shock at Bob's untimely death.

On November 18, Herb Caen announced, "After long investigation, District Attorney Joe Freitas has no plans whatever to prosecute him, so why does the Rev. Jim Jones continue to live in Guyana? It revolves around a five-year-old boy.... According to well-informed sources, the true father of the child is—Jim Jones." He was talking about John Victor Stoen, son of Tim and Grace Stoen. Jim now claimed John-John was his own son. It was still hard to believe that Jim Jones could stoop to such depths to hurt people. He had threatened that he wanted to kill Grace, but with this latest lie he had hurt her deeply.

Grace phoned and asked me, "Why would he say something so ugly? And why would Herb Caen print it without speaking to me?"

*   *   *

Christmas with Carl and Candy was delightful. Everyone went overboard getting presents for these children who hadn't celebrated a real Christmas ever before. Carl was doing better with his homework and Candy seemed to be earning—no longer buying—her friends at school.

Although all our hopes of exposing Peoples Temple and freeing the members seemed to have been destroyed, we hadn't given up. On New Year's Eve we promised Searcy, Ollie, Najah, Janet, Stephanie, Lillie, Beth, and Joey that we hadn't forgotten them. We silently sent them our love as we began the new year.

1978

Tim Stoen moved into the house next door to us. We talked about the frustrations we had experienced, trying to get someone to believe that Peoples Temple was a prison and not a church.

"My main concern, of course, is my little boy," Tim said. "If only there was some way to free him, but I've tried everything I can think of."

He had, too. Tim and Grace had already make a trip to Guyana, where the courts promised to reach a decision...sometime. Jim was still trying to cloud the issue by saying that he was the natural father, but in our hearts we knew that this was just another of Jim's many lies, just another way that he could hurt "traitors."

In the wake of the 1977 publicity, quite a few relatives of people in Jonestown had begun to ask how they could help to free the people who were being held against their will. In fact, so many people were interested in forming a group that we met and decided to call ourselves "Concerned Relatives." Fifty-four people signed a petition begging our government to consider the plight of these people who were being denied their basic human rights. On April 11, 1978, the group went to the gates of the San Francisco Temple and delivered a copy of the petition to the guards stationed there.

The following day Charles Garry told the press, "These accusations are a lot of bull." He said the followers in Guyana named by the group "don't want a goddamn thing to do with their relatives in this country."

We knew that the San Francisco Temple was communicating regularly with the group in Jonestown on a C.B. radio, and we thought we might try to obtain information about the goings on in Jonestown from someone with direct access to the radio talks. We were amazed as we were told about strategy planning among Temple leaders and Jim Jones himself.

We heard that they were spending large amounts of money for "goldfish" and "dresses," and, because of our other information, we were certain they were talking about gold and guns. We were told that they were having difficulty cashing Social Security checks. At first we would report what we heard to the San Francisco District Attorney's office, but it seemed that we were the only ones who thought it was important. They would thank us politely for the information but never ask for more.

We were actively working with the Concerned Relatives trying to get information to the State Department, the Guyanese officials, the Disciples of Christ Denomination, or to anyone else who would listen. A man named Leon, who had escaped a few months earlier, told us about torturous punishments and humiliations Jim was forcing his members to endure. "They have a big hole there and they make people stay in there in the hot sun for days at a time for discipline," Leon said. He showed us marks on his back where he had been beaten with a two-by-four because he didn't work fast enough.

Another family escaped and came to us. They told of watching as young people were forced to eat hot peppers or even have hot peppers put up their rectums as disciplines. They told of members who had begged for help to get out. In their fear, the family pledged us not to tell anyone what they had said. We also heard that parents were begging their children to come home for a visit. Pleas such as, "Your grandmother just died, can't you come to her funeral if I send you a ticket?" or "Your mother is in the hospital calling for you, won't you please come home?"

Again and again, we were told, the answer was: "I'm so happy here, it's so beautiful. I never want to return to America." But the speakers didn't sound happy.

As time went on we became more aware that something had to be done to stop Jim Jones. Everything we heard indicated that he was now almost completely crazy.

We organized a demonstration in front of the Federal Building in San Francisco asking Cyrus Vance to listen to our pleas for the safety of our loved ones. Al telephoned the TV stations the night before hoping we would get news coverage.

He called the newsrooms of the three major stations, but only at KRON did someone ask questions. "Where will it be? What issues are you planning to cover? Which politicians are you trying to get your message across to?" Al answered all the KRON news station's questions, but as he hung up he wondered why they had asked those questions.

The following day as we arrived at the Federal Building, the only station that wasn't there was KRON. And to make things even more suspicious, about fifty members of the Peoples Temple were there marching! The church had devised signs that indicated they already knew exactly what we had planned to say, and they had a printed brochure refuting the claims Al had made on the telephone to KRON the night before.

Tim Stoen and Steve Katsaris, father of Maria Katsaris, went into the office, demanding that the Temple marchers be cleared away. We'd made the reservation for that space first. The officials apologized, but said that, by some strange means, the church had also obtained permission to hold a demonstration, and that we would just have to march beside them.

It was, indeed, a strange combination. We carried signs saying "Free Our Families," and the church people carried signs with false accusations about members of Concerned Relatives.

I stood on one side and Tim Clancey stood on the other side—with the Peoples Temple. Tim and I had once worked side by side in the Publications Office!

*   *   *

When Debbie Blakey defected, she told us she had given information to Richard McCoy at the American Embassy in Georgetown as she left to return to America. We heard that two counsellors were sent to find her. Debbie couldn't understand why we trusted her without asking any questions. She had expected us to think she was an agent working for Jim. But we succeeded in convincing her that we had already received inside information about her defection and felt her to be trustworthy. We just hoped that she would not give in to Jones and return.

Her first reaction—much like the reaction of other defectors— was "I'd rather die than return; all I really want to do is die anyway. Life has no meaning." But after a few days of living a normal life, Debbie no longer wanted to die. She wanted to live—to make up for all the years she had wasted. She wanted to help her mother, who was dying of cancer in Jonestown, to get out before she died.

Debbie told us about "Bigfoot," a punishment that had replaced the "Blue-Eyed-Monster." "It's a deep well about forty-five minutes' walk away from the camp," she said sadly. "Counsellors have to sit in there, and when a child is to be disciplined they throw the child down the well. The kids would cry hysterically as soon as Jim would tell them they'd have to go visit Bigfoot. We'd hear them scream all the way there, and all the time they had to be down in the well, and by the time they got back they were begging for mercy. It was really awful."

"How many people do you think would leave if they had the opportunity?" Al asked her.

Debbie thought a moment and said, "I think if the people thought they would be safe that about ninety percent would leave today." She told us about the mass suicide drills and the inadequate meals.

Debbie was amazed at how much happier Carl and Candy were than when she had seen them in the church.

It was true, Carl and Candy *were* much better. But they were also more work than we were able to handle. Ann had been keeping in touch with us from time to time, asking how the children were. We had spoken with her about signing adoption papers, but we asked her attorney to stress to her that once she signed them the children wouldn't be hers anymore, and that if she wanted the children to come back to her she shouldn't sign anything.

Her attorney told her that she didn't seem very convinced about the correctness of giving her kids up for adoption and advised her to think about it.

At the same time, Al and I realized that the children were more than we could handle. The same friend who had once told us not to be afraid of Jim Jones now said something that really hit home: "You think those children need you. They would probably be much better off with their natural mother. There are blood ties and emotional ties that you will never have with them. The children don't need you, you need them. You seem to need to be the world's greatest mother, and until you realize that you're only a human being and not some kind of supermom, you will keep bringing children into your life."

The impact of her statement was shocking, to say the least, mainly because I knew it was true. These children wanted Ann, and they would never be happy with second best, me. One day I called Ann after Al and I had decided we weren't making the kind of progress with the kids that we should have been. "Ann, you know Al and I are really getting up in years," I began. I was only thirty-eight years old, but I felt like I was about seventy-five. I explained that the kids were a tremendous responsibility and that we were exhausted. I was just beginning, but Ann cut me off.

"Jeannie, are you telling me that you want me to take the kids back?" she asked.

"Yes," I admitted, half ashamed that I had to admit to my failure as a supermom.

"This is so amazing," she told me. "I've been reading a book that my attorney gave me, and I suddenly realized that my children are my life. I've been going all sorts of directions trying to avoid my responsibilities of motherhood, but now I know that I am ready to be the mother they need. I've been visualizing them living with me. I've already talked to the school and made arrangements for them to begin next September, but I just didn't want to hurt your feelings by asking for them back. And now you're saying you agree with me."

Relief swept over me. Ann explained that she had worked out her priorities: "I have two interracial children, and they are my statement to the world that integration can work," she said wisely. "I want to make that statement come true."

Al and I were ecstatic. We knew we had helped the children. They seldom, if ever, stole anymore. Carl was already into the third-grade reader, and Candy was doing very well in her classwork. They had learned to make friends in the neighborhood. Carl was developing a fantastic talent in drawing. Candy had actually been paid to model for a professional photographer. And now Ann was ready and eager to take up where she had left off.

Debbie Blakey was rapidly putting her life back together, too. She had found a good job and was ready to move. Before she left, though, I asked her about the time she and Christine had spied on our children so many years before.

"You know, that was so funny, Jeannie," she answered and smiled sadly. "We really were there on another mission. We had been parked in front of Julie Smith's house waiting for her to leave so we could get to her trash can. Jim wanted to have something on her so he could scare her into doing a good article about him."

Julie Smith *had* been the target of a lot of harassment. She later said, "I was bombarded with so many calls and letters while I was preparing the article about Peoples Temple that I changed the story I had planned to write. What I ended up writing was a goddamned valentine."

We got a telephone call from the Los Angeles District Attorney's office. They said they were investigating the lawsuit of Wade and Mabel Medlock and wanted to get enough information to find out if they could prosecute Jim Jones on charges of extortion, because he had threatened the Medlocks—an elderly black couple—with death if they refused to turn over their property to the church. The Assistant District Attorney asked if we would be willing to give their office information.

We'd already given the information to the Treasury Department, the State Investigator, the San Francisco District Attorney's Office, the newspapers, Joe Mazor, and the attorney who filed our lawsuit. We'd learned to do anything to help. By now we had our affidavits and evidence neatly catalogued and knew enough not to give out any originals. We decided to go with the L.A.D.A.!

We drove down to Los Angeles in July with our large stack of documentation, including proof of Jim's fear tactics, property swindles, brutality and other shady dealings. As we told the D.A. how many other times we had given this information to agencies—all to no avail—he assured us that he would proceed with this investigation.

Once again, we called all the people who would be willing to speak to him, and assured them that this time would be different—Steve Ramirez, who was with the Los Angeles district attorney's major fraud division, said that by mid-August he would try to have the case in court.

We learned that Jim Jones was sick—very sick. We heard that he had a steady 102 degree fever, and again, we hoped for his demise.

We were told that Temple nurses were ordering medical supplies, such as Haldol, Mellaril, and Thorazine in liquid form and in vast quantities. We wondered why. We spoke with a pharmacist who agreed that the requests were peculiar. "Those medicines are usually taken orally, in pill form. The only reasons anyone would need them in liquid form is if they were to be injected, or if a person were taking them unwittingly."

We heard that the counsellors had been discussing Jim McElvane, who was then still in San Francisco. Apparently, he was becoming discouraged and even hostile because of the secrecy surrounding the Jonestown mission. We heard his statement "Secrecy breeds paranoia," and we were told Jim's ominous instruction to the San Francisco counsellors was:

"The press has not been a good instructor" [referring to the newspapers], "the education [spanking] board will do better." A few days later, as the San Francisco counsellors said the matter had been taken care of, Jim was talking to another San Francisco counsellor saying, "I'm sorry you had to be a part of that."

Her response: "Whatever is necessary for the Cause."

We hoped and prayed that Jim McElvane would defect. He was a good man who had been brainwashed and had done some awful things. So had many of us. We had talked with many of his friends who were very concerned about his welfare. They remembered his sensitivity and his concern about the problems of society. Then we heard Jim's instruction to "keep him happy there until we can get him over here. We can do a better job of teaching here." Later Jim McElvane was sent to the "Promised Land"—never to return.

Al and I were in a pathetic position—to be hearing about the conversations between San Francisco and Jonestown, knowing as much as we did about the things that were happening in the jungle encampment.

When Debbie escaped, one of her public accusations about Jonestown was that people weren't getting adequate food. In order to refute this claim, the Jonestown residents began to brag to the San Francisco Temple members about the marvelous food they were eating. "We had fried chicken tonight. We just got through eating a big stack of hotcakes with ham and eggs." The empty boasts were taken seriously by the people in San Francisco, and they began to improve their own diet.

Often, I wished we could shout out a warning to the naive San Francisco members who believed they were preparing to go to paradise, when they were actually rushing toward their own destruction. But we knew that no one would listen even if we could do it.

*   *   *

We formed a new organization, a nonprofit corporation called the Human Freedom Center. If we couldn't stop this madness that was happening in Jonestown, at least we would be available to help people who escaped or who had found their way out of other cult groups. We remembered what it had been like coming out of the church—when no one believed our stories and we had no resources to start our lives again. We determined that any person who wanted out should have a place to go. Just in the act of putting the organization together we felt that maybe there was hope.

It was August, and Steve Ramirez told us that there was still no court date. We heard that the church was discussing the strategy to use to keep "Dr. Finkelstein" from trying to prosecute the church. We knew Dr. Finkelstein was the code name for Steve Ramirez.

Claire Bouquet, one of the members of Concerned Relatives, phoned to say that Congressman Leo Ryan was concerned about our loved ones in Jonestown and was planning to begin an investigation into their activities as soon as the November election was over. Again we felt hope. We had heard that he was a courageous man and that he had been concerned since the death of Bob Houston.

Bob's father, Sam, was a good friend of Leo's, and when Sam had told him about the mysterious circumstances surrounding his son's death, he decided that he would look into the matter. Another constituent had complained, and Leo decided he wouldn't put the investigation off any longer.

September came and went. No news from the L.A.D.A. It was an old, old story by now, and we weren't surprised. Disappointed, yes, but not surprised.

We got word that the Guyanese court had finally refused to rule on the case of little John Victor Stoen. Someone sent us a copy of the Georgetown newspaper. The headlines were "Judge Hits Out at Mean Despicable Acts, Declines to Hear Case." The article said that the judge had received so many threats and so much harassment that he was excusing himself from the case. He wasn't sure which side was doing this, but he didn't want to be a part of it any longer. Grace and Tim were right back at square one. They'd have to go through the legal battle again, this time with a new judge.

One of the first official actions of our brand-new Human Freedom Center was to help Will Holsinger, Leo Ryan's aide, to coordinate this official congressman's visit to Jonestown with a visit to many of the relatives of the Jonestown residents. We solicited letters and donations from people who had expressed concern about the welfare of their relatives, too. Many of the donations that came in were marked "anonymous." People were still afraid.

We held meetings discussing alternatives, possibilities, and problems associated with the trip. Steve Katsaris, Tim Stoen, Grace Stoen, and Beverly and Howard Oliver had all been to Guyana before and had been turned away. They were undaunted. They all sat with us planning to go again.

This time it was decided that only those who had relatives in Jonestown would go along. Actually I was relieved that I wouldn't have to make a decision whether to go with the group, since I didn't have any relatives there. We all knew it wasn't going to be a pleasant trip. The best we could hope for was the possibility that a few people might be allowed to talk to their relatives.

Others were also there helping coordinate the trip, including

Holli Morton, whose only connection with Peoples Temple was her friendship with some of the former Temple members, and Wanda Johnson, whose little boy, Tommy, had been forced to eat his own vomit by Jones as a punishment many years before and was now being held prisoner in Jonestown. Psychiatrists came and talked with us, explaining how to respond to the cold stare of the brainwashed. But never, in any of our meetings, did we think to discuss what to do if the Congressman and four of the newsmen were attacked. We were aware there might be danger, but we didn't believe that Jones would be so foolish as to hurt a government official.

* * *

And now Congressman Ryan...writers and photographers dedicated to their profession...and 912 from Jonestown...are dead. Thousands of people mourn the loss of their loved ones, and people all over the world mourn the tragedy at Jonestown. Investigations are now proceeding unhampered. People now want to hear the stories. Too late. The members of the church are not packing to go to the "Promised Land." It's too late to help 912 people, many of whom had begged for someone to free them.

* * *

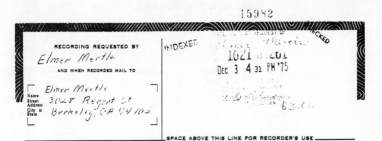

15982

RECORDING REQUESTED BY
Elmer Mertle

AND WHEN RECORDED MAIL TO

Name
Street
Address
City &
State
Elmer Mertle
3028 Regent St
Berkeley, CA 94105

INDEXED

CHECKED

AT THE REQUEST OF
Elmer Mertle
1021 201
DEC 3 4 31 PM '75

SPACE ABOVE THIS LINE FOR RECORDER'S USE

REVOCATION OF POWER OF ATTORNEY

KNOW ALL MEN BY THESE PRESENTS: That the *unlimited* Power of Attorney executed by *the undersigned* on the day of *undated*, 19 and recorded in Book, at Page *not recorded* of County, State of by which constituted *G. Donald Beck* Attorney for the purpose in said Power of Attorney set forth, is hereby wholly revoked, cancelled and annulled.

IN WITNESS WHEREOF, *we* *have* hereunto set *our* hand *s* and seal *s* this *third* day of *December*, 19 *75*

Signed, Sealed and Delivered in the Presence of

....

....

Elmer J. Mertle (SEAL)
Elmer J. Mertle

Deanna M. Mertle (SEAL)
Deanna M. Mertle

....(SEAL)

STATE OF CALIFORNIA } ss.

County of __Mendocino__

On __December 3rd, 1975__, before me, the undersigned, a Notary Public in and for said State, personally appeared __Elmer J. Mertle & Deanna M. Mertle__

known to me to be the person **s** whose name **s** **are** subscribed to the within instrument and acknowledged that **they** executed the same.

WITNESS my hand and seal

Mary Lou Firman
Notary Public in and for said State.
Mary Lou Firman

OFFICIAL SEAL
MARY LOU FIRMAN
NOTARY PUBLIC
MENDOCINO COUNTY
My Commission Expires May 18, 1976

Title Order No. Escrow or Loan No. _____

POWER OF ATTORNEY—REVOCATION
WOLCOTTS FORM 1404—REV. 8-62

This standard form covers most usual problems in the field indicated. Before you sign, read it, fill in all blanks, and make changes proper to your transaction. Consult a lawyer if you doubt the form's fitness for your purpose.

1021 201

15982

Here is the notarized form that wrested power of attorney from the Peoples Temple church after we defected.

Larry Layton marching in the counterdemonstration held by the church the day that the Concerned Relatives demonstrated at San Francisco's Federal Building in 1978. We were demanding freedom for our loved ones. Larry's sign says: "My sister, my mother and brother-in-law are happy in Jonestown." At the same time, his sister was trying to escape (and finally succeeded), and his mother was dying of cancer. (Photo by Al Mills)

At the same demonstration, Kathy Tropp, who had taken my position in the Publications Office, carried a sign that accused us of mistreating a teenager who had lived in our home in Redwood Valley.

Tim Stoen, another defector, speaking with reporters. His six-year-old son, John-John, died in Jonestown.

Steve Katsaris, father of Maria Katsaris, at the same demonstration, speaking to reporters.

The man holding the rifle in this photo, which is several years old, is Tom Kice. Tom was one of the men in the party of gunmen that shot and killed many of the people in Congressman Leo Ryan's group.

Jim tried his best to convert the members of Father Divine's Peace Mission. Here are several of them with Jim as host at a picnic. Most of them returned to their own church in Philadelphia. (Photo by Al Mills)

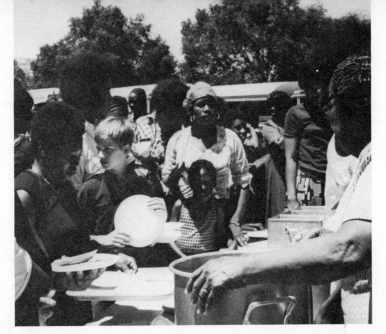

ABOVE *It was at a Sunday picnic, held in the parking lot of the Redwood Valley temple, just like this one, that Jim was supposedly "shot" by an enemy from the nearby hills.* BELOW, LEFT *After the "shooting," Jim became obsessed by the possibility of being killed by an assailant. He had this guard shack built—above the chimpanzee cage in his backyard. Since Jim trusted only his Planning Commission members to guard this important post, Al and I spent many cold, lonely hours up there.* RIGHT *Jim and some guards "looking for the enemy." (Photos by Al Mills)*

Jim loved to boast in his press releases about the temple's swimming pool. Here are members splashing about with their clothes on. That is because everyone <u>had</u> to jump into the pool when Jim gave the order.

One Sunday, Jim held a mass baptism for hundreds of members. Here he is, assisted by one of the Peace Mission converts, dunking someone.

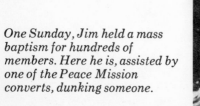

ABOVE *This was one of the first of hundreds of shipments of machinery and supplies headed for Jonestown, Guyana. (Photo by Al Mills)*

APOSTOLIC LIVING TODAY...

Larry Schacht and Jim Jones

Larry's Story

Study time is here again! The college students who have been helped by Peoples Temple are returning to the church-maintained dormitories for another nine months of study and fellowship together. Many of these young people have come from lives of drugs, crime and hopelessness.

Let's follow the life of one of our young students, Larry Schacht, as an example of the results of Apostolic Living. Larry heard about Jim Jones three years ago when he was living in Berkeley, aimlessly wandering around, his mind ruined because of the drugs he had been using for several years. He met one of the members of the San Francisco Peoples Temple. She talked with him about Jim Jones, a man who cared about him, even though Larry did not know him in person. Larry wanted to know more about Jim Jones and Peoples Temple, so he arranged to visit one of the services.

After hearing the WORDS OF LIFE that Pastor Jim spoke that day, Larry knew that he had reached a turning point in his life. He asked if he could move to Redwood Valley so that he could be close to the Temple Family and learn more about clean living and the Apostolic Principle of LOVE AND SHARING.

Larry moved in with the Assistant Minister and his wife who own a boarding home for the elderly. They knew that the best and healthiest life is a life of work and fellowship, so they gave him many jobs to do outside in the open air. His body became cleansed of the poisons that were destroying his mind and life.

Larry became a new man; his craving for drugs was completely gone. He found a job and began to think about his future. When September came he enrolled in school. Previous school years had been so marred by social problems that he had been an "F" student; now he was making "A's." He continued in college and graduated with honors.

Now Larry, along with another young man, Steve Buckmaster (who also had a background of drugs), is attending medical college in Mexico, sponsored by Peoples Temple. He and Steve have dedicated their lives to helping others. They plan to be doctors in a Peoples Temple Free Clinic as soon as they graduate.

Here are examples of two totally wasted lives redeemed and brought into wonderful fullness through actually living the Apostolic Teachings of the early Christian church.

This article was printed in one of the temple pamphlets. It is testimony about Larry Schacht. Larry was a doctor and was the person who mixed and administered the poison that killed 912 people.

TO WHOM IT MAY CONCERN:

Please be advised that Elmer J. Mertle and Deanna M. Mertle have my consent to take my daughter, Diana I. Mertle, with them in their travels outside of the United States anywhere that they wish to travel with said child in the world.

They are further authorized to procure any and all needed medical and hospital care for these children.

I further declare that Elmer J. Mertle has the sole and exclusive custody and care of the above-described child and is solely and exclusively responsible to make all decisions concerning her.

Dated:_____

ZOANNA M. KILLE

Subscribed and sworn to before me this ___ day of _____, 1973.

June B. Crym, Notary Public

JUNE B. CRYM
NOTARY PUBLIC - CALIFORNIA
MENDOCINO COUNTY
My Commission Expires October 3, 197.

TO WHOM IT MAY CONCERN:

Please be advised that Elmer J. Mertle and Deanna M. Mertle have my consent to take my son, Thomas E. Updyke, and my daughter, Daphene Marie Updyke, with them in their travels outside of the United States anywhere that they wish to travel with said children in the world.

They are further authorized to procure any and all needed medical and hospital care for these children.

I further declare that Deanna M. Mertle has the sole and exclusive custody and care of the above-described persons and is solely and exclusively responsible to make all decisions concerning them.

Dated: _____

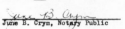
THOMAS E. UPDYKE

Subscribed and sworn to before me this ___ day of June, 1973.

June B. Crym, Notary Public

JUNE B. CRYM
NOTARY PUBLIC - CALIFORNIA
MENDOCINO COUNTY
My Commission Expires October 3, 197.

June Crym, who worked with the church's attorneys as a secretary, prepared these letters for us so we could take Diana, Eddie, and Daphene out of the country with us. Naturally, neither of our former spouses was to know that their signatures had been forged. We could never bring ourselves to do the forgery, even though June had already notarized the letters.

As the day approached for us to leave for Kenya, Bob Houston had us pose for our "official missionary picture." We were told that it would appear in the temple newsletter announcing our departure.

PEOPLES TEMPLE DOOR PASS

Internal Security. No Door
check necessary. Thank you.

This was the card that Jim's staff members carried. Having the card meant that you didn't have to be frisked at the temple door. Since I had access to the supplies used to make this pass, I quietly made one up for myself. That way I avoided the disgusting body search every Sunday.

FAIN   TINETRA
LAST NAME   FIRST NAME
1048 3/4 W. 42 ND
Address
LA   90037   231-3483
City   Zip   Phone No.
C 1268   11-8-58
Membership No.   Birthdate

Pd. $2.50

DOCUMENTS SIGNED

Information Sheet ___✓   Financial Release ___✓

Blank Statement ___✓   Sheet of Paper ___   5-3-75

Resignation ___✓   DATE

ABOVE *Every member was required to have an identification envelope for the files. It took care of everything—financial release, blank sheet (!) with person's signature, resignation, and an information sheet detailing name, address, and telephone number, and naming the members of the person's family.*

My Father
Pastor Jim Jones
Please don't let the
Bank of America
Savings + Loan
Foclose on my home
I will have the money
on this weekend Please
Father talk to Mr. Fleau
my Counselor 71 and I
promist I will not be
late again. Thank you
Father

Notes of faith such as this one came in every week from those who believed that Jim would take care of any problem.

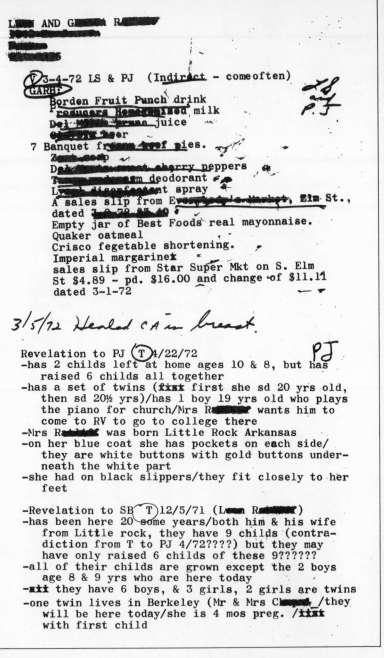

L█████ AND G█████ R█████

V 3-4-72 LS & PJ (Indirect - come often)
GARB:
    Borden Fruit Punch drink
    producers █████ised milk
    Del ███ ███ juice
    █████ ██er
7 Banquet fr███ ████ pies.
    Z██ ████p
    D██ ██████ █████ cherry peppers
    T█████████ ██ deodorant
    L████ disinfectant spray
    A sales slip from Ev████████ Market, Elm St.,
    dated █ █ 72 ██ ██
    Empty jar of Best Foods real mayonnaise.
    Quaker oatmeal
    Crisco fegetable shortening.
    Imperial margarinex
    sales slip from Star Super Mkt on S. Elm
    St $4.89 - pd. $16.00 and change of $11.11
    dated 3-1-72

3/5/72 Healed CA in breast.

Revelation to PJ (T) 4/22/72
-has 2 childs left at home ages 10 & 8, but has
  raised 6 childs all together
-has a set of twins (fixt first she sd 20 yrs old,
  then sd 20½ yrs)/has 1 boy 19 yrs old who plays
  the piano for church/Mrs R█████ wants him to
  come to RV to go to college there
-Mrs R█████ was born Little Rock Arkansas
-on her blue coat she has pockets on each side/
  they are white buttons with gold buttons underneath the white part
-she had on black slippers/they fit closely to her
  feet

-Revelation to SB (T) 12/5/71 (L███ R██████)
-has been here 20 some years/both him & his wife
  from Little rock, they have 9 childs (contradiction from T to PJ 4/72????) but they may
  have only raised 6 childs of these 9??????
-all of their childs are grown except the 2 boys
  age 8 & 9 yrs who are here today
-xxx they have 6 boys, & 3 girls, 2 girls are twins
-one twin lives in Berkeley (Mr & Mrs C█████ /they
  will be here today/she is 4 mos preg. /xixx
  with first child

This is one of thousands of files Jim used to get information for his "divine revelations." The codes on the paper indicate that the information was from a "V" (visit), and this visit was made by two of the staff members, one of whom was P.J. (Patty, Jr., Patty Cartmell's daughter). The information was gathered "Indirect" (without the person's knowledge), and the source of information was from their "GARB" (garbage can). The notation at the bottom of the information sheet indicates that on the day following the garbage can robbery, one of these people was "healed of cancer in the breast."

C 6/21/73 PC CARE RECENT TODAY
*B woman M█████ N███ told the Spirit she has a sister
Amenia ?7% S██████ who went on trip to California
-told Spirit had 4 sisters .5 including herself)
-on e broth er
-M██████ lives in Louisiana and has 6 childs .3 are
small yet;

This "C" (call) was made anonymously, much like the calls that Nita's son had received from a person "taking a survey." "P.C." (Patty Cartmell) indicates that she spoke with a woman who told the "spirit" (Patty) enough information about S.S. that Jim was able to use it to convince her she had passed a cancer. The pen scribbling on it is Jim Jones's handwriting, including the notation "Used passed cancer."

---

very enthusiastic when she
testified last nite/ came
here for an overhaul like
a mechanic would do with a
car

C 6/21/73 CRL CARE TODAY RECENT
-Mrs. S niece Pam-age 21█ speaking/ ████████████████████
███████████████████████████
█████████ Melvina also speaking/ ███████████ /think
Pam aunt is Mrs. S. daughter
-(basis of C giving away pupies--Mrs. S█████ wants a dog
Melvina says/

Another "C" (call), this time made by "C.R.L." (Carolyn Layton), to a niece. Again the information was sufficient to cause Jim to help her; as he notes in his own handwriting, "Passed female cancer. Had fibroid tumors." Carolyn's note CARE TODAY RECENT indicates that she had just made the call and Jim should take caution not to make her suspicious.

*A woman who had come all the way from Philadelphia to attend a
meeting in the Peoples Temple in San Francisco was convinced that she
had been healed of cancer. This release gave the church full permission
to use the information "any way they see fit."*

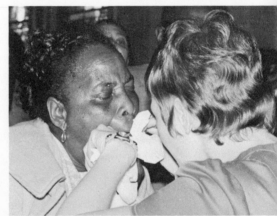

*In these two photos, taken within
a few seconds of each other, one
of Jim's assistants first inserts the
material (rotting chicken liver)
into the mouth of the gullible
"cancer" sufferer, causing her to
gag. When the material was spit
out (see second photo), she
actually believed that it had come
from her own body. The odor of
the material was revolting, and
Jim would shout from the pulpit,
"Stay away. That's a cancer!"
(Photo by Al Mills)*

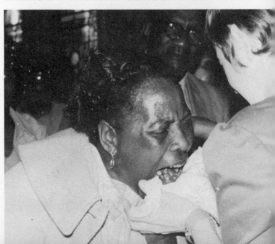

Rose Shelton was the person who most often assisted Jim with the "cancer healings." Here she is, standing beside a man who supposedly had just passed the mass of flesh that Rose is holding from his bowels. (Photo by Al Mills)

Jim is reaching from his platform to give an "anointed prayer cloth" to a woman who believed she was being healed by him. (Photo by Al Mills)

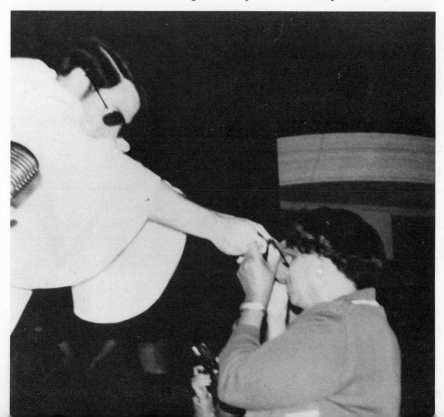

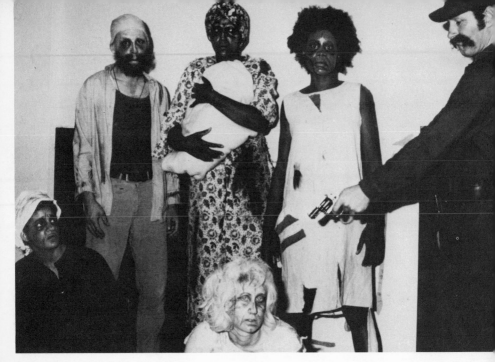

Jim Jones kept many of his black people frightened with frequent reminders of black oppression. He told us that he had a divine revelation that "all black people in America are going to be put into concentration camps or be hung— except for those who stay with me. I will protect you when that time comes." Plays like this one were graphic portrayals to those who remembered the days of slavery or who had heard the frightening stories of the midnight Ku Klux Klan raids. BELOW The many religious supporters of Jim Jones who publicly applauded his good works would have been horrified if they had seen him making fun of the "Sky God." Here is a photo of one of the plays the members performed during church services, poking fun at those who still believed in God. (Photos by Al Mills)

Every week the church was packed with people who wanted to hear Jim Jones preach. The balcony was filled with children who had learned to sit for as many as eight or nine hours at a time while the services were going on. (Photo by Al Mills)

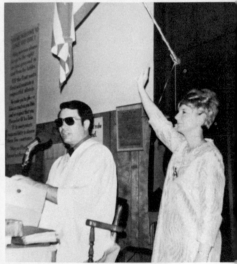

Photographs taken of Jim Jones and/or Marcelline Jones during the services. Most of these were later reproduced and sold at the picture stand during the church services. (Photos by Al Mills)

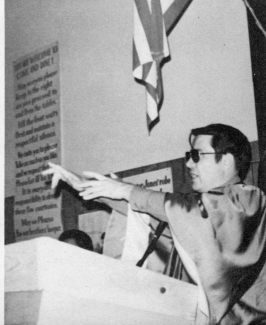

Jim had just "healed" this little girl of deafness, and her grandmother asked us to take a picture of them together. Jim smilingly obliged. (Photo by Al Mills)

Jim lovingly handed out allowances to the children in the early years. In later years, though, the allowances were given out by counsellors, and offering-takers would follow while Jim exhorted the children to "give your money to the Cause." (Photo by Al Mills)

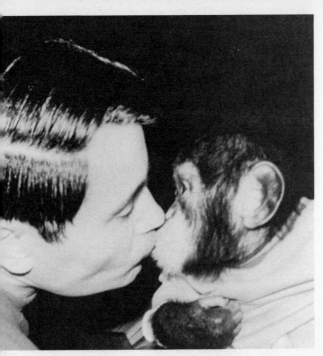

This photo was taken shortly after the church acquired "Mr. Muggs," a chimpanzee that had been destined to be used in scientific experimentation. Jim loved the little chimp at first, but later he began to teach Mr. Muggs to be mean. In Jonestown, Mr. Muggs received his cyanide along with everyone else. (Photo by Al Mills)

Here is a picture of Marcie Jones and her four sons. From left to right, they are Steven Jones (Jim's natural child), James Jones, Jr., Timothy Jones, Marcelline Jones, and Lew Jones. (Photo by Al Mills)

The Los Angeles Peoples Temple Church, on the corner of Hoover and Alvarado streets. (Photo by Al Mills)

The Redwood Valley Peoples Temple Church. To impress the neighbors, guards would often patrol the front of the church building. (Photo by Al Mills)

The eleven Greyhound-type buses made an impressive sight as they traveled up and down the freeways. People who saw these buses filled with smiling faces never realized the crowded, unsanitary conditions we were forced to travel in. Children were stuffed into the luggage racks, under the seats, and on the floors. There were usually more people sleeping in the baggage compartments underneath the bus. Occasionally spectators would ask why so many people were coming out of a small bus, but within minutes one of the counsellors would answer their questions by explaining that one bus had broken down a few miles up the road and the additional passengers had to crowd in for only a short time. (Photo by Al Mills)

Just a few doors down the street from the San Francisco temple the Black Muslims had their temple. Jim made strong overtures of friendship to this strong group, even sending large contingencies of our membership to attend their services, to which they responded by sending their members to our services. (Photo by Al Mills)

The apostolic guards. (Photo by Al Mills)

PART II

*

The Times That Try Men's Souls

I was born on July 2, 1939. My father left home when I was only a few years old, and my mother married a wonderful man who has been a real father to me to this day. Our family was deeply religious and belonged to the Seventh-day Adventist church. I went to their schools through my one year of college.

When I was twenty-one, I married a Seventh-day Adventist, and we had two children, Eddie and Daphene. After seven years, our marriage became untenable and we divorced. In order to keep in touch with people during this difficult period of my life, I joined a group called Parents Without Partners.

Al, my second husband, was born on July 28, 1928. When he was a year old—and his mother was bearing her seventh child—his father died. She raised all seven by herself. She was both mother and father to her kids.

As soon as Al finished college and army service, he married his childhood sweetheart, Zoe, and over the years they had five children. Al and Zoe were fervently dedicated to the principles of the Bill of Rights and worked steadfastly with groups to fight racism and inequality in the United States. Al marched in Selma, Alabama, with Martin Luther King, Jr.

Al and Zoe divorced after nineteen years of marriage. He then joined and became president of his local Parents Without

Partners. We met there in 1968. Al treated me like Cinderella at the ball; he made me feel wanted, comfortable, and like a princess. He was handsome, older, and more experienced, and he made me happy. I was confident that we would live "happily ever after" when we married not six months later.

By remarrying, my membership in the Seventh-day Adventist church would be revoked. To save me from the embarrassment of being voted out of the church that I'd attended all my life, a kind elder suggested I resign. I did just that. Because of my deep religious convictions, I thought that my resignation meant eternal doom in hell.

Al and I didn't have any friends in common to start with. The friends we'd had during our respective marriages had fallen away. Obviously, our common bond with the people in PWP was severed. We had our jobs, we had our home, we had each other. But, in time, we needed friends.

We were ripe for the Peoples Temple in 1969.

*   *   *

November 1969

Welcome, welcome all of you,
Glad you are with us,
Shake hands, no need to be blue,
Welcome to you.

He keeps me singing a happy song
He keeps me singing it all day long
For all the things that we drear
He is always near
And that's why my heart is always filled with song,
Singing, singing
All day long.
                    —from a Peoples Temple song

It had been a particularly trying day. Linda had admitted that she was using marijuana, Diana and Steve had been fighting, and Daphene was out in the barn doing heaven-knows-what with a naughty visitor named Freddie. Eddie, as usual, was up in his room all alone, reading. As I looked around at our family, I wondered if there was an encyclopedia that could tell me just the right words to say to each child to help them cope with the problems they were facing.

Al and I had been married for only one year. I had two children of my own: Eddie, who was eight years old, and Daphene, who had just turned six. When we got married, Al brought twelve-year-old Steve, ten-year-old Linda, and nine-year-old Diana into our home.

Al had to travel almost three hours a day to get to and from work, and I was on the road for an hour and a half each day. When we got home at night it seemed impossible to get all the chores done. To make matters worse, Al and I were discovering that we didn't have much in common. After a year of sometimes heated discussion, it turned out that our ideologies were very different.

The two things we did share, however, were our love for our children and our love for the goats we were raising on our small farm in Hayward. Al would get up at the crack of dawn to milk our old nanny goat and play with her kids. But this wasn't enough.

We had talked about going to a church, but every Sunday it

seemed we were just too busy to spend an hour away from the house, even though the church we had decided to attend was not far from home. We rarely bothered to socialize with anyone, but we knew we needed to discuss the changes our marriage was going through, so we decided to spend the evening with the minister who had married us and his wife.

Bob and Adele lived in the Berkeley hills. Adele opened the door and ushered us into their lovely living room with its big picture window overlooking the bay. The bright lights of the city were twinkling and there was a clear view of the Golden Gate Bridge and the Bay Bridge. After a pleasant dinner we sat down to discuss our problems.

"I met a most remarkable man recently," Bob said. "He is a minister of a small Disciples of Christ Church in Redwood Valley. This minister claims that he has helped thirty young people kick the drug habit." At the mention of young people kicking the drug habit, I began to listen intently.

Bob continued, "We are going to take a few friends to Redwood Valley this Sunday to one of his church services. Perhaps you and Jeannie would like to go along."

Al didn't reply, so I answered for him. "We really would like to see him." Bob smiled and we began to make arrangements to meet him at six o'clock the following Sunday morning.

"There'll be plenty of room," he assured us. "We have chartered an old school bus. The trip should take about three and a half hours, so be sure to be on time."

As we left, we promised Bob that we would meet with him at six o'clock.

At five o'clock the following Sunday morning the alarm went off. Sunday was our only morning to sleep in, and I found myself wishing I hadn't been so hasty in accepting the invitation. I almost hoped Al had changed his mind as I asked him, "Are you really up for a three-and-a-half-hour trip this morning?"

"Well," he answered sleepily, "we're awake now, so we might as well get up. Bob would be disappointed if we changed our minds." We had arranged for my mother to take care of our children for the day, and with all the chores we had lined up for our five children we were sure she wouldn't have much trouble with them. We grabbed a couple of cinnamon rolls, quickly drank some coffee, and headed for the parking lot where the bus was waiting. Bob hadn't been kidding when he said that the bus was old. It was ancient. The seats felt like boards. Instead of a "few friends," it looked as if there were already too many people there to fit into the little bus. I noted with discomfort that many of the "friends" were black, and, to make matters worse, there were several small children and even a crying baby. My dream of getting away from kids for a day vanished.

With poorly concealed bigotry I had always said, "I'm not a racist—*but.*" I had been brought up to think that black people were fine—in their own neighborhoods, in their own schools, and as far away as possible from me. One or two of them were okay and might be interesting to talk to, but once they were together in a group with me—well, I didn't know what then, but I didn't really want to find out either. I found a seat next to a window and beckoned for Al to sit next to me. I didn't want to sit beside a black person for three and a half hours!

Usually I didn't take time to think about black people. But here, in this crowded and noisy bus, I was forced to think about them.

I remembered the first time I had visited Al in his bachelor house. He lived in the heart of Richmond and was the only white in the neighborhood. It had never occurred to me that he might have voluntarily chosen to live there. I assumed that it was because he didn't have enough money after his divorce to buy a home in a "proper" neighborhood. Then I remembered that he had said something about marching in Selma, Alabama, with Martin Luther King. It suddenly popped into my mind that one of our first dates had been a very disagreeable evening when he had taken me to hear Bobby Seale preach. I had heard more profanity and ugly remarks that evening than I could remember in my entire sheltered life. I began to realize that I had been blinded by my physical attraction to Al, and that I hadn't realized what I was getting myself into. Maybe he and Bob had arranged this trip to force me to be with black people. "Oh, God," I thought. "What if this is a black church and a black minister?" I had never been in a black church before. Even when I went to hear Bobby Seale, the audience had been mostly white hippies and radicals. My thoughts were decidedly racist, and I felt ashamed. I reminded myself that I should treat "these people" kindly.

Al and I didn't talk much during the bus ride. The trip was unbelievably long. The children became cross and rowdy. Food was being passed back and forth among the chattering passengers, all of whom seemed to know one another. By the time the bus reached Redwood Valley I was out of sorts.

We drove past a big brown building that looked like a barn with a cross above it. We pulled in beside the barn and the bus noisily rolled over the large stones in the parking lot. There were grape vineyards on either side of the parking lot and a stone house behind the barn that I now realized was the church. It was even painted barn red. I wondered for a moment why anyone would want to make a church look like a barn, but then I became preoccupied with other thoughts.

As the bus pulled into the space I was relieved to see many white people walking around outside of the building. The bus was being parked quite a distance from the church and I realized, with disgust, that I was going to have to walk a long rocky path in my high-heeled shoes.

It was such a relief to get off the bus and away from the noisy passengers that I didn't notice a young woman walking toward us. "Hi, I'm Linda Amos. Jim healed me of stomach cancer. I had been told by my doctor that I would die within six months, and I had even tried to find another home for my children, but Jim healed me and now I am well."

Al's first thought was that Linda had escaped from the nearby mental hospital and had wandered onto the church grounds by mistake. I whispered a prayer of gratitude that we'd left our children home. As Linda walked away, Al and I exchanged puzzled glances.

"Do you think this preacher is supposed to be a healer?" I asked him.

"No, I think that woman is crazy," he responded.

Another girl came toward us. "My name is Christine Lucientis. My mind had been destroyed by using too many drugs. Jim gave me a reason to live and helped put my life back together. Now I'm helping other young people kick the drug habit in our Drug Rehabilitation Center." Her sincerity was touching, but, with a jolt, I realized that there was more going on here than we had expected. The other passengers from the bus were also being greeted by various church members.

Although I hadn't been inside a church for more than a year, I still held sacred my beliefs about God and the Devil. I began to worry about which of the two I was about to meet. I didn't have much time to wonder about this, though, because a comely young man was walking toward us. "I was in a car accident," he said with a warm and wonderful smile. "I was pronounced clinically dead. But when Jim touched me I came back to life!" It was hard to believe the stories these people were telling us, but each time there was another member beside the storyteller saying, "I was there and I saw it happen."

We were ushered into the church building where the first five rows had been reserved for our group. The church building was much bigger than it had appeared. A large indoor swimming pool took up the back third of the building. The rest of the auditorium was filled with folding chairs, and I was surprised to notice that all the seats were filled. People were even sitting behind the swimming pool.

Brightly colored posters were on the walls and the American flag was proudly displayed in the front beside the speaker's platform. We could see women bustling around the kitchen taking platters of food from various members.

The people attending the church were dressed casually. Most of the girls, and many of the women, were wearing jeans and slacks. It seemed more like a P.T.A. meeting than a church service.

The members all looked normal. In fact, they were the happiest and most wholesome-looking people we had ever seen. Several of the people already seated came over to welcome us, and a few even embraced us. I was still concerned about the strange stories we had been told as we walked into the church, and I whispered to Al, "He might be the Devil." Al didn't even smile. He agreed that this was all strange.

We couldn't help feeling intrigued by what we were seeing and feeling. We watched the young people's choir walk in. All the women were dressed in sleeveless dresses and the men wore black pants and ties. Black and white faces made a checker-board pattern that was pleasant to watch. Throughout the room, black and white people were seated together. We saw white parents holding black children, and white children sitting on the laps of black parents. There seemed to be no racism in this atmosphere of peace and love and I began to relax. A young black woman flashed a smile at me as though she could read my thoughts. I returned her smile and decided to start being friendly with black people.

The choir's music was professional and inspiring. When the young people finished singing, they sat down and a blond man asked the children to come forward. More than fifty youngsters, from tiny toddlers to eleven-year-olds went to the front of the room. The sight of these black and white children smiling and holding hands was strangely satisfying. I had never before witnessed the warmth and love I was seeing in this totally integrated group, and their songs were sweet and simple. This made a strong impression on me. Our children were so wrapped up in their own problems that they could think only of themselves. Here were children learning about social justice and singing songs about love and freedom. Their radiant faces conveyed the message of the songs as eloquently as their voices. As they finished they went back to their seats in a group. These young children sat through the remaining hours of the service much more patiently than I was able to.

A tall, good-looking man smiled as he stepped up to the

microphone. "Now you can have the opportunity to tell about the wonderful things you have experienced." I was familiar with giving testimonies about answered prayers and I wondered if I had recently had any prayers answered. I couldn't think of any, so I didn't raise my hand. An hour later I was going to be thankful I hadn't.

About twenty-five people stood up, as if on cue, and formed a line in the front. "There is a three-minute time limit on what you say, so please be brief," someone admonished the people standing in line.

A large, elderly black woman stepped up to the microphone, smiled, and began. "My pastor, Jim Jones, healed me of cancer. I had suffered for years with pains in my stomach. Two months ago I spit up a cancer right here in this room. I am so thankful for my healing that I want to sing a song." She immediately began to sing a beautiful Negro spiritual. The audience joined her in the chorus, and I realized that she must have sung this song before. Everyone knew when they were supposed to join in without any prompting.

Another woman stepped up and testified, "My pastor saved my life. I was in a car accident and should have been killed but because of the love of Jim Jones I was able to walk away from the scene of the accident." This was a middle-aged white woman who had been sitting next to Al earlier.

I found it disconcerting that these people, who seemed to be so devoted to their pastor and to have so much respect for him, found it comfortable to call him by his first name. In my church the ministers were always called Elder or Pastor. No one dared address them with this kind of familiarity.

Linda Amos, the first woman who had greeted us in the parking lot, stepped forward and walked to the microphone. "One day Jim was in a council meeting with several of us and we were discussing church business. Suddenly he said, "Someone needs me." I rushed out to the car with him and he drove directly to a house I didn't recognize. We ran to the door and a crying woman answered. He walked past the woman and into their dining room. There, lying on the floor in a pool of blood, was a man with a mark on his forehead that looked like a bullet hole." Linda took out her handkerchief and wiped the tears from her eyes as she continued, "Jim lovingly picked up the man's head and put his hand on his bleeding forehead. I thought the man was dead, but as Jim held his lifeless head in his lap the man's eyes seemed to come back into focus and he started to smile. As Jim lifted his hand up the bullet fell out of his forehead and onto the floor. The man stood up and looked around as if he was trying to remember what had happened. He asked Jim what we were doing there and Jim just shook his hand. He told them both about our church and our humanitarian works and we left. This is only one example of the hundreds of times Jim has reached out with compassion to help people he doesn't even know. He is always concerned about people who are suffering."

I asked Al why Linda would have gone with Jim. Al thought Linda must be one of Jim's most trusted workers. I noticed that throughout the rest of the meeting Linda was speaking to different members. She seemed to be giving them messages. The people she spoke to never answered her, they just nodded their heads.

I calculated that each testimony was taking about five minutes. There were still twenty-three standing in line. I was already bored and there were almost two hours of this testifying left. More testimonies about healings and miracles were related, some by weeping women and some by children. A few men also told about personal miracles they had experienced through Jim's ministry.

After each testimony the members of the church applauded. In the church I had attended the loudest noise anyone ever made was an occasional "amen" and even that had sounded out of place. It took some time before I could bring myself to join in the clapping because it seemed sacrilegious, but when I finally did I found it pleasant to be able to participate in the service.

Fortunately the next twenty-two people weren't as long-winded as the first three, and within forty-five minutes the last person was through. I was trying to visualize myself testifying about an answered prayer when I suddenly realized that not one of the twenty-five people had mentioned prayer, God, or Jesus. Each of them had given all the praise and glory to Jim Jones. I mentioned this to Al.

"Yes, it is strange," Al agreed. "I really don't know what to expect next." As we were whispering to each other Jim quietly took his seat behind the pulpit and as we looked up he was already sitting down.

Jim Jones was sitting on a high, barber-type chair behind a large custom-built pulpit. This pulpit was constructed with many shelves on each side and a well top so that neither the audience nor the people seated in front could see his notes. Behind him was a beautiful stained-glass window with a large, many-pointed star design and doves flying through the star. With the American flag on one side of him and the framed Declaration of Independence on the other side, it made a very unusual setting for a minister. I wondered why he was seated.

His appearance was striking. He was wearing large dark

glasses and a maroon turtle-neck sweater. With his jet black hair and long sideburns he didn't look like the typical minister.

Al whispered to me, "He looks like a humble man. I'm sure all this praise and worship is offensive to him. He'll probably tell these people that they should be giving God the glory."

I searched the minister's face for any frown of disapproval toward those who had heaped all this praise on him, but instead I saw a self-assured smile. It seemed strange to look at a preacher who was wearing sunglasses. My mind began to wander and for a moment I thought about Alice when she stepped through the looking glass and suddenly nothing made sense. That's the way this church seemed.

I'd never heard of a church where black and white people intermingled freely. I had never seen a minister sit at the pulpit. Who ever heard of a pulpit where the minister's notes were hidden? The choir was singing popular songs of the day instead of traditional hymns. Instead of organ music we were listening to a band that should have been playing at a dance. Instead of children sitting restlessly beside their parents, these children were sitting quietly and respectfully together. The young people, instead of clustering together and breaking off into moony-eyed couples, were singing in the choir or talking comfortably with visitors. In any church I had ever visited no one spoke to the visitors, except perhaps a specially assigned "greeter" at the door, but here I had been made to feel like I was a part of the church family on my first day.

My wandering thoughts were interrupted by Jim Jones's powerful voice. "Thank you, and bless you all," he said, nodding to the congregation of people who had risen to their feet and were clapping at his arrival. Al looked at me strangely.

"He seems to be accepting all this praise for himself," he observed. We both realized by this time that Jim Jones was not going to give God any glory. He obviously felt he deserved it all himself.

A funny thing I've noticed about human nature is that when someone feels he deserves respect, he usually gets it. I couldn't help but be awed by his confidence and even his arrogance. Once again I had the feeling of jumping through Alice's looking glass. This man was dressed so casually that he appeared to be humble and unassuming; yet his words commanded the attention and respect of every person in the room.

Jim began to speak now and the atmosphere was electrically charged. He seemed to be speaking to each person individually. There were more than 500 people in the audience and not a whisper could be heard throughout the building. His message was filled with love, and with fire. He explained why he was seated: "You're sitting down, why shouldn't I?"

He was saying things that neither of us had ever heard before. He wasn't making any claims about having supernatural power or explaining why he felt he deserved all this praise and adoration, but he was eloquently telling the people in the room the things he didn't believe in. "The King James Bible is full of contradictions and errors," he said angrily. "The slave owners forced black people to take the King James religion and forsake their own beautiful African beliefs. Any black person who still believes in the Bible is a sellout." He quoted several contradictions in the King James Bible, throwing out texts as proof for people who were still perverse enough to believe in the Bible. "Copy these texts down and check them when you get home if you don't believe me," he threw out as a challenge. I glanced around trying to find a Bible so I could look up these texts to prove him wrong, but again I was to be surprised. There wasn't a Bible in sight. Not one person had brought a copy along, and there weren't any Bibles on the shelves around the room.

He was still shouting about the errors in the Bible, and he began to throw in a few spicy swear words to make his point perfectly clear. I was shocked and offended. "How can he say things like that about God's Holy Word and get away with it?" I asked Al in a whisper.

As if he had heard my words, Jim smiled and said, "If there were a God in Heaven, do you think he would let me say these things about His Holy Word?" and looking up toward the ceiling, he shook his fist violently and challenged, "If there is a God in Heaven, let Him strike me dead!"

I waited. I'd had a fundamentalist upbringing, and I visualized Jim clutching his throat, unable to breathe, writhing in pain all over the floor of the podium. I was certain a bolt of lightning would come out of heaven and strike him, but nothing happened. The room became silent as Jim grinned and said, "Someone in this room is waiting," and the entire audience, with the exception of a few of the visitors, burst into laughter. My faith took a sharp nose dive and I braced myself for what was still to come.

Jim had just begun. The two hours that followed were like a roller-coaster ride for my emotions. This man believed the exact opposite of everything I had ever been taught. He said things like "The only people who are practicing real religion outside of our church are the Black Panthers." I remembered the foul-mouthed Bobby Seale and tried to fathom how Jim could call that religion. Then he said that prostitutes had more love and compassion for the poor than any minister, with the exception of himself. He preached on and on...and on. He talked about the current political problems, the war in Vietnam, which he claimed to have prophesied, the government-supported drug racketeering in our country, the social injustices committed against the minorities, the religious hypocrisy in every church but his, and then he finally got around to telling the audience the secret he had been hinting at throughout his sermon.

"I have seen by divine revelation the total annihilation of this country and many other parts of the world. San Francisco will be flattened. The only survivors will be those people who are hidden in the cave that I have been shown in a vision. Those who go into this cave with me will be saved from the poisonous radioactive fallout that will follow the nuclear bomb attack. This cave is what led our church to migrate to this little valley from Indianapolis, Indiana. I have been shown that this cave goes deep into the earth. All the members of my church will stay in it until it is safe to come out. We have gathered in Redwood Valley for protection, and after the war is over we will be the only survivors. It will be up to our group to begin life anew on this continent. Then we will begin a truly ideal society just as you see it here in this room today. People will care about one another. Elderly people will be made to feel needed and will be allowed to be productive. People's needs will be met because they are loved, and not because they have money. This church family is an example of what society will eventually be like all over the world. There will at last be peace on earth. I have seen this all by divine revelation."

Jim asked those in the congregation who had been told the exact year, month, day, and minute to raise their hands, and about twenty hands went up. These people nodded their heads indicating that they had indeed been told the exact time this holocaust was going to take place. "My prophecy included thirteen time cycles," Jim said ominously. "We are entering the twelfth cycle now. The thirteenth cycle is very close."

My logical, rational mind didn't want to believe any of this nonsense, but in November 1969, talk of bombs and war was very prevalent. Radio and television broadcasts were interrupted a couple of times each day with the words "This is a test. If this had been an actual alert you would have been told to tune in to..." The war in Vietnam was in the news every day, and we all lived one day at a time, never knowing when some power-crazed leader would take all our lives into his own hands to prove that his country was stronger than any other country.

Every person seems to have a built-in desire to live out her or his natural life span and I was no exception. I forgave Jim for his arrogance, his profanity, and his interminably long sermon, and began to feel some respect for him. He was the first person I had heard who seemed to have a method of salvation from the bomb that I had been fearing for almost twenty years. I still didn't want to join his church but I thought I would put our names on his mailing list. Jim promised that the people who were on this list would be notified two weeks in advance of the actual bomb attack so they could join his members in the cave.

Now Jim stopped speaking and nodded to his organist. Soft religious music filled the air and in a very quiet voice he called out, "Hendricks. Is there someone here named Hendricks?"

A man near the back of the room stood up. Jim asked, "Do you live in a white house with red cement steps and green shutters?"

"Yes, I do."

"And is there an elderly woman who would be sitting on a rocking chair and rocking back and forth right now on your front porch?"

"Yes, there is! That's my mother." Astonishment and anticipation were written on his face. He waited, hardly breathing, to find out what else Jim could see by revelation about him.

"Is your mother's name Isabella?" Jim asked, "and does she have a red shawl that she sometimes wears on windy days?"

"Yes, yes, yes!" the man shouted.

"I am being shown that tomorrow morning at about seven-thirty, when you would have been leaving for work, you would have had an accident and died, but since you came here today you will not have that accident. You will live!" Jim dramatically took a small red cloth from his pulpit and held it out in front of him. "Take this red cloth and wear it on your body for the rest of this month and you will also be relieved of that pain you have been suffering in your side."

"Oh, thank you, thank you, God!" Mr. Hendricks was crying real tears as he walked up to the front. He took the prayer cloth from Jim's hand and clutched it to his heart. The audience clapped their hands as the organist pealed out a song of praise.

Jim looked around the room again and in a loud voice called out, "Wilson." The room became silent.

"Yes?" This time it was a middle-aged black woman sitting near the front.

"You have been having a dull pain in your stomach even as you sit here today."

"Yes."

"To give you more faith I want you to know that I can see a bottle of aspirin in your bathroom medicine chest. It's sitting beside a prescription bottle that was given to you by a Dr. Edwards."

Mrs. Wilson, who had been speaking softly, suddenly shouted out, "Yes, Lord!"

"Who can know these things?" Jim asked with a sweet smile.

Tears were flowing down her cheeks as she answered, "Only God could know."

"You have a cancer in your stomach. You don't even know it is there but by the power of love I will make it pass."

Mrs. Wilson went into the restroom with one of the women that Jim indicated was a nurse and a few minutes later they returned. The nurse was holding a mass of smelly flesh covered with blood in a handful of tissues. Jim asked the nurse to take it around to show those who might be skeptical. He took his dark glasses off for a moment as he looked lovingly at the woman and said, "This is the cancer that left your body, and I tell you that it will never return. Praise God!" And praise she did, along with everyone else in the room. But the praise was not for God, it was all directed toward Jim Jones.

As I watched all this, I was perplexed. I had never heard of a church where people were healed. In my church, miracles were something that had happened in biblical days. My mind swirled in confusion, speculating that they might be phony displays, but on the other hand the people seemed to be so thankful when Jim healed them that I also believed they might be real.

The healing service went on for another hour and a half. I was getting hungry and bored, and Al told me that he was ready to go home, too. We looked around to see if everyone else was getting tired of sitting so long, but the members of the church were still enthusiastically praising as Jim healed others, so we waited. At five o'clock in the afternoon, the meeting that had begun at eleven o'clock that morning finally came to a close, or at least it appeared that it was over.

A hot meal was quickly set up on some tables in the rear of the room, in front of the swimming pool. Ushers took the chairs to the side of the room and we noticed that each member, including the children, picked up his or her own chair and put it in the racks provided. Within a few minutes the church had been turned into a dining hall with paper tablecloths and decorations on each table. The long rows of tables were set up so that every person seated could still see the front of the auditorium, where Jim was sitting before the pulpit. He announced, "Guests will be first in line, seniors and children next, and members last." No one grumbled about being hungry and not one child tried to push in front of the line.

The dinner was delicious We were beginning to enjoy our meal when someone at the microphone shouted, "Everyone please be quiet. Jim has something to say." Jim began and droned on and on. Throughout the meal all the people were quiet and respectful so they could hear each word. As the meal ended the ushers began to set up the chairs again for another meeting that was about to begin.

Bob gathered the passengers for our bus together and asked if anyone wanted to stay for the evening meeting. The vote was unanimously against. Everyone was anxious to leave. A few people admitted that the sermon had been interesting, but no one wanted to sit through any more. Al and Bob explained to one of the ushers that it was late and the bus had a long way to go.

Jim could see that we were leaving and he called out a cheery good-bye from his seat. "I want to extend each of you an invitation to return whenever you wish," he called out as we left.

During the long bus ride home there was a lot of conversation. A woman sitting behind us was talking to her friend. "I'll never go back there. That man sounds like a communist to me."

Bob and Adele decided that they had seen enough and weren't going to return. Bob confessed, "I hadn't been aware of some of the more bizarre aspects of the church such as the healings and the hero worship."

Another woman commented dryly, "He may be doing a lot of good things, but I don't think a person should swear at God. It's dangerous." Most of the people on the bus agreed that this church was a place they never wanted to visit again.

Al and I, too, had decided that even though it had been an interesting experience we would never return. The service had been a physically and emotionally draining experience. I was frightened by some of the things I had heard and I decided to put the church and this strange preacher out of my mind forever. By unspoken agreement, neither Al nor I mentioned Peoples Temple again for the next two days.

Then letters began arriving at our home, as well as at the homes of all those who had visited the church that Sunday. Several of the letters we received were long, but most of them were short, only a few sentences. They all said essentially the same things. The members wrote that they had enjoyed our visit and hoped we would return. Each letter related one miracle that the writer claimed to have personally experienced, and every person praised the miraculous power of Jim Jones. A box of homemade candy arrived the following Saturday with another cordial invitation to return sometime. It was difficult to forget Peoples Temple when every day I found another reminder in our mailbox.

At first I refused to touch the candy. But when I saw Al and the children enjoying it, I finally relented and had some, too.

Al began to dream about Jim Jones. He would wake up restless and try to put it out of his mind, but he began to seem so troubled that I asked what was bothering him. He told me about his strange dreams, and I had to admit that I was having similar dreams. In fact, twice while I was at work, I had actually felt as if Jim Jones were in my head and I was looking out at the world through his eyes. I never before had such an eerie experience, and it frightened me.

I was more sure than ever that Jim had to be the Devil. Al and I began to have long discussions about the church. Neither of us could explain what we had seen and heard or why we were having these disturbing dreams.

In one of my dreams, Jim was a giant whale swimming frantically around in a little pond. The whale found two little fishes (which I thought represented Al and me) and protected them from any harm. As a rule, I wasn't able to remember most of my dreams but this one was so frightening that I recalled it vividly.

The letters continued to arrive, sometimes as many as five in one day. The writers informed us of the amazing healings they were witnessing and the blissful lives they were living, and about their leader, Jim Jones, who made certain that their every need was met. One writer boasted, "There is no sickness here, no hunger and no death. In fact, this church is the closest thing to paradise on earth."

Al called one of the men who had visited the church with us that day, to find out if they were getting as many letters as we had. He said that he and his wife had already received forty-two letters and the box of candy, but that his wife just threw them all away. The man indicated that he was disturbed by the volume of letters, but more by his wife's extreme fear of Jim Jones. "I'm not sure about those miracles either," he said suspiciously. "Either Jim has a lot of power or he has a lot of people lying for him."

I was beginning to wonder if I might have been wrong in my first judgments of him. The Bible text "By their fruits ye shall know them" kept ringing in my ears. I realized how cold and unfriendly most churches were, especially compared with the warm, loving people we had met at Peoples Temple. I was able to see black people in a new light. They were no different than I was. Why, I wondered, hadn't anyone ever shown me that before?

Our children seemed to be more difficult than ever now, in comparison to the cherubic youngsters we had seen listening intently for six and a half hours while Jim preached. I thought about their friendly smiles as I watched our children bickering. When Steve grumbled about his food, I thought about the rows of children we had watched eating every morsel on their plates without a murmur. As I mopped up Daphene's spilled milk, I remembered seeing a six-year-old girl in the church run into the kitchen for a cloth to wipe up some punch an adult had accidently spilled. Instead of fading into our memories, Peoples Temple was becoming a big part of our daily thoughts.

As Al and I continued to discuss Jim and his church, we were becoming more and more aware of how different our fundamental beliefs were. I was still a "Bible-toting Christian," and Al considered himself to be an agnostic. He didn't know if there was a God and he really didn't care.

I had to honestly admit that I wouldn't feel comfortable in a church with so many black members, but Al had always been a crusader for the rights of minorities.

"I'd enjoy the integration," he said, "but I wouldn't want to sit in a meeting for that many hours again." Already we were moving closer to the time when we would join the church, but neither of us would admit it, even to ourselves.

We began to talk about this unusual church to our friends at work and one man asked if he could go see for himself. Six weeks had passed since our first visit and we had talked so much about the church that our children wanted to see it, too. We agreed to take Al's friend the following week but we explained that we were going to take our five children, too.

As our station wagon drove through Ukiah it began to feel as if we were driving toward a family reunion. This church and Jim Jones had become so much a part of our thoughts and our conversations that I was actually looking forward to our return. I wondered if the people would be as friendly to our family as they had been to us when we were a part of the large visiting group. The man we were bringing was asking a lot of questions and we found ourselves explaining and defending the bizzare things we had seen there.

I had almost forgotten the long hours we had sat just six weeks ago. Somehow the hunger, boredom, and hostility that I felt then had disappeared and I was only remembering the love and warmth that we were greeted with that Sunday. Instead of thinking about the puzzling miracles, I was recalling the beauty of black and white people living together without any barriers between them.

*   *   *

Our car was pulling into the rocky parking lot. This time I had worn sensible shoes because I knew what to expect. Smiles of recognition greeted us as we walked toward the church. By the time we entered the building, all our children had been invited by other children to sit with them. People we didn't remember seeing during our previous visit came up and talked to us, calling us by name. We hadn't written to tell anyone we were returning and I couldn't believe that so many people would remember us.

As we stepped inside the church, Jim Jones walked over to us. He was dressed casually and didn't have his dark glasses on. His warm smile and extended hand made me forget some of my earlier antagonism. He looked directly into my eyes as he said, "I'm so glad you returned. We were all hoping you would."

He smiled at Al as though they were sharing a common secret and said to me, "Some people confuse our communal way of life with communism. Actually it has nothing to do with politics. If everyone would live as we do here, there would be no need to fear a communist takeover in our country. Our church could be this country's answer to fight communism." Either Jim had a psychic ability or he was one of the most sensitive persons I had ever met. He seemed to sense that this was one of the things that bothered me most. I relaxed. As long as I knew that Jim wasn't trying to threaten the democracy I loved, I would listen to whatever else he had to say.

Once again the singing was inspiring. This time there were only a few testimonies and Jim's sermon was fascinating. Now that I had stopped trying to find fault with him, a lot of the things he was saying made sense. When he talked about the errors in the Bible, I agreed. I had looked up each of the texts he had quoted and, to my amazement, he was right. The Bible was not perfect. Not only had I found errors, but in one of the reference books he suggested I had found that the God of the Old Testament was a cruel tyrant. My mind was open to hear his message because my own beliefs had become very shaky.

Jim told the congregation that he had the answers to the world's problems. If each of his members would follow him in complete faith, the church could end poverty, racism, political oppression, hunger, and even death. Who could resist such a panacea?

Although Al's friend was not impressed, our children loved every minute of it. We were happy to see them smiling and associating with wholesome-looking friends. Each time we looked over to where they were sitting, we saw them looking at Jim with rapt attention. Their new-found friends answered all their questions and begged them to come back again, often. My thoughts meandered back to my own childhood. In all the years I attended church, I never felt the warmth and friendliness that our family was being shown here as visitors.

As the service was ending, Jim asked all the small children in the audience to come forward and he gave each one a sweet hug. All our children, except Steve, the oldest, went up and enjoyed Jim's embrace. I had never seen anything so beautiful in my life.

All the way home our children were bubbling over with enthusiasm about the wonderful time they'd had. "Please, Dad and Mom, could we join this church?" they begged. We had to admit that we enjoyed the service more this time and we told the children that we'd think it over. Somehow, though, we knew that it was only a matter of time before we were going to become members of Peoples Temple.

*   *   *

1970

My desire is to love you truly,
And to do your holy will,
To be whole-hearted, consecrated,
Self-denying and real.

It's true, I never knew,
That I'd be living in heaven today,
Living with God in a body,
Who's ruling and reigning and having his way.

Mind and attention,
Love and devotion,
Ideas and opinions
All directed to you.
                    —from a Peoples Temple song

Every Sunday the seven of us would drive 120 miles to church. We began to appreciate the long meetings, because we were told that spiritual growth comes from self-sacrifice. Jim's sermons no longer seemed long or boring. Now we listened to every word he said so that we could learn to make the world a better place for everyone.

It took a few months for us to sell our lovely farm home in Hayward and find a farm in Redwood Valley. Jim put us in contact with a real estate agent who found us a large farm only seven miles from the church. Things went so smoothly with this transaction that it seemed to confirm the correctness of our decision to join this church family. Our new home was more beautiful than either of us had hoped.

It was a rambling five-bedroom house nestled at the foot of a hill with the beautiful Russian River winding through the center of the lot. There was a massive living room walled by floor-to-ceiling glass doors and windows, and a lovely stone fireplace.

A small A-frame cabin was on the other side of the circular driveway. It was perfect for my parents. There was also an acre across the bridge where "Grandma," as my mother was called, would be able to plant her garden. Our children fell in love with the new home as soon as they saw it, and we couldn't think of any reason to say no. We put a down payment on the property and began to make preparations to move.

Now that we had signed the escrow papers, we knew that our decision to move was irreversible. It was time to quit our jobs. Jim had extended the same promise to us that he did to every new member. "If you will move to the valley, I promise that I will find you jobs. Your family will always be provided for, and your bills will always be paid." Led on by this security, we quit our jobs and moved.

Happiness flooded our lives. The guarded words of caution from our well-meaning friends fell on ears that could only hear the promise of Jim: "I will take care of my family." We had enough money to live on for several months and we knew that in time Jim would provide jobs for us.

* * *

From time to time Al and I would ask one another, "What did we do with our lives before we joined this group?" and we would answer that life hadn't seemed worthwhile until Jim instilled a sense of purpose in us and gave us a reason to live. We wanted to please him because we believed that he loved us. We were certain that as long as we stayed in his group our lives would continue to be blissful.

My parents were unhappy about our move at first. They had been living in a one-bedroom trailer house on our farm and we assumed that they would want to move where they could have the lovely cabin. Grandma was uneasy about living so close to a church that she didn't believe in. "What if Jim Jones decides that he doesn't want us around?" she asked.

"Oh, Mom," I answered, "you don't need to worry about that. Jim is a very loving man and told us it would be fine for you to live with us. We will need you more than ever now to help us with the cooking and the care of the animals. Please don't worry." I was sure that once my mother met Jim Jones she would never worry about anything again.

Grandma continued to be uneasy, though, until she actually saw the beautiful cabin that was ready for her and Grandpa. Then she relented. She looked at the garden area and felt as if she was returning to the mountain home she had lived in as a young girl.

Without any doubt, we knew now that this home would bring happiness to every member of the family. We packed our belongings and began to move. The truck, the car, and a rented trailer made several long trips back and forth. Charlie, our rapidly growing calf, was the hardest animal to move, but with the help of several neighbors we finally got him into the trailer. All the rabbits, chickens, ducks, cats, dogs, birds, and, of course, our beautiful goats, were transported to their new home. Without a backward glance, we at last made our trip. Finally, late at night, every animal was in its assigned place and all our children were settled into their bedrooms.

A few days after our move, Grandma noticed a bad odor coming from our front yard. Al called a sewer inspector to come to see what the problem was, and after an inspection he told us some very bad news. "Your leach lines are all clogged. You will have to have new lines dug immediately, and it will cost about five hundred dollars." Al mentioned this to one of the church counsellors, and he told Al not to worry.

Al didn't understand why until the next morning. As we were finishing our breakfast we looked out the kitchen window and saw two carloads of church members and a large dump truck driving toward our house. The men had picks, shovels, and wheelbarrows with them. In one day fifteen men dug an entire new leach-line system, hauled in the gravel, and re-covered the yard. When Al offered to pay them for the work, they laughed.

Grandma and Grandpa couldn't believe their eyes. They had never seen a church that was so willing to respond to members' needs. The men ate Grandma's delicious hot lunch and thanked her. They said they didn't get much home cooking and Grandma, whose cooking is superb, felt an immediate kinship with them. Over the years she was affectionately called "Grandma" by the hundreds of church members who visited our home. Neither she nor Grandpa ever joined the church, but they both accepted the church members as a part of their family.

Each morning I would scan the classified ads in the Ukiah *Daily Journal* for jobs. One day I found an ad that sounded perfect. "Executive secretary needed for small, one-girl office. Must have knowledge of full bookkeeping procedures. 600 dollars per month." I telephoned and made an appointment for an interview. All the other jobs I had read about were paying between $400 and $500 a month, and I knew we would need more than that. The job was in an electronics shop a little more than a mile from our home. Since we lived fourteen miles from Ukiah, it was unusual to find any job near us, and to find one that paid well was nothing short of a miracle. With a confidence inspired by Jim's promise that we would find jobs, I applied knowing that this job was for me. The man liked my qualifications and hired me immediately. I thanked Jim for his spiritual help and made arrangements to begin work the following day.

One of the church members was working at Juvenile Hall in

Ukiah and helped Al get a job as a counselor working a week each
month. With two salaries and three weeks of unemployment
checks, we would make enough money to pay our bills and take
care of the children's needs. It never occurred to us to give
anything to the church. We gave our time and Jim didn't ask for
more than that.

Jim promised us utopia and in return asked only that we give
our time and energies to his worthwhile projects. We felt there
wasn't enough we could do to help him. Our lives revolved around
the church's activities, and I waited impatiently to be assigned
some task for the Cause.

*   *   *

On Wednesday nights there was a meeting for members only at
which people ironed out their personal problems. Jim called this
process catharsis. We went to our first Wednesday-night meeting
totally unprepared for the rigors of this type of confrontation.

Jim began the evening by calling Martha Cole, a young woman
who directed the junior choir, to the front of the room. He read a
letter he had received from one of the other members accusing
Martha of "compensating" with Melvin.

At the mention of his name, Melvin jumped out of his seat and
made his way to the front of the room beside Martha. They made
an unlikely couple. Martha was fair, with neatly coiffed, golden
brown hair, while Melvin showed the results of years of street life.
As Jim began to talk seriously to Martha, I quickly learned that
"compensating" meant encouraging someone of the opposite sex
to start a relationship with you. Since Martha and Melvin were
both divorced, I couldn't understand what they had done that was
wrong, but I could tell that Martha had broken one of the
important rules of this church.

"Martha," Jim began in a stern voice, "is it true that you sat on
the piano bench beside Melvin and asked him to take you out for a
hamburger?" I almost smiled at the serious look on Jim's face. I
thought surely he must be joking! All this fuss because she had
asked him to get her a hamburger? But I realized he wasn't joking
as I saw the looks of disapproval on most of the faces in the room.

Martha hung her head. "Yes, Jim, that's true. I get so lonely
sometimes and Melvin is a lot of fun. I just wanted a chance to get
acquainted with him."

"Don't you realize that Melvin is really just off the streets? If he
hadn't come here he would have gone to jail because he had been
caught pushing drugs for the third time. Do you know what
happens to a three-time loser? They usually throw away the key
and forget him. He is here to straighten his life out. How do you

think we can help him if you are inflating his ego and making him think he's a superstud?" Jim asked her.

"I'm sorry, Jim. I was thinking of myself. I'm sorry, Melvin, for causing all this trouble." Martha looked as if she was about to cry. I couldn't help feeling sorry for her, but now I was beginning to understand what Jim was trying to teach her. Flirtations certainly weren't going to help Melvin right now.

Several other church members began to form a line near the microphone. A few children ventured forward to stand in line, too. Jim looked at the people as they came forward and said, "It looks like some of the other members have a few things to say to you, too."

A counsellor named Karen Layton stepped forward. "Martha, you always say you're sorry and won't do it again, but just a few months ago you were compensating with another man. Your children need some stability from you, but it seems that all you want is to find someone to jump into bed with." Jim motioned for the boy holding the microphone to turn it off as he called Linda up to the pulpit. He whispered something to her and she went directly to Martha's three boys and led them outside where they couldn't hear what was being said.

"Now we can continue. It isn't good for your young children to hear some of the things that might be said tonight." Jim was showing a sensitivity toward the children that reaffirmed my belief in his compassion.

"Thank you, Jim. I appreciate that," Martha said earnestly.

"You may go on," he said, indicating to the boy at the microphone that he could turn it back on.

The woman in line continued, "I just wish you'd learn the lesson, Martha, so we wouldn't have to keep reminding you to leave the men alone."

Martha didn't answer. She stood there with her head hung low as Jim called the next person forward.

"Martha," the second woman was speaking now. "Every time you bring your boys to the church they look dirty. They look like you don't take care of them, but I notice that your clothes are always pretty and your hair is always fixed nice. I wonder if you love your boys as much as you love yourself." There was a lot of derision in the voice of the speaker. This was the first time I had heard anyone talk like that in this church, and I was surprised.

Martha became defensive. "Look, I try to do the best I can with my boys. Sometimes, I can't take care of them by myself. I get them cleaned up and then they go and start a fight or something. Then when they get to church they look like I never take care of them. It's not my fault they're so rowdy, you know."

Jim interrupted her. "I can understand what Martha is saying. I remember when my boys were that age. They were forever getting into some dirt or tearing their clothes or something. I must admit that her boys usually look clean when she first gets here." Martha's oldest son was only five and most of the people in the audience could empathize with her problem. Her sons were little "tough guys," always trying to start a fight with one another or with the other children.

Jim continued, "Martha's husband left her because she refused to leave this group. It isn't her fault she's alone."

As he finished speaking, the next person in line stepped forward. This time it was a young boy about seven years old. "Martha, whenever we have junior choir practice, you always say things that scare me, like you're going to beat us up, or you're going to kill us or something. I don't like it when you say those things."

Martha looked at the young speaker. "I'm sorry, Joey, really, I am. You know, sometimes you kids get so rowdy that I don't know what to do with you. I'm the only adult there most of the time and I don't have any help. When you all start screaming, I don't know what to do."

A little girl stepped forward. "Sometimes when the boys are making noise and the girls are being quiet, you still yell at all of us and say we're all being bad. I don't think that's fair to us girls."

As the other children in the audience heard the bold complaints of the first two, a few more came forward. I looked at the line of children waiting to confront Martha and my heart flooded with compassion for this lonely woman who had been singled out for attack because she needed companionship.

Martha had a difficult job trying to supervise the children's choir without any help. I thought about offering to assist her, but as I looked at the line of mischievous children, each one telling about Martha's shortcomings, I changed my mind. I had to admit that I couldn't take the kind of confrontation that she was being put through.

The children continued to tell Martha about other mistakes she was making and Martha patiently listened to each one, apologizing. Before the evening was over I knew in my heart that Martha would never return.

The following Sunday morning, as we walked into the church, I glanced toward the junior choir section to see who was taking Martha's place. To my amazement I saw her sitting there, smiling as though nothing had happened. The very children who had confronted her just a few days before were sitting beside her as though the encounter had never happened. I wondered if I would be able to go through a session like that, and I hoped that if I ever had to, my turn would be many years in the future. I was impressed by Martha's courage but I wasn't ready to help her out of her predicament. Someone else would have to volunteer. I'd wait for a task that didn't require so much patience.

When Jim's sermon was over, he began his healing service, which I watched closely. I was determined to learn to feel empathy. I was disgusted with myself because I hadn't felt the concern and love that I knew Jim was feeling with each healing. Tonight I silently vowed to myself, "I am going to feel their suffering and feel their joy as they are healed."

Jim asked the organist to play some soft music and he began to call out some prophetic warnings. I quietly took a pencil and paper and wrote them down. From now on I was going to remember these important "words of life" that he gave to us in love.

"No one is to use Crest Toothpaste. The only toothpaste that will make your gums resistant to atomic radiation is Phillips Toothpaste." He paused for a moment before he continued, "If you see a ladder with a spot of red paint on it, you are to put the ladder out of sight for two weeks. No one is to ride a motorcycle for a month." I was beginning to believe that it was a miracle to be with a man who could save us from disaster with such simple, easy-to-follow rules.

Next, Jim called a man forward. "Aaron James."

I had taken a seat in the front row so I could see everything that happened. From the back of the room I heard a man answer, "Yes?"

Jim glanced over his dark glasses to see where the voice was coming from, and said, "You have been thinking about money problems and wondering how you were going to pay all your bills this month."

"Yes, Lord!"

"Your wife's name is Sally, and you have two children who are not with you today."

"That's right!"

"You're thinking right now that you have another child living in Texas by a previous marriage," Jim said with a mischievous smile.

"Yes, Lord, and no one here knows that but me!" The man had come to the front of the room now and was crying.

Jim stood up with a solemn look on his face. "Who can know the thoughts of your mind?" he asked sternly.

"Only God can know," the man said, weeping freely.

"Since you have so much faith I am going to heal you of a

stomach cancer that has been causing you pain for many years."
Mr. James looked perplexed and shook his head as if to indicate he
didn't understand what Jim was talking about.

Jim sternly reprimanded him, "You know you have been
wondering about that pain in your stomach that comes and goes."

"Yes," Aaron James said emphatically.

"If you will go to the restroom with the nurse, I will make you
pass that cancer that has been causing pain in your stomach."
Mr. James walked to the restroom with Rose Shelton, the woman
who often helped Jim with the cancer healings.

The guards made certain the restroom was empty and stood
outside the door while Rose and Mr. James went inside.

For the first time I wondered what was happening in that
restroom. Before, I had taken it for granted that the person would
come out with praise on his lips, and the nurse would be carrying
his cancer. This time, though, I wanted to understand how the
cancer was actually passed.

Within a few minutes they came out, just as I knew they would,
with Rose carrying the smelly mass of flesh. I looked at it carefully
and noticed that it was a light-colored material covered with
blood. At that point, Jim shouted to me "Not too close! That's a
cancer!"

When the meeting ended I made my way to Mr. James. After I
hugged him and told him that I was grateful for his healing, I
asked him how the cancer actually came out.

"I'm not really sure," he answered, shaking his head. "The
nurse had me sit on the toilet and try to strain to make the cancer
come out of my bowels. She gave me some kind of an enema and
something did come out but I didn't feel any pain. Jim made that
cancer come out painlessly! And you know, the most amazing
thing is that I never even knew I had cancer."

That night Al and I talked about this healing. I told him how
Mr. James had described passing a cancer that he didn't even
know he had. Al looked serious. "If I were here because I thought
Jim was a healer, that description might make me wonder about
him. But I've always told you I'm here because I believe Jim has
the knowledge and ability to make this world a better place. This
is the only place I've seen true integration practiced. I believe that
the confrontations are a healthy way for people to interact
honestly. I like the family structure with the children relating to
many people as parents. These are the things that are important
to me and certainly not the healings."

I tried to put my doubts out of my mind. The man had passed
something and was certain it was cancer. Who was I to question

Jim's healings? Al seemed to be following my thoughts as he answered, "I only know that Jim is doing more for humanity than any person I've known."

If I did have any questions, they abruptly vanished the following week by what I felt was a miraculous healing of our eight-year-old son, Eddie.

Eddie had never been very healthy. For a few days he mentioned to me that his chest hurt but I thought he might have fallen and didn't give it much thought. One day he came into the house and collapsed on the floor. "It hurts right here," he said, pointing to his heart. I listened to his heartbeat and knew that something was very wrong. The beats seemed irregular. I had Grandma and Al listen, and they heard the same thing.

I was frantic. I tried to call Jim, but his wife, Marcie, told me that he was out of town for a few days. I called a local physician and made arrangements to bring Eddie into the hospital immediately. Al carried Eddie into the car and I began to drive, silently asking Jim to heal my little boy. I visualized open heart surgery and the possibility of my first-born son dying on an operating table. Then, as if Jim had put the answer into my mind, I began to talk to Eddie. "You know, son, every week we watch people get healed by Jim. He doesn't have to be there when he heals, all we have to do is ask him. I know he can help you." Eddie and I each fervently pleaded for Jim's power to heal his heart.

When we got to the Ukiah General Hospital the doctor was waiting. I carried Eddie into the emergency room and laid him on the table, holding his hand. The doctor came in, smiled a greeting at my son, and took out his stethoscope. I hardly breathed waiting to hear his verdict. He turned to me and asked, "What did you say was the matter with his heart?" I explained what his heart had sounded like to me. He handed me the stethoscope and I listened. Eddie's heart pumping regularly and strongly, without skipping a beat.

"Is it possible that it could have been so irregular just half an hour ago, and sound like this now?" I asked him.

"Well, I guess anything's possible, but his heart sounds fine. The only problem I see is that Eddie looks a little pale. Why don't you try giving him some iron pills to see if you can get some color into his face?"

Eddie got up from the table, and we went home praising Jim. From that day forward Eddie was able to play as hard as any other child. We forgot about the iron tablets because within a few days Eddie's complexion was rosy for the first time since he had been six months old.

I called Marcie and told her about the miracle. I asked her what

I could do to help the Cause, to show my appreciation. She told me to call Linda Amos and ask for a work assignment. Linda assigned me to the letter-writing project.

All of us who were on this letter-writing crew were expected to write at least twenty letters a day. I was also told to read newspapers and magazines for people to congratulate in the name of Jim Jones and the church for anything praiseworthy they might have done. Many of our letters were written to visitors who came each week and I noticed the resemblance in the letters I was writing to the ones we'd received after our first visit to the valley. These letters were all copied from the same format. I began to realize that this was a mass manufacture of letters. We just had to write our twenty letters and we wrote whatever we were told.

In the name of Jim and the church I wrote some time-worn sentences about the wonderful works our church was doing. Most of the letters would begin, "Our church and our wonderful pastor, Jim Jones, want to express gratitude for [whatever it was] that you have done in your community." Then we were to describe a miracle we had personally witnessed, such as Eddie's heart incident, and we would close our letters saying, "Our pastor has taken in hundreds of children and senior citizens because he cares so much for people. He loves animals, too. In fact, he has erected a beautiful animal shelter behind his own home. Our pastor wears only used clothing because he doesn't want to spend any money on himself that could be used to feed the hungry...." Each letter sounded like the one before.

Though it was tedious writing the same things over and over again, I believed in the things I was saying, and I remembered how impressed we had been by the flood of letters we had received. I could understand the wisdom of sending so many letters, and whenever I felt the work load was too great, I would remember Eddie's healing and work with renewed vigor.

Not to be outdone by my dedication to the Cause, Al asked to be assigned to a project, too. He was put in charge of a small construction crew. A few days later this assignment gave him an opportunity to experience his first catharsis. One of the men, Hugh, had gone home early, leaving most of the work for Al and Chris Lewis to do. When Al asked Hugh to stay and finish the job, he ignored him and left. Al dutifully turned his name in to Jim.

That night Jim read the note and called Al and Hugh to the front of the room. "Hugh," Jim said sternly. "Al has reported that you went home early today and left the hard work to be done by the others."

"That's not true, Jim," Hugh said as he tried to appear to be telling the truth. Jim started to smile but became serious.

"Hugh, how can you look so innocent when I know you aren't telling the truth?"

Hugh shook his head. "I am telling the truth. I did work."

"I didn't say you didn't work, Hugh, you're twisting my words. I said you didn't do your share of the work."

"Well, that might be the truth, sir, but I did work."

"Al, did Hugh do any work?" Jim asked, motioning for Al to step toward the microphone.

"Hugh did do some work, but when the hard work started, he left."

"Did you ask Hugh to help you then?" he asked.

"Yes, but he was already leaving."

Jim started giggling. It was obvious to Al that Jim wasn't taking this issue seriously, and he began to get angry. "I don't see anything funny about Hugh cutting out when the hard work needed to be done," he said.

"No, I'm not laughing about that, Al. Don't be so serious. I'm laughing at Hugh. He always manages to get out of work and every time he is confronted he has the same lame excuses. We all know that he's lazy but he keeps trying to convince us that he's not."

Al was still angry. He thought Jim was making fun of him for expecting Hugh to do his share of the work. "This is the first confrontation I have been in but I don't think you're taking it seriously."

Several counsellors angrily jumped forward. Jack Beam was the first to speak. "How dare you speak to Jim like that?" he shouted at Al.

Al had committed treason, although innocently.

Before he had an opportunity to respond, Karen Layton, another counsellor, ran forward. "You seem to think you're great because you're working on the construction job. No one here is dedicated enough to question Jim's motivations. What makes you think you can tell Jim when he should be serious and when he can laugh?"

Al was shocked. Where was all the fairness he had seen in the previous confrontations? Suddenly it dawned on him. He had questioned the leader and made him appear unsympathetic in the eyes of the congregation. He knew that a leader must maintain an image in order to command the respect of his followers. He had learned that in the army. Several more counsellors were shouting now, but as soon as he had the opportunity Al went to the microphone.

"Jim, I'm sorry I said what I did. I know you are fair, and I had no right to question you. I should have seen the humor in the situation, too, but I was so involved with my problem that I couldn't understand what was happening here. Please forgive me."

Jim benevolently forgave him. He smiled as he excused the men from the platform. Karen suggested that they hug each other to show that they held no animosity. As Al hugged Hugh he realized that he was no longer angry.

On our way home Al commented, "Before I came to this church I would simply avoid a person I had a difference of opinion with. Here we are learning how to work out our problems with other people."

"I know," I answered. There was a new softness in my husband that I hadn't seen before. He had apologized even though he didn't feel he was wrong. I was so proud of him that I felt like singing.

That catharsis meeting between Al and Hugh was the first of several public confrontations for our family. We were no longer new members. It was flattering to feel like part of the trusted members, but it wasn't fun to be in front of a crowd having our faults exposed.

1971

We've found joy in sharing,
Sharing what we have with one another,
And we've started caring,
Caring what becomes of our brother,
And the world needs us all,
To do what we can, big or small.
Don't you hear the hungry people crying?

Let's keep on sharing,
And doing good, for others in our world!
Let's keep on living a better way
So that others
Will change their minds and follow, too.
Yes, the world is changing... will you?
　　　　　　　　　—from a Peoples Temple song

One morning Rosalie called me on the phone. "I have a young man in my home who is very unhappy," she said. "Roz brought Larry Schacht into the church last weekend and placed him with me, but he doesn't want to conform to our house rules. I know that sometimes you and Al help with new kids and I was wondering if I could bring him over to you." It was a challenge that I accepted.

Larry was a good-looking young man from Berkeley. Little did we know then that he would one day become the church's doctor. Now he was just a confused and frightened boy of about eighteen years. He had all his possessions in a backpack which he wouldn't put down for fear someone might try to take it away from him. Larry stood in the doorway without moving.

"Larry, would you like to see the rest of our house and our animals outside?" Al asked him.

Larry agreed to look at the house but he still wouldn't put his backpack down. After about twenty minutes Larry had agreed that he would like to live with us, especially after he saw the beautiful dinner Grandma had prepared.

That evening Larry shared his "treasure" with us. It was a plain, cloth-bound book called *I Ching*, which he claimed had tremendous power. "This book gave me the message to come to the north to meet a man that has divine truth," he said solemnly.

I had to admit the passage was impressive as he read it to us. We promised him that we wouldn't ever take this book away from him, and only then did he trust us enough to put it under his bed. He'd had a few rough times during his brief time "on the streets" and had lost much of his willingness to trust others.

As the weeks passed, Larry became a much more happy and outgoing person. He loved our family and our animals. He and Grandma developed a warm friendship.

He wanted to be loved and accepted in return, and as long as he lived with us he seemed happy. Unfortunately, a couple of months later, a counsellor named Archie decided that Larry had become a good worker and took him away to work for him. We sadly watched as Larry learned to conform to the church's rules, rules that didn't match his sensitive and gentle disposition. We never again saw the look of happiness that he had when taking care of our animals or talking with Grandma about her poetry or her garden.

We began to hear rumors that Al's friends, Nita and John, were getting a divorce. Nita had been on the bus trip with us when we first visited Peoples Temple and she had made it clear that she wanted nothing to do with Jim Jones. But now, in view of her family crisis, Al thought it might be a good time to invite her to return to the church for another visit.

Nita and John had seven children. As a contractor he had been able to buy a lovely home in an expensive neighborhood for his family, but Nita, who had been his child bride, had never learned to manage either money or time. Al and I suggested that she would have a difficult time managing her children alone, and we began to describe our church family in glowing terms.

"Each of your children will be given an education through college," I told her.

"And you will have friends, people who will care about you and the children," Al added.

"Please come to visit, Nita," I said, trying to pressure her into making the decision. "Jim Jones has helped hundreds of people and I'm sure that he could help you now, when things seem so depressing."

Nita admitted that she had felt on the verge of a nervous breakdown. The following Sunday morning, Nita and her children were ready when Al drove by to pick them up. Since it was summer, and the children wouldn't have to go to school, Al suggested they get some clothes together and stay through the week so they could know what it was like to be a real part of the church family. Her children were thrilled at the prospect of spending a week on our farm.

As I sat beside Nita in the service, I felt sorry for this frail woman who looked ten years older than she was.

During the service Jim called out Nita's name. She stood up and went to the front of the room. He told her about her life crisis and said that he understood what she was going through. "I was with you this week and you knew it, didn't you?" he asked lovingly.

Nita couldn't answer him. She simply nodded her head while tears spilled down her cheeks.

Al and I were elated about this meeting. Jim had impressed Nita. We fervently hoped that she would decide to join the church.

The next morning, though, we received a shock. Nita's oldest son, Sam, phoned her at our house. Nita talked to him for some time, and we could tell by the look on her face that she was hearing some distressing news. When she hung up she looked at us solemnly and said, "I don't understand what's happening, but Sam told me that yesterday morning he got a call from people who said they were doing a survey. They asked him a lot of questions about me and the children here. Sam thought that Jim Jones might have had someone call to get information for his revelations. This really frightens me!"

We didn't understand it either, but we knew it was important not to upset Nita's faith any more than it already had been.

Al said that perhaps Sam had made up the story to discourage Nita's faith. He added, "Nita, many things will happen to test your faith in this group. The main thing you have to do is judge for yourself. Don't let other people persuade you against your will. Jim wants you to think for yourself. You know Sam would like to talk you out of joining this church."

Although we had rationalized the incident, I still wanted to be sure we had figured it correctly. We had been told to tell Jim about any unusual or perplexing things that happened to us so I wrote him a long letter telling him about Sam's phone call to Nita. I ended the letter saying, "I don't understand how this could have happened, but I know that you can find out by using your metaphysical gift. The call really perplexed us."

It was a three-page letter and I quickly put it into an envelope and put the envelope in my purse so I wouldn't forget it the following Wednesday night.

My doubts were pushed aside the following morning. I was driving into Ukiah to purchase some supplies when I suddenly saw Nita in my mind. I also saw that she was contemplating suicide. I was certain I heard Jim's voice saying, "Go home and tell Nita that those who commit suicide are forced to come back to this earth again and again, until they conquer the urge to solve their problems by ending their lives. Tell her that she will one day work for this Cause and that her life will have great purpose. There will be a time when she will be able to give her life for this Cause and at that time her death might help hundreds of people to be set free. Above all, tell her that I love her." This was the first time I had ever received a telepathic message, although Jim had mentioned others that he communicated with this way. I had no conscious awareness of Nita's considering suicide, but I was compelled to return home immediately to tell her. I headed back toward our home. When I walked in Nita was making lunch for the children. "I have to talk to you right now," I announced dramatically.

"This morning when I was driving into town I received an urgent telepathic message from Jim that you were contemplating suicide," I said, sternly looking at Nita.

"That's amazing," she answered, shaking her head in disbelief. "This morning, as I was lying in bed, I thought about that telephone call from Sam. Jim Jones has helped me so much since I've been here that I decided if he's a phony I don't want to go on living."

I nodded my head, trying to conceal my own amazement at having received such a clear message. "Well, he must have known what you were thinking, because he impressed this message upon my mind. I just drove straight home." I went on to relate the entire message to her. "I don't understand some of these things," I confessed, "especially about your death possibly helping hundreds of other people, but I do know that this is what Jim wanted me to say."

"I understand it perfectly," Nita said, smiling. "Now I know for sure that Jim Jones is more than a prophet. He even knows my thoughts. Jeannie, thank you for telling me this. I don't feel the need to take my life anymore. I don't understand Sam's telephone call but it isn't important now." Thus, Nita made her decision to join the church and move her family to Redwood Valley. Of course, we told her they would be welcome to live with us until they found a home.

The following Wednesday I almost forgot about the letter, but after I arrived at church I noticed it in my purse. Jim was standing outside the building, and I casually handed it to him. I expected him to put it into his pocket and read it later but he immediately opened the envelope. I was about to walk away, but he asked me to stay so he could answer it right away.

His face turned pale as he came to the end of the last page. "This is the second time this has happened to me," he said solemnly. "I am certain that someone is conspiring against me. They must be bugging my services, and when they hear me calling someone by revelation they immediately telephone the person's house. People want to make it appear that I don't have a divine gift."

I was anxious to help him unravel this mystery, so I pointed out that Sam had said he got the call before the service even began. Jim thought for a minute and came up with another answer.

"I often have revelations about people early in the morning. I write the information that comes to me on paper at my desk. Someone must have copied my notes so they could discredit me. You know people always try to tear down what is good."

Jim's answer satisfied me. I was sure he was telling the truth, because he had often talked about the forces of evil that continually tried to discredit him. I briefly wondered why he couldn't use his power to discern who had been sneaking into his house, but I didn't ask. I didn't want him to think I was questioning his gift. He seemed so upset by my letter, and I wanted to give him some good news.

I told him about the message I had received in my mind for Nita and how much she said it had helped her. "Yes, I gave you that message, Jeannie, and I was certain that you would relate it to Nita. It has helped her a great deal. I am so thankful that I can count on you to convey messages for me this way." I beamed at his words of confidence and praise.

"I'll do anything you want. I'm thankful that I can help you in whatever way you choose," I volunteered.

I stayed up all that night writing my letters. A strange combination of pride and humility mingled in my soul as I rededicated my life to Jim Jones and his Cause. He had used me to save Nita from suicide! This was only the beginning, I assured myself. I would become indispensable to Jim Jones. I visualized the time he would casually beckon to me, as he did to Linda Amos, to take his secret messages to people. Jim Jones knew that he could trust me. My letters that night were masterpieces as I poured all my energy into them.

We were writing letters opposing G. Harrold Carswell's nomination to the Supreme Court. Jim said that Carswell shouldn't have the post, so he set a goal of 50,000 letters for our church members to write and mail. The entire church membership was being asked to write twenty letters a day for this endeavor. Everyone was instructed to use Christian (which meant false) names on their letters. The instruction sheet given to every member said, "You can write several letters to each legislator alternating your handwriting with printing, typewriting, writing backhand, using different stationery, etc. This way every politician will think he is hearing from hundreds or even thousands of people."

I put the stamps on my fifty letters and left them unsealed so they could be checked. I knew that the boxes of letters gathered at the weekend meeting would be sent all over the United States to be mailed from different post offices so it would appear the whole country was opposed to Carswell's nomination. It was difficult for me to justify this practice, so I asked Linda. She assured me that it wasn't illegal. "We only do this because so many people outside of the church are too lazy to write even though they feel as we do. You are actually writing their letters for them."

We were learning a new set of ethics from Jim: "The ends justify the means." He also called it "situational ethics." The way it was translated to the church members was "You do whatever Jim says because he knows what is needed for the Cause." Whenever he suggested something that sounded a little dishonest, he would lovingly remind the congregation of the Cause and tell us not to worry. He knew we were doing the right thing.

Since Nita had decided to join the church we drove to her house the following Sunday to pick up the rest of their clothes and belongings. Our two back porches were converted into extra bedrooms and the old house trailer where Grandma and Grandpa had lived in Hayward was utilized for two more sleeping quarters. By adding an extra table in our dining room we had made room for two families, and none of us thought about its being inconvenient. This was what the church was all about—one big happy family.

I was amazed at how little disagreement there was between the members of this church. Before we joined the church, Al and I couldn't even agree on whom to vote for in the presidential election. Now that we all belonged to a group, family arguments were becoming a thing of the past. There was never a question of who was right, because Jim was always right. When our large household met to discuss family problems, we didn't ask for opinions. Instead, we put the question to the children, "What would Jim do?" It took the difficulty out of life. There was a type of "manifest destiny" which said the Cause was right and would succeed. Jim was right and those who agreed with him were right. If you disagreed with Jim, you were wrong. It was as simple as that.

At night, though, when Al and I were in bed together, talking quietly about our own thoughts and ideas, we made a personal commitment to each other. Al said, "I believe in this Cause but I want you to promise me something. We joined because we felt it was right. If either of us decides to leave the group, let's leave together."

My love for Al was growing as we worked together for the Cause, and the thought of losing him was terrifying, so I solemnly promised that I would stay with him whether we stayed in the church or left it. We also promised each other never to betray confidences to Jim or any of the other church members so that we would always feel free to talk to each other. These promises proved to be a slim thread that connected us with reality in later years and eventually helped us to find the strength we would need to break away from the stranglehold that Jim Jones was getting on our lives. However, that night we only thought of it as our personal secret. It was a way of saying "I love you more than I love anyone or anything else."

*   *   *

The following Sunday Jim instituted a new rule. No longer would visitors be allowed to come freely into church services as they had in the past. He explained that some agency or group was trying to discredit him, so he had to be careful who we let in. "In the future, if you want to invite someone into our services, you have to notify me first," he said sternly. He asked each member to write a letter about the proposed visitor, telling the person's name, address, telephone number, and place of employment. "I will use this information to determine by revelation whether the person is a spy or not," he said convincingly.

If this seemed strange to anyone, no one mentioned it. I smugly smiled, understanding that he didn't want the forces of evil to play any more dirty tricks on him like the telephone call that Sam had received.

That evening the entire church heard the results of our long hours of letter writing. Someone brought a radio in so we could hear the announcement that was being repeated every hour. "All the previous polls had indicated that Carswell would be confirmed, but at the last minute many of the legislators changed their votes due to the flood of mail they received from all over the United States. Carswell has been defeated." Now we could understand why thousands of our letters had been mailed from other states. No one could possibly know they all originated in the tiny hamlet called Redwood Valley. The meeting that evening was a celebration party. Jim's wisdom and ability to sway politics had been proved in a powerful demonstration that no one could dispute.

Now that I understood the importance of the letters, I wanted to be able to write more. I found that I had some extra time at work, so I began to use some of my working hours to write these assigned letters. My employer was already upset with me because of the number of personal telephone calls I received and because I was tired much of the time.

One day he walked over to my desk and I knew he was upset. "I saw a list of names in your drawer the other day, Jeannie. I also saw a pile of letters that looked like they had been typed on my typewriter. l wasn't snooping. I was looking for something when you stepped outside, but since I found them I want to know what they are."

I stammered as I tried to find an answer. "Well..."

"I also want to know why you're always so tired when you come to work. Don't you get enough sleep at home? I've noticed that sometimes you take a nap during your lunch hour."

I knew I had to come up with a good answer, but I wasn't accustomed to lying. I knew I couldn't admit that I was writing assigned letters for the church, because we had been instructed to keep our church membership a secret from people we dealt with in the community. "I'm sorry" was all I could think to say.

"I think you'd better look for another job. I'm not going to pay you to take care of your personal business on my time."

I tried to mumble an answer, but as I stood there, my only concern was what Jim was going to say about my losing my job. "You're right," I admitted. "I've been tired because of personal problems at home." He had me prepare my final check and a few minutes later I was walking out, stunned. I was trying to figure out where things had gone wrong. I knew I shouldn't have left those letters in my drawer. "If only I had locked that drawer," I reprimanded myself.

On the way home I was rehearsing the words I would use to explain my irresponsibility to Jim and the church. I had seen one man severely reprimanded for losing his job in a recent confrontation meeting, so I braced myself for the worst as we drove toward the church that night.

Jim read my note about being fired and asked me to come to the front of the room. For the first time since we had joined the church I knew real fear. Jim encouraged me to "Explain to the members what happened at your job today."

"I lost my job," I began. The words were difficult to get out. "My boss found some letters that I was writing for the church and he overheard some of my telephone calls from other members, so he fired me. I know I should have been more careful, and I'm sorry." There, I breathed a sigh of relief. I'd said it. I was prepared for the worst, but instead Jim referred the case to a private counselling session.

The following night at eight o'clock, I paced back and forth in the empty church building. I had been told not to be late. I waited patiently for the counsellors to call me into the small counselling room behind the kitchen. I could hear people shouting at each other. Since this was the first time I had been asked to come in for private counselling, I wasn't sure what to expect. I remembered hearing one girl tell a friend about being "grilled" for two hours about her sexual activities, and I began to wish that I could just disappear. At 9:00 one of the counsellors stepped outside of the room and told me to be patient, they would be ready for me shortly. At 9:45 a woman came out of the room crying and the first counsellor said they would call me in just a few more minutes.

At ten they finally ushered me in. I glanced around to see the expressions on the counsellors' faces. They seemed to be relaxed and comfortable. This wasn't the scene I had expected when I saw the other woman who left crying. Several people in the room were munching on apples and grapes. They were sitting around a long table that nearly filled the small room. There was one vacant seat and they motioned for me to sit. Shelves of food lined one wall and cardboard boxes were stacked at the end of the room. Two of the counsellors were perched high on the boxes. I wished desperately that Al were with me. I felt very alone and frightened.

Jack Beam, Jim's assistant minister, was the first to speak. "So you lost your job?" he asked caustically. He was a fat white man who was nearly bald. As I heard the sneer in his voice I instantly disliked him.

"Yes."

Clarese, a fat white woman with a soft face, was next. "Did your boss know who you were writing to?" She reminded me of a "Jewish Momma" and I hoped that we would be able to be friends.

"No," I answered her, "he just saw the pile of letters and noticed that they had been typed on his typewriter."

"Are you sure he didn't know what the letters were about?" Clarese asked me again. I realized that this must be important so I took a little time before I answered.

"I'm certain he didn't get an opportunity to read them. They weren't disturbed and I was only outside a few moments. It isn't possible that he saw what was in the letters." I waited for the next question.

Jack spoke again. "It's a good thing he didn't see the letters. We have all been instructed never to take our church work to our jobs. If anyone saw what we write, they might not understand our reasons and might try to cause our church some trouble. Apparently no one has told you this before, so we will excuse you for the mistake this time."

The counsellors began to talk among themselves. They seemed

to agree that since no one had seen the letters there was no serious problem. The immediate problem was to find me another job. Jane had an idea.

"Jeannie has been doing an excellent job with letter writing and Jim has been trying to find another full-time church worker. Maybe she should work for the church instead of trying to find an outside job." She looked directly at me and asked, "What do you think of that idea?"

"We couldn't afford to support our family on Al's salary alone," I said honestly.

"Well," Jane answered, "sometimes when a person works for the church, we give them additional assistance to pay their bills." She looked around at the other counsellors in the room waiting for their response to this idea.

Jack agreed. "With her talents we need to have her work full time for the church." The rest of the counsellors nodded in agreement, and I was officially made a church worker.

It was midnight when I finally got home. I was so excited that I had to wake Al to tell him about my new position in the church. He was pleased but a little apprehensive. "How can we support our children on the little money I make?" he asked.

"They said they will help pay our bills as long as I work full time," I answered. The following Sunday, church held much more meaning for me. Now I was intent on using all my time and talents for the church. I really wanted to understand Jim's teachings fully so that I could help him serve humanity.

*   *   *

There were more people than usual at the Sunday service, and for some reason the church members hadn't brought enough food to feed everyone. It became apparent that the last fifty people in line weren't going to get any meat. Jim announced, "Even though there isn't enough food to feed this multitude, I am blessing the food that we have and multiplying it—just as Jesus did in biblical times."

Sure enough, a few moments after he made this startling announcement, Eva Pugh came out of the kitchen beaming, carrying two platters filled with fried chicken. A big cheer came from the people assembled in the room, especially from the people who were at the end of the line.

The "blessed chicken" was extraordinarily delicious, and several of the people mentioned that Jim had produced the best-tasting chicken they had ever eaten. One of the members, Chuck Beikman, a man who had come with Jim from Indianapolis, jokingly mentioned to a few people standing near him that he had seen Eva drive up a few moments earlier with buckets from the Kentucky Fried Chicken stand. He smiled as he said, "The person that blessed that chicken was Colonel Sanders."

During the evening meeting Jim mentioned the fact that Chuck had made fun of his gift. "He lied to some of the members here, telling them that the chicken had come from a local shop," Jim stormed. "But the Spirit of Justice has prevailed. Because of his lie Chuck is in the men's restroom right now, wishing that he was dead. He is vomiting and has diarrhea so bad he can't talk!"

An hour later a pale and shaken Chuck Beikman walked out of the men's room and up to the front, being supported by one of the guards. Jim asked him, "Do you have anything you'd like to say?"

Chuck looked up weakly and answered, "Jim, I apologize for what I said. Please forgive me."

As we looked at Chuck, we vowed in our hearts that we would never question any of Jim's "miracles"—at least not out loud. Years later, we learned that Jim had put a mild poison in a piece of cake and given it to Chuck.

*   *   *

We needed extra income, so Al and I decided to have the boys who were sleeping in the trailer move back into our house so we could rent the trailer.

Within a few hours after our ad appeared in the Ukiah *Daily Journal,* we got a telephone call from a young teacher. He said that he and three of his friends were looking for a place to rent in our neighborhood because they were opening a small alternative school just a mile down the road from us. "Would you consider renting your trailer to four people?" he asked.

Of course we would, we assured them, as long as they had fifty dollars for the month's rent. The four young teachers moved in the next day.

They were delightfully unobtrusive neighbors and we felt fortunate to have such nice people next door. They enjoyed talking with Grandma occasionally, but aside from that we seldom even saw them. It was Grandma who told us about their teaching methods, and we asked them to tell us more.

They told us about the small classes where the children were allowed to progress at their own speed and were encouraged to help the teacher design their education program. The teachers also told us that they had been talking with Jim and some of the church's counsellors about the possibility of enrolling some of the church's slower learners into their school.

It had always required more than usual patience to try to teach Eddie math and science, and Steve had a serious problem of daydreaming at school. This school seemed to have the perfect answer for both of our sons. Al and I told them we would like for our sons to be able to attend their school but that we didn't have enough money for tuition.

The teachers were very understanding. They agreed to enroll both of our sons in exchange for free rent. It was more than a bargain and we accepted their offer gratefully.

Somehow word got back to the church that we had enrolled two of our children in the Woodland School.

"Jeannie and Al are to stay after service tonight for a counselling session," Jim announced.

As soon as the meeting was over we met in the little back room with Linda Amos, Jack Beam, and several other counsellors. Al explained that we couldn't stay long because we had to drive our children home, so Linda made an appointment for a few of the counsellors to visit us at home the following day.

Linda was the first to arrive and she asked if we could be in a private room where we wouldn't be disturbed. Soon Jack Beam, Carolyn Layton, Linda Amos, and Archie Ijames arrived and we all sat on our children's beds to begin the discussion. Neither Al nor I had any idea what we had done wrong, so we waited with blank expressions on our faces to hear what they had to say.

Archie began, "I understand that you folks have enrolled two of your children in the Woodland School without asking for permission," he said, scowling at me.

"I didn't know we had to ask permission to send our children to school," I answered him defiantly.

Linda responded, "No, you don't, as long as they are attending regular schools. You know most of the other church members can't afford to send their children to private schools, so it's not fair for your children to be allowed this privilege."

This was a new angle that I hadn't considered and I needed time to think about it. Al answered, "It's not costing us any money. The teachers are letting them go free in exchange for rent."

Now Carolyn spoke. "Have you looked into this school carefully? Do you really know what they're going to be teaching your children?"

Actually we hadn't asked that many questions. Our only concern had been that our boys would receive individual attention.

Al was becoming a little angry. "I heard that Jim thought about enrolling some of the other church children in this school, so

I didn't see anything wrong with enrolling our kids there."

Jack seemed surprised that Al knew about this and he said, "Well, yes, that is true. But that was before we looked into the backgrounds of these teachers. Did you know that several of the teachers use marijuana?"

Now I became defensive. "I don't care what they use, that's their own business. These teachers live next door to us and I know they are fine people. I'm sure they won't be smoking marijuana in the classrooms."

It was a mistake to become defensive and I realized it instantly. All five of the counsellors began shouting. Al and I just sat there, amazed at their irrational anger.

"You want your children to be special but that's not fair to the other children," Carolyn said.

Linda added, "You think you're too good to ask for permission like everyone else."

"You don't understand the basic concepts of our church."

It was hard to believe! We hadn't intentionally done anything wrong. Our only concern had been for our two sons who were having a difficult time in the public schools, and yet we were being yelled at as if we were their enemies.

Al had never been able to remain calm when people were yelling at him, especially if the situation was unfair. He stood up and shouted, "All of you get out of here, unless you can talk rationally like reasonable human beings. We don't have to listen to a shouting match."

Archie calmed down. "I understand, Al," he answered. "We'll just let Jim know how you feel and see if he wants to say anything else to you."

The four counsellors left. As they drove out of the driveway Al and I stood looking at each other in amazement. "Do you think Jim is going to get mad if we send the boys to that school?" I asked.

"I don't give a damn," Al answered. "They're our kids and we'll send them wherever we want."

Jim's sermon the following Wednesday night could have been titled "The Joys of Equality and the Evils of the Woodland School." Without ever once mentioning the heated controversy that had taken place in our home a few days before and without looking at either Al or me once during the entire evening, Jim got his point across—several times.

"There are people in this congregation who think their children deserve special treatment. They believe that because they come from white, privileged backgrounds, they should send their children to private schools. People don't realize that a small band of hippies are operating the school. These men and women are all pot-smoking sexual deviants. The poor children at that school are subjected to their strange and bizarre beliefs and teachings. One father who sends his children there is a marijuana-smoking white racist bigot. This is a perfect example of the type of people this school attracts."

As if it weren't enough to have an entire sermon directed against us, several of the counsellors, including Linda, who had always seemed friendly, now turned their backs on us. It was more than I could stand and I left the church crying. I went out and sat in our car until the service ended and we were ready to drive home.

The following Wednesday night Jim was going to hold a special meeting in San Francisco and take a busload of people with him. We had just finished bagging a large mailing at Publications that day so I made arrangements with the bus driver to take me to the post office in San Francisco after he dropped everyone else off for the service. Al and the rest of the family stayed to attend services in Redwood Valley.

I got to the meeting almost an hour late. I smiled at Linda and she turned her back on me. I couldn't stand getting the cold shoulder, and by the time the meeting was over tears were streaming down my cheeks.

On the bus I sat near the front—still crying. For some reason the bus didn't take off when it should have. We just kept waiting. I looked up at some commotion near the front door and saw Jim walking in. He came over and knelt in front of me. In a whisper he asked if I would like to ride back to Redwood Valley in a car away from all these people.

Jim had never shown me any personal attention before and I was skeptical. I thought he might be embarrassed because I wouldn't stop crying and that he just wanted to take me out of the sight of the other members. Anyway, I reasoned, I certainly didn't want to stay with these people who didn't like me anymore.

I got into the back seat of a luxury Cadillac beside Jim. It was the car of a wealthy couple who lived in San Francisco, members who I knew contributed a lot of money to the Cause. Instead of driving toward Redwood Valley, we went to a very expensive restaurant where Jim told me I could order anything I wanted.

I had finally been able to stop crying, and Jim still hadn't asked me what was wrong. As I glanced at the menu I was astounded. Jim was going to eat here? After all his sermons about poverty?

He whispered that the couple we were with were paying the bill, so we didn't need to worry about the prices. We had steak with all the trimmings.

Later in the car Jim asked why I had been crying, and I began to cry again as I explained how unfairly I thought we had been treated with regard to the Woodland School issue. "We didn't know we were supposed to ask for permission to send our kids to a private school, and we don't understand why everyone got so angry."

Jim patiently explained that he had investigated these teachers and found them unable to teach the values and ethics he believed in. He apologized for the unfair treatment we had received and asked me to reconsider our decision and voluntarily send our children to public school. By the time we arrived back home I had agreed to do as he wished. I hoped that Al would understand.

By this time Eddie and Steve were very aware that they were the center of the controversy and asked Al to let them continue in public school. Al decided that since it was causing so much friction it wasn't worth making an issue of.

We explained our change of plans to the teachers and they seemed to sense that we had been pressured enough. They didn't even ask us why we reversed our decision. They wrote out their rent check without comment.

But we were still on edge. A lot of the contradictory things that we had accepted about the church were beginning to bother us. One Sunday morning a young woman named Phyllis Houston approached us. "We're going to have a pancake breakfast next Tuesday in Ukiah. Every family has to sell ten tickets."

Al took the ten tickets she was holding out and asked, "What if I can't sell them?"

Phyllis answered, "Then you just turn in fifteen dollars and do whatever you want with the tickets. You can use them for your own children."

Something in the tone of her voice caused Al to get irrationally angry. He handed the tickets back to Phyllis, grabbed my arm, and walked out of the building with me. "I'll be damned if any church is going to force me to pay for tickets if I can't sell them," he said angrily. "Let's quit."

It wasn't this incident alone that prompted his decision. All our little conflicts and disagreements with the church had come to a head. With a smile of relief I said, "I agree," and we got into our car and drove home. We decided that we would return to church after the evening meeting, but for now we were free.

"I'm glad you see it my way, Jeannie," Al said. "Maybe we made a big mistake joining this church. It isn't the utopia we thought it was."

We spent the rest of the evening composing a letter to notify Jim about our decision to leave the group. We realized it would be a major change in our lives, but we were ready for a major change. We still hadn't decided whether we would make our children quit or allow them to continue going until they became disillusioned. "Let's take it one step at a time," Al suggested. "We'll send Jim our letter first and see what happens."

"Dear Jim," our letter began. "We have decided that we are going to quit attending the church. We see so many inequities in the way people are treated. You announced that none of the men or women could have their hair done professionally and yet your wife goes to the beauty parlor every week. You make all the men in the congregation shave the hair off their faces, and yet your sons continue to wear mustaches. You even go so far as to pencil in your own long sideburns.

"You praise Patty Cartmell for her dedication to the Cause, and yet she sleeps at work and expects other members to do her job for her. You say none of our children can participate in sports at school, and yet your sons are in the high school's competitive games. You even go with them to the school games, but you say the other members can't go. We joined your group because we were concerned about the welfare of the poor and oppressed, but so far all we have seen is a lot of people being made poor by your excessive offerings and being oppressed by your disciplines. Sincerely, Al and Jeannie."

When we went to pick up our family we handed our letter to Linda. She promised to take it directly to Jim.

We told the others in our household about our decision and they were shocked. Eddie and Daphene were the only ones who were happy. They said they wanted to quit, too, but the other family members felt that we were betraying the Cause.

Friday evening Eddie and Daphene stayed home with us and we went for a long walk up the country road in front of our house. "Such a wonderful freedom," we laughed with each other as we walked in the center of the deserted mountain road. "We haven't had the time to see our neighborhood before. I feel sorry for the people who are sitting in the meeting, probably listening to Jim take a long offering right now." As we breathed the sweet air we decided we would take our other children out of the church the following day.

Jim had anticipated this and spent the entire evening talking earnestly with the members of our household privately. He had someone else conduct the service for him. "Your parents don't realize what they are doing. They have been looking at very petty problems that can be ironed out. Just give them lots of love now because they are confused. Above all, remember that the Cause needs you and your parents. Please don't let them influence you into quitting." It was a rare privilege to speak privately to Jim, and when he spent the entire evening with them they felt quite honored.

The next day the children wouldn't listen to anything Al or I had to say. The older ones had even talked Eddie and Daphene into changing their minds. Jim called us later in the afternoon and we listened on the extension phones. Item by item Jim went over the points we had made in our letter.

"You are only seeing one side of things and are judging me without knowing the facts," he began. "Yes, Marcie does go to a beauty parlor, but she gets the work done free. My son wears a mustache because he has a rash on his upper lip and is so self-conscious about it that I have insisted he keep it. My other son is wearing a mustache so that Steve doesn't feel like the only person allowed to keep his. I pencil in my sideburns because I have a skin condition which makes my hair grow unevenly on one side and I must maintain an image for the group. My sons are involved in school sports because it is good public relations for our church. They are so good in sports that the schools would become angry if I were to make them quit. As far as your criticism of Patty, you have no idea how much work she does for the Cause. Our members who work with her know this, and they have asked to be allowed to do her work for her.

"I don't like to have to defend my actions like this, but for the sake of your precious children I felt that I had to make this call. I resent the implication you make that I am unfair. If you really believed in the Cause you would accept my decisions about these things and not expect me to explain them." He talked as though he were reading notes.

I was the first to answer. "I'm sorry you are so angry. I don't know why you are upset. I didn't ask you to call us. We quit the church and you are treating us as though we were up for confrontation. All we have asked is to be left alone."

Al added, "We are letting our children make their own decisions but we are quitting. Your explanations haven't changed our minds."

"I'm sorry to hear that," Jim said sincerely. There was still an angry tone in his voice, though. It wasn't often that people became this bold with him. "I want you to know that I still care very much about both of you, and I want you to take time to think over what I have said. No one in the group will know that you have quit. I will tell them that you are on an important mission for me." We said our good-byes and hung up.

I burst out laughing. "To think we've been afraid of him! He sounded pathetic with his excuses and explanations."

Al was laughing too. He mocked Jim's voice as he said, "My son has a rash on his upper lip." We had a glass of wine to celebrate our freedom. We were sure we would be able to persuade our children to quit, too.

Now that we weren't members anymore I wasn't going to be getting money from the church. I began looking for a job, but it was a slow time of year and jobs were scarce.

We took the money from stock that Al had accumulated during his nineteen years with Standard Oil, along with a deed of trust that my mother let us use, and put a $20,000 down payment on a tract of nineteen homes in Willits, a few miles north of Redwood Valley. The two- and three-bedroom homes were old, but they could be a nice source of income and a good investment for the future. We still had $4,000 left, so we put a down payment on a lot with two houses and a barn that would also produce a monthly cash flow. With careful managing we knew we could get along until I found a job.

We hadn't fully calculated Jim's persuasive ability. Our children were unmoved by our arguments. Jim had gone over our letter with them and explained his answer to every question. Moveover, he had said, "Remember, your poor misguided parents need you to be strong now. They will be killed when the atomic war comes if they don't have my protection."

For almost a month we watched our children go to the services with members who came by to pick them up, and we realized that our family was becoming divided. We didn't seem to have anything in common with them anymore, and they were showing their keen disappointment in us. One day Al tried to talk to them. "You know your mother and I are still very much concerned about helping the poor and oppressed, but we are going to do it in our own way."

"What are you doing to help?" our daughter Linda asked. Al didn't have an answer. As he thought about her question he realized that we had been enjoying our freedom, but he couldn't think of one thing we were doing to help anyone but ourselves.

Eddie asked a question that made us reconsider our decision. "If you really care about the poor and oppressed, why don't you come back to the group and help us do something for them? You can't do anything by yourselves, you know."

His words rang true. What could two people alone do to change the world? Whether we liked Jim's methods or not, we had to agree that a group of concerned people working together could accomplish a lot more than two people alone. We didn't know any other group that was even trying to help improve the lot of minorities. The following night we returned to the church.

Jim had kept his word. Not one member asked where we had been. Nita and all the children had kept their promises to Jim and told everyone that we were on a mission for him. We were greeted with warm embraces as we walked through the door. We decided that it was time to overlook the things that had disturbed us and get down to the business of helping Jim make the world a better place.

It was almost summer again. With eleven children and three adults living together, our house was beginning to seem crowded. Jim announced that he was going to take all the young children with him on a vacation trip to Oregon, and I was delighted. It would be wonderful to have the children gone for a week and a half so I could catch up on my letter writing and housecleaning. When Jim asked adults to volunteer to go along, I looked the other way.

Nita nudged me and whispered, "I'd love to go along to watch our kids, wouldn't you?" I was filled with guilt about my selfish desire to be alone, so I raised my hand. Jim acknowledged our hands and asked Linda to talk with us. She took us immediately into the counselling room. I supposed that we were going to make plans for the trip.

As we walked into the small room I saw several people sitting at the long table quietly discussing something. Nita and I sat with Linda at the other end of the table.

Linda Amos smiled condescendingly as she said, "Jim appreciates your offer to go with him on the vacation, but he asked me to explain that he won't need you this year."

"Why not? He asked for volunteers, didn't he?" Nita asked, obviously hurt.

Jack Beam, the assistant minister, was at the other end of the table and he overheard Nita's question, so he came over to answer her. "Yes, he did call for volunteers," he said, trying to be tactful. "But you are both overprotective parents and Jim feels that your children will learn more if you two are not along."

Linda added, "Jim wants you to understand that he appreciates your offer but he does know what is best for your children."

We both knew better than to disagree with the decision that Jim had made, so we didn't argue, but Nita was heartbroken. A few days later, as we watched our children leave, she had a hard time concealing her disappointment.

A week later a letter arrived from Daphene. As Nita and I read it we were dismayed to hear that the "wonderful vacation" seemed more like a nightmare.

"Dear Mom," the letter started in her childish scrawl. "We left on the green bus. They had painted crosses on the sides of the bus so it would look like we were Christians. There's mostly kids here.

Parents probably didn't want to interfere with our fun. We sang songs on the way here.

"After we got here we put all our things in the big building, then we lined up outside with our supervisors for a night hike. As we walked we felt around us so we wouldn't bump into anything because it was dark and cold. When we reached the river we were told to take off our sandals and walk through the freezing cold water. I heard the other children crying because it was so cold. We had to strip to our underwear and try to swim. Jim was in the water shivering but he scolded us. He said, 'If I can do it, you can too,' but I thought it wasn't fair because he's much older than us.

"We all cried and yelled as we were pulled into the freezing cold water. Hours later they let us go back to the building to rest. We had to use our blankets to dry ourselves and keep us from nearly freezing to death. They made a large fire outside and everyone crowded around it to keep warm.

"This morning practically all the kids, and some of the grownups, have bad colds and runny noses. We aren't allowed to be lazy at all. We had to get right up, get dressed, and go outside in our play clothes. We used the same clothes we swam in. If we have to go to the bathroom they have a place in the bushes where we all go. Love, Daphene."

"Doesn't that sound too strict?" Nita asked as we finished the letter.

"Yes," I answered. "Now I understand why Jim didn't want us to go along. We wouldn't have been able to watch those children screaming in the cold water."

"Do you really think it's necessary for him to make them do all those things?" Nita asked skeptically.

As I thought about her question I realized that it was important not to shake her faith. The wrong answer might be reported to Jim and I would be in trouble, so I piously answered, "Who are we to question Jim? He's always right. We are overprotective parents, you know." Nita knew better than to argue with that statement and risk questioning Jim, so we let the subject drop.

A few days later, when the children returned, Daphene confidentially whispered to me, "You know that letter I sent to you? Well, I wasn't supposed to mail any letters, but I went with the bus driver to get some gas and put it into the mailbox without anybody knowing." I was surprised that Daphene confessed to breaking a church rule, but I was so happy to have received her letter that I didn't ask any questions.

Janet, Nita's youngest daughter, had quite a story to tell: "Little Tommy Kice was acting spoiled. He wouldn't eat all the food they put in front of him. Jim said he had to eat it because everyone had to eat all the food on their plates. He made Tommy eat it but then he vomited it up into his plate. Then Jim took a spoon and made him eat the vomit. Tommy threw it up again and Jim made him eat it again. Tommy was screaming and yelling but Jim made him eat it anyway." Janet made a face and Daphene spoke up.

"The food really looked nasty by the third time, but Jim made him eat it anyway." As I looked down at these two little girls, both eight years old, both with long blond hair and big brown eyes, I felt a rush of anger toward Jim. Their wide-open eyes and serious faces expressed the horror they had watched Tommy endure.

I cautiously asked the girls, "What did you think about that?" They looked at each other suspiciously because they knew better than to criticize Jim and yet they knew what they had felt.

Finally Daphene answered in a very small voice, "I didn't really think it was fair."

Janet added, "I know Jim did what he thought was best, but I sure wouldn't want him to do that to me."

We never mentioned this incident again because we knew it would be treasonous to criticize Jim's teaching methods. We did notice, however, that the children who had gone on a trip no longer grumbled about cleaning up their plates....

The summers in Ukiah are very warm. This year was no exception. As we were sizzling in the middle of a heat wave our swimming hole became one of the most popular spots in Redwood Valley. Dozens of the church's children came to swim; some came for an afternoon, some stayed overnight, and some would ask to spend a few days. Although our house was crowded, there was plenty of room for the children to run and play on our six acres and on the uninhabited mountains behind our house. Sometimes the ducks and chickens that roosted on our parking lot at night would have to share their sleeping quarters with as many as a dozen children in sleeping bags.

It was a warm Sunday afternoon and everyone brought food for a picnic lunch. After the meal, people were milling about, talking quietly, when suddenly three shots were heard from a wooded area nearby. Jim slumped over and the nurses ran to his side. After a few minutes he dramatically began to stand. His face was contorted with pain and each word was labored, but we heard him say, "I'm not ready to die yet. My people need me."

We were all rushed inside the church, and a few minutes later Jim walked in. His steps were slow and it was obvious that he was still in great pain. "I hope you will always remember this day," he said. "I could have died but I determined that I would remain here with you."

Jim never went to a doctor. He explained, "I have neutralized the bullets in my body. Lenin died with a bullet in his body, and someday so will I."

*   *   *

Nita and her children were beginning to long for a home of their own. She had started taking on a lot of the responsibilities for running the household, and her children were even helping her. We realized that she would be able to make it on her own now. We submitted a request to council to allow Nita to take her children to a small house she had found in Ukiah, and the council approved the move. The only one of her children who didn't want to leave was Janet. Nita knew how close I felt to her, and so when Janet begged, she was allowed to remain with us.

The church was going to have a small group go on an evangelistic tour for a few weeks, and Nita, Al, and I had all been asked to help organize the trip. Nita postponed her move until the trip was over.

Janet was so pleased that she was going to stay. She and I had often talked about how much we loved each other. Janet was so special. She was only eight years old and yet she had more sensitivity and empathy than most adults. When she heard people talk about pains they were having or a cruel thing they had seen at school, Janet would weep for that person. If anyone in the house cried, Janet would cry, too. Daphene and Janet were inseparable, and now, with this promise that they could be together "for always," they became even closer.

The trip was enjoyable. Since there was only one bus and Jim was on it, we had good food and conversation. We stopped in each city for only one meeting and usually had pleasant sleeping accommodations. In fact, several of the cities had planned parties and entertainment for us. It was a real vacation, the only one we were to have during our entire six years in the church.

On the way home the bus was crowded because many of the people in different cities had decided to pack their things and move to Redwood Valley. Twelve people were added to our church, and when we returned we were told to wait until the counsellors decided where these people would live.

Finally, Patty Cartmell, one of the counsellors, stood in front of the room and went through the list of people waiting. Jim introduced the new members one by one. Patty read my name and I walked over to the group that was gathering. Linda came over and whispered to me, "Since Nita and her children are moving out of your house tomorrow, we thought you might be able to take

Betty and her four children into your home." She pointed to four children who were hovering around their mother looking very small and frightened.

"Oh well," I said, with a shrug of my shoulders, "I guess it's okay. I had been looking forward to some peace and quiet, but I do like small children around the house." Linda took me over to meet Betty and her children.

She was an attractive black woman whose husband, Cy, was in jail. She had come to hear Jim preach in Philadelphia and he had offered to help free her husband. When Jim offered her a place to stay in Redwood Valley until her husband was freed, she gladly took him up on his offer. She had been having serious financial difficulties and was deeply appreciative of the kindness he extended to her family. She shook my hand warmly and said that she was grateful for a place to stay. "I'll do whatever I can to help you," she said, "but you should understand that I don't have any money at all to repay you."

I smiled. "Jim Jones has taken care of all that. All we want you to do is enjoy our country home. I'm sure your children will like our animals and the swimming hole." One of her little boys opened a sleepy eye and looked up at me when he heard about the swimming hole. He grinned and went back to sleep.

Al came in looking for me and walked over to meet Betty. I introduced him and he offered to take Betty and her children to the car. "You came at a perfect time, Betty," he said with a smile. "A family that was living with us just moved." He looked at me and said, "That's where I've been, moving Nita's things to her new home."

"Good," I said happily. "Now we have plenty of beds for you and your children. We're happy to have you stay with us."

It was after three in the morning and Al and I were the last ones into bed. I looked at him with a tired grin. "I thought we were going to have a peaceful household for a while, but I guess we have children again." I thought about my childhood dream to have twelve children, and with a quick count I realized that we were getting close to my dozen.

The next morning the children woke up early and went outside to play by the river. These small children from the big city of Philadelphia had never seen a goat before, and this was the first time they had even had the opportunity to run free. It was beautiful to watch them enjoying the fresh country air. Betty spotted our piano right away. "Do you mind if I play?" she asked almost bashfully.

"I'd love to have you play," I answered. "I used to play the piano but I don't have much time anymore."

Betty sat down at the piano and sang while she played. Her voice had a soulful quality that made me feel like crying. My heart went out to this young mother who had been transplanted to a strange church group with a white family. I felt that I was helping Jim do something to alleviate suffering.

When I told Jim about Betty's musical talents, he asked her to play a song at a service. Once again her fingers brought a piano to life. The members of the congregation joined her and sang as they had never sung before. Jim was amazed. Betty was more than a good musician, she played from something deep within her and was able to bring a genuine response from people. As she finished her song he asked if she would help the organist from then on.

Two wonderful months passed and Jim announced that the church had accomplished what he'd promised Betty. Cy had been freed from jail and was on his way to Redwood Valley. Betty was elated, and her children couldn't talk about anything but their daddy, a man of whom they were fiercely proud.

Cy was an outspoken man with deep convictions. His gratitude to Jim and to us was deep and sincere. He agreed to stay in Redwood Valley long enough to find out what Jim was teaching before he decided whether to take his family back to Philadelphia.

Jim asked me to explain the errors in the Bible to Cy and I tried to do as he requested. But Cy knew so much more about the Bible than I did that I wasn't able to make any headway. I would show him one of the carefully marked contradictions that Jim had shown me, and he would show me another text that seemed to explain the original contradiction. I told Jim the problem I was having and he said he'd take care of it in the next sermon.

It so happened that the next sermon fell on Thanksgiving Day. The church had provided a lovely turkey dinner and we were all told to take our seats for the evening service. That night the sermon was about the errors in the King James version of the Bible. Cy listened to the entire sermon without once interrupting Jim. Jim searched his face for a response, but Cy's expression never changed from the polite interest he had exhibited when the sermon began. Finally, after two hours, Jim became exasperated and blurted out, "Well, Cy, I'd like to hear what you have to say about all this."

Cy stood up. "Jim, I must thank you, first of all for what you have done for me and for my family. I don't know if we will ever be able to repay you. When I was in jail I was so worried about Betty and the children that I couldn't sleep. Then she came to your service and you took her and the kids in, and wrote letters to the parole board on my behalf. I want you to know that I deeply appreciate all these things. However, you have asked me a fair question and I must answer you. I have listened to everything you have said, but I disagree with you. I have talked with Betty at some length about the things she has seen and heard here, and I must also tell you that I don't agree with the hero worship that you have tried to instill in her and in our children. People here are looking to you as some sort of God, and I still believe that God is in the heavens. Betty and the children are going to be leaving with me tomorrow, and we will try to send you some money to repay you for your kindness." As he finished his speech he sat down.

The silence in the room was stifling. Few people had ever dared to speak so honestly to Jim. Cy had been courteous, but he had contradicted Jim publicly. It was apparent that Jim was trying to control the urge to scream at Cy.

He took off his dark glasses and glared. "You ungrateful bastard," Jim said, spitting the words out like they were poison. "We got you out of jail and took care of your family—for nothing, mind you. We don't want any money from you. In fact, we don't want anything from you." He stood up and looked at Betty's children, who were beginning to cry. Jim was screaming now. "I am not going to give another penny to support you or your children. I am sorry for your family, but they seem to have chosen to stay with you, so I will not help them either. To give you any financial help now would only help you go back to hell. But I want you to know that if you take Betty and these four little children away from the protective atmosphere of this church, one of your children will be dead within a year. You will be back in jail with no hope of parole and nothing but pain and sadness will follow you for the rest of your life." He tried to regain control of himself as he looked at Betty. "Is it true that you have chosen to leave this church and take your children away from my protection to follow this—um—man?" He said the word *man* as though he were saying *dog*.

Betty stood up. "Jim, I understand that you are angry and I am sorry. You have done a lot for our family, but Cy is my husband and these are his children. Yes, I have decided to stay with him."

Jim gave her a look of disgust and with a deep sigh said, "Then go, damn you, take your children to hell. I withdraw all my protection from you and your family forever!"

I will never forget the horror that followed Jim's tirade. All four children were weeping hysterically. They had been in the church long enough to believe that Jim had enough power to cause the terror he had just predicted, and yet they loved their daddy. Betty was crying as she and Cy walked out with their children.

Jim asked Al to stand up. "Take that ungrateful family to the nearest Greyhound station. Do not give them one penny. They are

going to have to take care of themselves. They'll have to beg on the
streets to get back to Philadelphia."

"All right, Jim," Al answered obediently. The Thanksgiving
meeting ended and everyone went home in silence. This was the
first time most of us had seen Jim show this kind of anger and
hostility. It had been painful to watch the suffering and fear in the
children that we had come to love.

Al and I drove Cy, Betty, and the children to the Santa Rosa
Greyhound station. As instructed, we dropped them off on the
sidewalk with their suitcases and sleeping bags. It was almost
two o'clock in the morning and the four little children were still
whimpering.

Cy asked me to give him enough money to call his relatives. "I
just got out of prison and all I got was a plane ticket out here. I
don't have a dime," he pleaded. Jim had pointedly told us not to
give him one cent, so we sadly refused.

As we drove away I felt a deep surge of hate for Jim Jones. I
tried to rationalize that Jim was doing the best thing to help Cy
realize that he was unable to take care of this family on his own.
But it broke my heart to see these little children that we had grown
to love sitting there with no place to go in the middle of the night.

Once again we had more beds than children. Jim had been
asking all of us to get foster home licenses so we could take in
children from the Bay Area. "There are many black children in
Oakland who cannot find foster homes. Most of these children
will never have the opportunity to enjoy the fresh country air
unless we are willing to take them in," Jim had said.

Since we had the space, and one of the members had been
assigned to do most of the paper work and negotiations with the
placement workers, the only thing I needed to do was volunteer
our home. Two days after I told Carolyn Layton that we would
take a child, a placement worker brought Andre to our door.

Andre was nine years old, very black and very hungry. We
didn't know anything about taking care of a black child and
Andre wasn't prepared to teach a white family the things they
should know about special hair and skin care.

But after many months we all learned, through trial and error,
how to enjoy each other, and I proudly showed him off when I
went into town. The shocked stares of small-minded racists in the
community only added to the feeling of oneness in our church
family where all people were accepted, regardless of color.

*   *   *

When most Americans were writing Christmas cards to their
friends, we were writing letters to people who Jim felt could give

him support. His instructions were: "Every letter is to be written with one thing in mind. I want to have letters in my file praising our group or praising my ministry." He encouraged us to write to politicians who might be running for an important office in the future. "Try to find out what each politician is interested in, and include that in your letter."

We anxiously waited to see how many people would respond to the "bait" they had been sent. When we received the appropriate response, Jim would file it for future use. Some of the letters sounded as if the writer could be encouraged to say more, so Jim would assign one of his staff members to write another letter. Again, these responses were filed for future public relations work.

In our small community it was likely that the candidate Jim endorsed would win, so he was courted by them all. After they would take him to dinner or to a party, he would come back bragging that he had extracted promises from each of them by pledging his vote. The fact that Jim had made the same promises to the opposing contenders didn't bother him at all. When the loser asked Jim why he didn't keep his promise, he answered, "Well, you know, I can't force my members to vote the way I do."

Actually we hadn't discussed any political issues in the church because we didn't have to decide whom or what to vote for. The night before voting we received a telephone message telling us how "Jim was going to vote." We copied Jim's suggested list when we went to cast our own ballots.

*   *   *

As my work pressures increased I was having to spend more and more time at the Publications Office. Since Al worked only one week each month, he was confined to the house most of the time, doing the things that a mother usually does. I would get home from work just long enough to eat dinner and *maybe* talk to the children for a few minutes before I had to leave again to get back to work or to a church meeting.

Al finally asked me if I could spend a little more time with the children. He didn't realize how much it hurt me that I wasn't able to. The Cause was demanding more and more of my time.

We had almost forgotten that we were in a holiday season. We certainly weren't in any mood to celebrate. We remembered the Christmases before we joined the church. They had been filled with joy and happiness. This year each child was going to be allowed presents worth exactly sixteen dollars. All presents were to be given out by Jim Jones and none by the parents.

Instead of parents enjoying Christmas shopping, a "Gift

Committee" would select the gifts based on the age and sex of each child. The children would be permitted to submit recommendations to the Gift Committee.

By midnight, when Jim finally finished his Christmas sermon, all the children, who had been eyeing the presents, had fallen asleep. Now they were prodded to go up front so "Uncle Jim" could play Santa.

The presents were wrapped in newspaper and string. Children who had been raised in the church had no other expectations; this was all they had ever known, or they had forgotten the thrill, from many years before, of colored paper and pretty ribbons. But our children were keenly disappointed. In fact, the only one who would even open her presents was Daphene, and she was disgusted to find that all her toys were for children much younger than she was. She handed the entire pile of "baby things" to a small child sitting near her.

Daphene and Janet came over to me with tears in their eyes. "Is this all we get?" I whispered in their ears that we would be going to a store the next day to enjoy the after-Christmas sales.

We secretly had our own Christmas one day late. I couldn't make my children sacrifice everything for the Cause that I had chosen.

*   *   *

*

1972

I thank you Jim, I thank you Jim,
I thank you Jim, I thank you Jim,
For you've been so good to me,
Yes you've been so good to me.

You've been a healer in the sickroom,
You've been a lawyer in the courtroom,
You've been a mind healer and a mind regulator,
Made a way out of no way.

You've made the blind to see
And the lame to walk,
Even made the dumb to talk,
Oh Jim, I thank you Jim.
                    —from a Peoples Temple song

It was a long, cold winter, and we were in the middle of one of the heaviest rains that anyone living there could remember. The Russian River, which was a beautiful winding stream during the summer months, had become a raging torrent. The teachers living in the trailer house began to worry as the rains continued day after day. The river rose to within a foot of the bank, and they decided that it was time to find different living quarters. They realized that with just twelve more inches of rain they might be floating down the river in the trailer, along with the large logs and other miscellaneous things that went rushing past them every few minutes.

We couldn't blame them, for we were a little frightened ourselves. Three days after they moved out, Roz, one of the church members who wasn't afraid of the high water, moved in. We never could figure out why Roz had decided to live in the country. She was deathly afraid of poison oak and of touching anything that might have touched poison oak, including cats, dogs, or wandering children.

Roz would occasionally come over to our house to eat with us, bringing a bottle of rubbing alcohol with her. She would carefully wipe her chair, the table, and anything else she might touch, with this alcohol, "to destroy any poison oak germs" that might be waiting for her. In spite of this odd habit, we loved her. She brought art and beauty to our family and filled our children's evenings with drama lessons and fascinating stories.

In addition to the pleasure she brought into our home, Roz was probably the most powerful public relations person in the church. Through her efforts alone more than a score of new members were added.

It seemed that each time there was bed space available in our home, a new person would come along to claim it. Now that Betty's family had moved, I wondered who would be next. I didn't have to wonder long, though, because the following week Joanne came to visit Grandma, and when she saw our beautiful country home she asked if she could share it with us.

Joanne had been a member of the church for more than a year. Her husband had left her because he didn't want to live under the strict rules of the church. Joanne had a year-old baby named Gwen and she was also taking care of Julie, the spunky daughter of a handicapped mother. Gwen was a picture-book baby, the kind that a mother would order if it were possible to list all the characteristics you wanted in a perfect child. She was beautiful, loving, cuddly, and very, very good. Julie, on the other hand, was a gangly, noisy, hyperactive child with a lot of emotional problems from having been raised with very little supervision. Joanne loved her two daughters equally and showered as much attention on Julie as she gave to her own little baby. We were impressed by her fairness and compassion, and we knew that she and her little family would be pleasant additions to our home.

About two weeks later, Tina arrived. She was a red-haired, freckle-faced girl in her late teens. Tina came down our hill one day, just as Grandma had prayed for God to "please send someone to help mend the goat's fences." Grandma looked up after she finished her prayer and there stood Tina at the end of the garden path.

"I just asked God to send someone to help mend the fences," Grandma said, knowing that Tina was His answer. She spent the next two days with Grandma.

Grandma introduced her "angel" to us. We liked her instantly and asked her if she'd like to go to a church service with us the following Sunday. Within a week, Grandma's "angel" had become a member of our church.

We asked Tina where she was living and she showed us her "home," a funny-looking, homemade camper shell on the back of her old truck. She gladly accepted our offer of a real bed and a ready-made family.

At the time Tina was moving in, a young man, Len, was traveling from Philadelphia to Redwood Valley. He had heard

Jim preach in his city, and one day as he was enjoying a marijuana high he had gotten the "message" to go to Redwood Valley to be with God. Len hitchhiked with his backpack all the way to our church and got there in time for the next Sunday service. Tina took one look at Len and fell in love.

Len had a long, messy ponytail but a warm and wonderful smile. "Could he please come to live with us? You know, he doesn't have any place else to live," Tina begged. I told her to ask him if he wanted to come to our house and she brought him home with her.

Len was happy to be offered a home. Tina made no secret of her open admiration for him. When Tina would become too forward, though, Len would tell her about his girlfriend, Meri, who would probably be coming up from Los Angeles soon.

Two weeks later Meri arrived in search of Len and in search of God, who had told her where the church was. She arrived early one morning. Meri was half starved, and she shook from both malnutrition and drug abuse. Len had gone by the church grounds on his way to a job he had just started in Ukiah. He saw her there, and told her to wait in Al's car until Al got off work later in the afternoon.

Meri later told us that she'd sat in his car for several hours, hallucinating, with no idea of how many hours had passed. She also told me that when a white dog had walked past the car she thought it was the "God" that Len had told her about.

Later that afternoon Al was shocked to see this trembling waif sitting in his car.

"What are you doing here?" he demanded; Meri trembled more.

"Len told me to wait here and someone would take me home," she answered.

Because he didn't know what else to do, Al brought Meri home with him. She moved in, bringing her lice, "crabs," and dysentery. Her hands shook so hard that she wasn't able to do any chores even though she wanted to be helpful.

Once again our home was filled. Al and I looked at our "family" sitting in the living room and I proudly whispered to him, "Aren't they beautiful?" Our five children, Andre, Joanne, Gwen, Julie, Tina, Len, and now Meri. With a quick mental count, I realized that I finally had the dozen children of my childhood dreams.

One day Len asked me to cut his hair and I gratefully stopped what I was doing and got my scissors. When I finished with Len, Meri asked me to cut hers. With haircuts they were both good-looking people and seemed to feel more like a part of the church family now that they had shed their "hippie" clothes and appearance.

We didn't know, at first, that Meri had dysentery. We thought that her continuous diarrhea was a result of malnutrition. But suddenly the rest of our household started to get high fevers and diarrhea, too. We took several of them to the doctor and when we told him how many people were in our home he prescribed a quart jar full of tetracycline pills. He notified the Health Department and our home was quarantined. The doctor said dysentery was a highly contagious disease and we weren't to come in contact with anyone until we were all well. Health Department officials came out twice to inspect our well water, but they were finally satisfied that Meri had brought the disease from another city. Our well was given a clean bill of health.

While we were battling the dysentery, Meri was fighting a private war with her crabs and lice. She bathed her hair and body every day with a special shampoo, would think they were all dead, and then would find a survivor. Amazingly, she didn't spread them to anyone else. When the last one died she hung her sleeping bag out in the sunshine before getting it cleaned. Finally the dysentery epidemic ended, the quarantine was removed, and we were able to go back to our jobs and the church meetings.

When we returned to the church Jim was pleased to see that Len and Meri had gotten their hair cut. They looked so good that he decided to institute a new rule. "It is counterproductive to have long hair. People who wear their hair long are just on an ego trip. Only people who want to serve their own selfish interests will keep their hair long. People in our community judge our group by your appearance and our image suffers if your hair is long." He had built an entire evening's sermon around the evils of long hair and everyone who was still wearing long hair began to fidget uneasily.

Jim looked proudly at Len and Meri and praised them for having their hair cut on their own. Then he looked at Roz with her beautiful long black hair. "Are you willing to have your hair cut, Roz?" he asked her.

Roz looked frightened as she said, "I really don't want to cut it. All my life my hair has been the only thing that makes me feel good about myself." She explained to Jim and the rest of the congregation that her hair was very important to her self-image. As a child she had been told that without long hair she would be ugly. She offered to wear it on top of her head or under a wig, but Jim had no mercy. She was told to have her hair cut before the following weekend.

Roz was not the only person upset by this new rule. In retrospect, it is a little strange that people reacted so violently. We had all pledged our lives to this church, but hair was such a personal thing.

True to his word, the following Sunday Jim had several

amateur barbers ready to help the members conform to the new image he wanted us to project. Throughout the entire day and into the evening counsellors would tap one offender after another, and direct them to stand in line for a haircut. Men, women, and children were all subjected to the same rule. Many of the young girls with beautiful long hair were standing tearfully, obediently waiting for the unmerciful shearing that Jim had commanded.

Meri and I were becoming good friends. We would talk for hours, sharing our dreams and our questions. Meri had come from a military family and, to my surprise, I was finding out that she was a genius. She had walked away from a mathematics scholarship into a life of drugs and rebellion. As the drugs began to leave her system, it became more and more apparent that she was a very unusual person with great abilities.

She and Tina both loved Len, but Meri felt that she had the first claim on him. He enjoyed the attention showered on him from both of these women, but he made it very clear that he wanted to keep a safe distance. Meri, using her prior relationship with him as a lever, moved her sleeping bag into his room and slept on the floor beside his bed. She finally realized he wasn't going to share the bed with her and moved out.

As Meri became more comfortable with us, she confessed that she had a little medical problem and should see a doctor. I made an appointment for her and drove her into Ukiah for an examination. The doctor told me she had colitis and couldn't eat anything but strained foods for several months. More than that, though, Meri had a serious case of venereal warts and needed an operation to have them removed. As Meri and I talked about the doctor's findings she cursed the man she had been living with in Los Angeles who had given them to her.

We knew that Meri would have to get a job to help pay for this operation, and she found a good job in Ukiah working as a technician in a local television station. Her new job, though, presented a very big problem. Meri didn't have a car and had never learned to drive. We would have to leave at 5:30 A.M. to get her to work on time. It was a fourteen-mile trip along a winding mountain road with many dangerous curves on it, and Meri was afraid that she wouldn't ever be able to drive by herself on this road.

After several weeks of driving her to and from work each day, I realized that, afraid or not, she would have to learn to drive. Al tried first, but every time he told her she was doing something wrong she would start to cry. Al realized that she was still too nervous to be criticized, so he asked me if I would try because I was a little more patient.

Offering to help Meri learn to drive was one of the most dangerous things I had done in my life. Her reflexes were slow, probably because of her years of drug use, and her nerves were constantly on edge. She couldn't drive moderately. She had only two speeds—bat-out-of-hell fast or stopped. She couldn't judge the position of the car on the road and kept drifting into the lane of oncoming traffic. If I calmly suggested that she had wandered into the wrong lane, she would swerve the car into the gutter of the lane and cry because I was so critical.

After six weeks of this punishment, Meri finally passed the driver's test. We gratefully loaned her the money to put a down payment on an old used car. I sent a prayer to her guardian angel and left Meri's fate to a higher power.

* * *

Jim was making inroads in San Francisco, trying to start a congregation there, looking forward to the possibility of purchasing a church in the near future. He was trying to obtain more money and started taking more and more offerings. "We need more money to extend our human service ministry into the Bay Area and eventually down to Los Angeles," he said, as he took another offering. "I feel that there are thousands of people in the metropolitan areas that need to hear this message before the bomb destroys them. We need to purchase more buses so that you can all travel with me from city to city giving the warning so that many can be saved." The ushers passed the buckets for the third time in one service.

We believed that Jim needed money, but it was still emotionally draining to listen to him begging for the people to give everything they could. Some of the members began to have garage sales and other moneymaking events to help purchase the buses that Jim wanted.

He asked the members for new ideas to use as he took the offerings. One woman stood up. "When I was in the Baptist Church," she volunteered, "our pastor would have us form an offering line. He would ask us to put the money directly into his hand. The members gave more because they knew that he was watching how much they gave."

Jim tried this new approach the next meeting and found that the members did indeed give more. Later in the same service, he had every person touch his robe as they gave another offering. The church was changing, but the changes were so gradual that we hadn't really noticed the difference.

Another summer was approaching, and Jim began talking

about the "Divine Movement" in Philadelphia. I had never heard of Father Divine, but Jim was becoming obsessed with the idea of taking a trip to recruit the members of Father Divine's church, the Peace Mission. Father Divine had died, and Jim was upset. He patiently explained his concern.

"Father Divine failed his mission and now that he has died, it is up to me to finish the work he began. There are many wonderful people still in the Peace Mission and I want to go show them that the Divine mantle has been placed on my shoulders."

Jim sent letters to Mother Divine and to some of the members of her church requesting the privilege of spending a few days in the Mission.

Mother Divine opened the doors of the Peace Mission to Jim. As soon as he received her invitation he began to prepare some young people for their visit. "You always have to say 'thank father, thank mother' for any courtesy extended to you," he explained to them. "Everyone has to dress nicely and all the women have to wear dresses or skirts. The Peace Mission doesn't allow women to wear slacks." The young people laughed together over the silliness of saying "thank father, thank mother." Little did any of us dream that we would soon be saying the very same words to our pastor and his wife.

The buses traveled day and night stopping only when necessary for refueling. The young people ate, slept, and lived on the bus for three days. They stopped a few miles outside of Philadelphia to get cleaned up so they would look refreshed when they arrived.

Mother Divine ushered them into the waiting room, and our people reported being amazed at the splendor of the furnishings. Beautiful gold-framed pictures of Mother and Father Divine hung in almost every room.

As they were ushered into the dining hall, they were even more impressed. Crystal, silver, and beautiful china adorned the splendid table, which was covered with a lace tablecloth. At the head of the long table was the most beautiful setting of all, with a gold goblet. Someone whispered that it had been Father Divine's place and that no one was allowed to use it.

The members of the Divine Mission were friendly to everyone from Peoples Temple and they invited Jim to speak that evening. He spoke eloquently, mentioning to the assembled group that Father Divine had begun a great work and that he, Jim, was practicing the same teachings that Father Divine had taught. There was no word to indicate to Mother Divine that he had planned to try to take the members away from her. After the meeting Jim and Mother Divine spent the evening together.

The meeting must have been friendly because the following day they seemed to be on cordial terms with one another. Later that evening Jim was again invited to speak. This time, though, his sermon was much different. He began to criticize the expensive furnishings of the Mission and say that the ideals of Father Divine had been betrayed. He performed a couple of miracles to prove that he had the same gift that Father Divine had possessed and quickly invited the members of the Peace Mission to come to Redwood Valley where they could once again practice the true apostolic socialism that Father Divine had taught while he was alive.

The meeting was brought to a close when Mother Divine abruptly asked Jim and his group to leave immediately. Some of the members of the Peace Mission had been impressed by Jim's miracles and about a dozen went to California with Jim.

A few days later the travelers returned. Jim had a message telephoned to all the members giving us a new set of church rules, ostensibly to help the new members from the Divine Mission feel more comfortable. "There will be no more swearing. Women cannot wear slacks or jeans to services, only dresses. No one is to call Jim anything but Father." The message continued, "You must all begin to show Father a great deal of respect because this is the way the Divine members have been trained. We want them to know we respect our leader as much as they respected Father Divine."

At first it was hard to remember to call Jim "Father," and it seemed silly. Most of us assumed it was a game Jim was playing to placate the Peace Mission members until they understood the fact that you don't have to give a person a title to show respect. We all hoped that within a few weeks these temporary rules would become a thing of the past.

The Divine members proved to be more difficult to indoctrinate than Jim had expected. He first tried to destroy their belief in Father Divine, but every time Jim would say something unkind about their leader, a Divine member would jump to his defense.

Jim tried a new approach. One of the Divine members had told Jim privately that Father Divine had come into her bedroom one night and asked her to make love with him. Without warning, in the meeting next night, Jim asked this sister to stand up. "This sister was approached by Father Divine in the middle of the night and he tried to force her to have sex with him," he said, pointing his finger at the shocked woman. She was aghast that Jim had turned her private confession into a public indictment of Father Divine.

Instantly another Peace Mission member shouted at her, "I

don't believe you. You've always told lies and I think this one is the biggest lie of all." Jim assured the woman that he knew by revelation that this story was true. "I have absolute evidence that Father Divine was having sex with many of his members, both men and women, before he died," he said with a tone of authority.

The following night, at a special meeting, Jim explained to us why he wanted to take in these members, most of whom were old. "It may seem strange to you now that we would be bringing older members into our church," he began. "They serve several functions that will be very helpful to us in the future. First, if we are ever trying to escape into another country the border guards will see all our old people and assume that we are a humanitarian group. Also, no border guard would want to detain buses that are loaded with elderly people who might have heart attacks or strokes. But more importantly, if we are ever to relocate in another country these people's Social Security and pension checks would follow them. In a communal situation in another country, where the cost of living is lower, our entire group might be able to survive on these checks until we are able to find other means of making money."

But Jim was having problems convincing the Divine followers that he was the person who had been chosen by God to take Father Divine's mantle. He performed amazing healings and gave them frightening predictions of coming gloom, but he still couldn't measure up to their memory of Father Divine.

Jim also told us that he'd have to tear down the image of Mother Divine, who was the acting leader of the Divine movement. He announced to the Peace Mission people: "When I went into her room with her she tore her blouse open and begged me to make love to her. She flaunted her sagging breasts in my face but I wasn't tempted. I wouldn't do it, no matter what she offered me. She even begged me to join her and help her lead the Divine movement, but I refused her every wish for any amount of money or power."

The faithful members of the Peace Mission were not convinced and many of them left that night to return to Philadelphia. A few decided to stay because they believed some of Jim's miracles. They hoped to stay on and see if he was actually able to raise the dead as he had promised.

Jim expected that most of the Divine members would follow the first group to Redwood Valley but obviously he was to be disappointed. One by one those who had come became disillusioned and left our group. They didn't want to believe that this vulgar man had taken Father Divine's mantle. As they returned to Philadelphia they warned the other members not to pay any attention to the letters they were receiving from Redwood Valley. The doors of the Divine Mission were locked against Jim and any member of Peoples Temple from that day forward.

One of Jim's most avid supporters in Ukiah was Walter Heady, a man who headed the local branch of the John Birch Society. It was a strange combination—Jim Jones, who admitted to being a socialist, and Walter Heady, whose organization was decidedly right-wing in its beliefs. But Jim nurtured this relationship, successfully, glossing over their differences in philosophy as only his silver tongue could do.

One Sunday Walter Heady dropped in on our church service unexpectedly. Within moments the word went around from member to member: "Just follow Jim's lead."

As Jim walked to the front of the building he whispered to the organist. A few moments later she began to play "The Star Spangled Banner," and we all stood and joined in the song. Then we followed his lead in pledging allegiance to the flag.

The sermon would have delighted me at my first meeting in 1969, but now it seemed totally out of place. The same man who had been screaming about the injustices in our society and the inequality of capitalism was just as sincerely preaching about the glory of America and the wonderful people in our community.

The following day, Heady told someone, "I've heard some strange things about Peoples Temple and I went to check them out for myself. But now I am satisfied that he isn't just putting on an act to fool me. After all, the whole program couldn't have been changed just because I was there." Little did he know.

*   *   *

The plans for opening a church building in San Francisco were progressing nicely. Jim had found a large three-story building on Geary Street that had a vacant lot behind it which could be used for parking. Along with the negotiations on the building, Jim was trying to purchase three Greyhound-type buses to help transport the members between Redwood Valley and San Francisco.

As he explained the need for the buses he said, "It will be easier for me to protect you on the road if you are all together rather than spread out in separate cars. Your personal safety is the only thing that is important to me."

Now that the San Francisco members were going to have their own church, they didn't have to be begged for offerings. They began to volunteer for many different moneymaking projects in their homes and in the church.

For some time now Al and I had been operating a concession stand in the church, selling Jim's anointed pictures.

It had started with one photograph, blessed for healing, which sold for five dollars. By now our product line had expanded to include holy oil, prayer cloths, and a wide assortment of pictures of Jim Jones, which were blessed for every conceivable need. We were bringing in several thousand dollars a month at this table, which all went to help the Cause.

I knew, too, that San Francisco would provide me with a whole new group of people who wanted to buy Jim's anointed picture, so I began to make lockets, key chains, and other trinkets with his picture in them for people to use as charms to ensure their health and healing.

As Jim looked forward to expanding his congregation he began to change his image even more. He was becoming infatuated with his new title of Father and the respect that it demanded. Most of the Peace Mission members had returned to Philadephia, but he kept the name he had assumed for their benefit. He didn't allow anyone to call him Jim now, not even his closest staff members.

Jim was becoming more preoccupied with the fear that someone was going to kill him. He knew he had made enemies at the Peace Mission in Philadelphia when he was there and again when he told the crude lie about Mother Divine. He also told us that there were people in Indianapolis who hated him because he had brought their relatives to California.

He chose six men he felt he could trust and assigned them the duty of protecting him whenever he appeared in public. Those who had been chosen were honored to be appointed to guard the leader. He dubbed them "guards," and several were issued weapons permits along with weapons to carry at all times. None of us questioned Jim's need for guards. We were grateful that he wouldn't have to worry any more about the threat of being killed.

He began to hint broadly that he was none other than "God Almighty." In a secret meeting he told us that he knew his previous incarnations. He bragged that he had been Buddha, the Bab, Jesus Christ, and, most recently, Lenin. "Of course," he warned them "this is highly confidential and you aren't to tell anyone else. The members might not understand, especially about that last incarnation."

When he realized that his staff members were awed by this revelation, he decided that the rest of his members would probably be impressed, too. In the next Sunday service he announced that he was going to tell those who were present one of his greatest secrets. With a great deal of ceremony he announced, "I have lived on this earth before. I have come for a special mission and you who are following me are my chosen people. Most of you have been with me during some of my previous incarnations. I lived thousands of years ago as Buddha. Then I spent a short incarnation as the Bab, the person who founded the Bahai faith. I have lived on earth as Jesus the Christ, and my last incarnation was in Russia as Vladimir Lenin." He spoke with such authority and sincerity that we all believed him.

It was a wonderful secret and we felt privileged that he had shared it with us. "We are so fortunate to be able to follow him" was the sentiment expressed by most of the members. I'm sure that if Jim had known what was just around the corner he wouldn't have been so anxious to make these astounding claims. He was openly bragging that he was God Almighty by the time the San Francisco temple was ready to be used as a worship center.

The church's construction crew had worked for several weeks modernizing the interior of the church and building the pews and pulpit. Finally, in September, the building was ready. We had purchased our first three buses for the members to use to attend the first service in our new church.

Then, like a thunderbolt out of the sky, Lester Kinsolving wrote an article in the San Francisco *Examiner.*

On September 17, 1972, the Sunday paper had a front-page headline that proclaimed "The Prophet Who Raises the Dead." Before Jim had an opportunity to react to this first article, another one was out in the Monday paper, "Healing Prophet Hailed as God at S.F. Revival." Newspapers across the nation began to pick up the sensational story that included a graphic tongue-in-cheek description of the "dead" people Jim had revived.

Jim was stunned. He called his staff together to discuss the strategy they would use to try to undo the damage Kinsolving had done to the image of the church. The next morning we got an emergency message that we were to meet at the Redwood Valley Church parking lot dressed warmly. Most of us hadn't seen the San Francisco paper, so we didn't have any idea why we were being called to gather at the church. The only members who didn't have to go were those who had jobs that they might lose. Even the schoolchildren were to stay out of classes for the day to join the members at the parking lot.

We were rushed into buses, still without being told where we were going or why. Finally, a rumor started circulating through our bus that the *Examiner* had printed an unfavorable article and we were going to protest.

It was still early when we arrived in front of the *Examiner* building and began our march. Several people were handed signs which had been hastily made the night before. The only instruction we had was: "Keep marching, and don't talk to anyone. If a reporter tries to get you to talk, point to Bonnie or Carolyn and let them do all the talking."

Lunchtime came and went and we were all getting hungry, thirsty, and tired, but we were told that we were still going to march for several hours.

Television news stations, newspaper reporters, and radio announcers came to cover the story of Jim Jones's "devoted flock" who so faithfully marched from early morning until after dark. They were unaware that we weren't even sure what we were marching for. None of the reporters stayed around to watch the pathetic dinner we were finally given: a dry peanut butter sandwich on partially frozen bread and a small drink of Kool-Aid, which we had to consume while we continued to march. Not one reporter commented about the fact that the marchers couldn't answer even the simplest question without pointing to a spokesman. It didn't occur to the reporters that the young children marching with us should have been given some time to rest. We were all aware of the counsellors watching us to be sure we didn't talk to anyone.

The same church member who had paid for my steak dinner a year before was marching with us. He was a prominent businessman in San Francisco, and he didn't want any of his business associates to see him there. Several of us noticed that he dodged the many TV cameras as they panned our group, and one of the counsellors reported this to Jim. Jim had Bonnie ask one of the camermen to make a special point of getting his face on film, which he obligingly did. His picture was flashed on millions of television screens that night on the news broadcast.

We marched for two more days until our feet became numb. The food didn't improve, and neither did our dispositions. Finally, though, Jim had stirred up enough public sympathy so that the *Examiner* stopped its articles and gave him the opportunity to tell his side of the story.

In a taped interview Jim told the press what he wanted them to print, and they promised to use the entire interview without cutting or editing. One of the first questions he answered in the interview was about the forty-three resurrections he had bragged about. Although he said that all forty-three people had subsequently been sent to a physician, he did admit that he had, indeed, raised them from the "apparently dead" state.

Late that afternoon as Jim was telling his attorneys about the taped interview they suggested that there might be legal implications that would be unfavorable about his claim to be able to restore life. He decided that it might be better to have the newspapers remove that particular sentence from his statement. The newspaper refused to take this sentence out, so he tried a desperate strategy. He had the counsellors spend the remainder of the night making threatening and then pleading calls to the editor, publisher, and owner of the newspaper. The management of the paper had already been angered by the adverse publicity it had received when the church picketed, and the new harassment made it worse. The interview was published exactly as Jim had given it.

Amazingly enough, the church did not lose a single member because of the Kinsolving exposé. In fact, as Peoples Temple got nationwide attention, hundreds of people wrote asking for more information about the church. Several new members joined, hoping that a man who could raise people from the dead could also help them with their physical problems.

Taking courage from his triumph over Kinsolving and the adverse publicity, Jim decided that he would begin a church in Los Angeles. He found a beautiful building that was ideal for the members who had been faithfully attending services in a rented hall.

Now Jim had three churches over a 700-mile spread. He finished negotiations on seven more buses and now he had a fleet of eleven buses, plenty to carry all his members from one end of the nation to the other.

We were about to begin a weekly schedule that seemed impossible to keep up with. One weekend the eleven buses would take us to San Francisco for the Friday evening service, and when that service ended, we would board the buses and travel all night to Los Angeles. We arrived in Los Angeles by 11:00 A.M. the next morning, giving us time to eat breakfast, get our church clothes on, and be at service by 2:00 P.M. The afternoon service ended at eight in the evening. On Sunday the Los Angeles service would last from eleven in the morning until about four in the afternoon. Then we would quickly eat our dinner, board the buses again, and arrive back in Redwood Valley by 6:30 Monday morning. It gave us enough time to get home, eat, and leave for work or school.

On the alternate weekends we would have Friday-evening service in San Francisco which usually lasted until two Saturday morning. The Saturday service, also in San Francisco, would last from seven in the evening until about two on Sunday morning. On Sunday there would again be a service from eleven in the morning until about 2:00 A.M. Monday. We would arrive back in Redwood Valley at about 5:00 A.M. Monday, giving us a few minutes in our own beds before we had to be up again.

It was a grueling schedule, and many of us were bitter about the fact that we had no time left for ourselves or our families. No one complained aloud, though, because Jim explained that the Cause must be served first. "Besides," he explained, "hundreds of these people will be saved when the atomic bomb falls just because we bring them this message now." We were becoming fond of a lot of the San Francisco and Los Angeles members by now and were grateful that their lives would be spared when the bomb came.

The school year had begun a month before, and our children were gone most of the day. Joanne was able to stay home to take care of the domestic needs of our large family, and I felt good knowing that she loved the children and would see that their needs were met.

Our daughter, Linda, started bringing one of her girlfriends, Nichol Johnson, over to visit us quite often. She and Linda were both thirteen years old and they would sit in the bedroom and have long, serious talks. Nichol made no pretense about liking Peoples Temple. Her mother had joined the church a couple of years before, and Nichol and her two brothers had come along. All three of the children were resentful.

Nichol was an angry person. She confided that she hated her mother's emotional outbursts of temper and wished she could move. The church tried to move her several times and she complained about being shoved from place to place and being forced to live with people she hated. As she told me about a friend of her mother's who had made sexual advances toward her, I could feel that these hostilities were only the tip of the iceberg.

After several visits she asked me if she could come to live with us. "I can't stand it at Karen Layton's house anymore," she said. "Nobody really wants me to live with them anyway." I made a quick telephone call to her mother to ask permission and she said she would be glad to have Nichol stay with us.

Meri was also still with us, and we were becoming very good friends. I enjoyed talking with her because she was intelligent and extremely interesting. I had found a friend that I felt I could talk to about things I didn't dare discuss with anyone except Al. She began to talk about wanting to make a bigger contribution to the Cause. One day she said, "The thing I want more than anything else is to be on Jim's staff. It would be a real thrill to work that close with him."

"I've found that in this church you can have almost anything you want, if you're willing to work hard for it," I told her. "If that's really what you want, then you should start working with the people close to him." A few days later she was helping one of the attorneys, Tim Stoen, and she confided, "I think I'm on my way, he's been praising my work."

Meri Crawford was indeed on her way up and, eventually, made her way right to the top.

*   *   *

In the wake of the Kinsolving articles our church became the target of several investigations by reporters who thought there might be another "story" in the church. One of the reporters was Mark Duffy.

He was a young, good-looking, and very intense man. He came to criticize and stayed to help. He was so impressed by Jim Jones and the other members of the church that he immediately sold his fancy car, gave up his job, and moved to Redwood Valley to follow Jim's Cause. Because of Mark's background, Jim immediately appointed him the church's representative to the media.

*   *   *

Christmas 1972 was nearly upon us, but I knew it would be another disappointing day. I told the children that if they asked for their sixteen dollars in cash, I'd take them shopping the next day. At least that way they could get whatever they wanted.

*   *   *

This photograph of Jim blessing the children was taken in the spring of 1972. It picked up an aura of light from Jim's heart to Dorothy Buckley's head. Jim immediately dubbed it his "Shekinah Glory," claiming that the camera had captured the love that he had been projecting toward Dorothy at that very moment. The photo became an instant bestseller in the church. (The "aura" really came from a tiny slice in the negative.)

This image of Jim as loving father has now become macabre. The boy on Jim's right is Philip Lacy who lives in San Francisco. His mother and sister were both poisoned in Jonestown. Next, going counterclockwise, is John-John Stoen, who at age six died in Jonestown. Holding John-John is Kim Uneii, whose corpse was shown on the cover of Newsweek.

Danny Beck was adopted by members and was their pride and joy. He was murdered in Jonestown while his parents were in Redwood Valley managing Jones's farm. Next, Steve Burnham, is still alive. After Steve is Martin Amos, who had his throat slashed by his mother the night of the Jonestown murders.

Danny Pierson is somewhere, but no one knows exactly where. When his parents tried to quit the church about four years ago, his father, Dennis, was beaten so brutally that many have assumed he is dead.

Darrin Janaro was murdered in Jonestown.

Darrin Swinney was also murdered in Jonestown.

The next child is the daughter of a defector who was harassed unmercifully by Jim after her escape. She is living her own quiet life now, grateful that the nightmare she lived through has finally passed.

The last, the recipient of Jim's "Shekinah Glory," Dorothy Buckley, is dead. She was poisoned in Jonestown.

PASTOR
I HATE
JIM
JONES

SCHOOLTEACHER, FORMER HUMAN RIGHTS Commissioner, Grand Jury foreman, present president of Legal Rights Foundation, and

- **Christ-like leader** of Peoples Temple, who supports the cause of **peace** and social justice,
- who **adopted a black son** and five other children of different races,
- will be conducting his unique **prophetic healing** message to the public. Miraculous healings of growths, crippling diseases, etc. occur before your eyes in every meeting.

PEOPLES TEMPLE IS A TOTALLY INTEGRATED church near Ukiah, California,

- which operates a **drug rehabilitation** center, animal refuge, two **college dormitories**, and senior citizens' home, that serve all races and creeds.
- Our healing ministry **in no way** opposes the work of medical science. In fact, due to the insistence of our pastor, 82 people went to their doctors, who found diseases which would have led to their early demise. They went to doctors, and through treatment they have now completely recovered.

Until his attorneys told him that he could get into some legal difficulties, Jim never hesitated to advertise his ability to perform "miraculous healings of growths, crippling diseases, etc. [that] occur before your eyes in every meeting."

THIS? **OR THIS?**

PLACE STAMP HERE

TO:

This was one of the money appeals we made up at Publications for our mailing list. On the left is our daughter Daphene, portraying a slum child. It was particularly poignant to me that we didn't have to costume her for the role of the neglected child. Most of the children on the right—the happy ones—are listed as dead at Jonestown. (Photos by Al Mills)

SPECIAL LETTR TO GO OUT - EVERYONE MUST WRITE!!!

Write a short letter thanking Vice-President Rockefeller
for giving such a superb speech. Our Pastor, Jim Jones,
thinks so very much of you (respects you, etc.) and
appreciated all that you said at the Religion in American
Life dinner the other night. Some say that Pastor Jones told
you about his great speech.
You can also say things like:

     - I think you are a great vice-president

     - I wish you the best of success

     - All of our members at Peoples Temple Christian
          Church think the world of you

     - We need great leaders like you in these times

     - Pastor Jones has always taught us to appreciate
       and respect our governmental leaders, and has
       praised you often for your concern for people, etc.

     - It is important to see leaders in government taking an
       interest in (and honoring) our nation's religious
       leaders.

     - We've looked to you often for wisdom and guidance
       and have found you to be a tremendous inspiration

     - I want you to know that whoever Pastor Jim Jones
       respects, I respect. And he thinks the world of
       you. You have done so much for the country, and
       for the office of the Vice-President

     - You have shown courage and wisdom in so many issues, etc.

Do not seal your letter. Please have it done by tomorrow night's
meeting. It can be short. Put it in a stamped envelope, and address it
to:

               Vice-President Nelson Rockefeller
               Washington, D. C.

Put your return address on the letter. Use a previous address if you
wish.

Some can use a variation on this address - Say Vice-President
Rockefeller, or Nelson A. Rockefeller. Some can put on his
address Office of the Vice-President, or Vice-President of the
United States. XXXXXXXXXXXXXXXXXXX

*This instruction sheet was handed to every member of the church because
Jim wanted to impress then Vice-President Rockefeller. Such campaigns
were Jim's most effective means of gaining prominent and powerful
supporters.*

PEOPLES FORUM

Statement Of Support

We applaud Peoples Temple for taking the initiative to call for a thorough police investigation of the alleged break-in at the office of a local magazine.

We are familiar with the work of Reverend Jones and Peoples Temple and have no hesitancy in commending them for their example in setting a high standard of ethics and morality in the community and also for providing enormous material assistance to poor, minority and disadvantaged people in every area of human need.

Willie, Brown, Assemblyman
Rev. Norman Leach, San Francisco Council of Churches
Cecil Williams, Glide Memorial Methodist Church
Jane Fonda, actress/activist
Yori Wada, University of California Board of Regents
John Maher, Delancey Street Foundation
Julia Hare, radio commentator
E. Robert Wallach, attorney, professor of law
Rev. Dr. John V. Moore
Will Battle, President, Officers for Justice
Mrs. Franklin (Joan) Brann
Rev. William P. Clancey, Jr.
Rev. J. Alfred Smith, Allen Temple Baptist Church
Enola Maxwell, President, Portrero Hill Neighborhood Assn.
Paul Avery, author/investigative journalist
Mimi Silbert, Dr. of Criminology
Rev. Lynn Hodges, former Executive Director of No. Calif. Ecumenical Council
Vincent Hallinan

Howard Wallace, Gay Action
Bishop Karl Irvin, President, North. Cal./Nev. C.C. Disc. of Christ
Tom Hayden
Joe Hall, President, San Francisco NAACP
Mervyn Dymally, Lt. Governor, State of California
Rev. Gerald McHarg, Regional Pastor, So. Cal. Dis. of Christ
Rev. Dr. A.C. Ubalde, Jr., Bethany United Methodist Church, S.F. Housing Comm.
Albert Kahn, author
Sylvester Herring, San Francisco Human Rights Commission
Dave Jenkins, I.L.W.U.
Jack Weintraub, Local 85, IBT
Rita Semel, Conference on Race Religion & Social Concerns
Ray Yaeger, Co-ordinator, Inter-Faith Communications Comm
Mike Fairchild, Exec. Direc., San Francisco Educational Services
Dr. Nathan Hare, Clinical Psychologist
Harvey Milk
Paul Jacobs, author/journalist
Terrence "Kayo" Hallinan, attorney
Francis Huff, African-American Historical Society
Steve Kahn, Community-Action Co-ordinator
Connie Williams, Connie's Restaurant
Rev. Glenda Hope, Director, Genesis Church & Ecumenical Ctr.
Patricia Tunison, artist
Mrs. Charles R. Garry
Dave Whittaker, Haight-Fillmore Community Research Action
Claude Wynne, Gay Action
Charles Briody, Bay Area Ecum. Comm. Concern for Chile
Ceasar Smith, Street Peoples Committee
Margie Baker, San Francisco Unified School District
Gloria Davis, teacher
Ruth Kadish, San Francisco Airport Commission
Vivian Hallinan, President, Feed the Cities
Irma Tuominen, World Peace Council
Thomas Fleming, Editor-in-Chief, Sun-Reporter
Art Agnos, Assemblyman
Grandvel Jackson, 1st V.P., NAACP
Dennis Banks
Gil Graham, lawyer
Yvonne Golden, Principal, Opportunity II High School
Joan Byrnes, San Francisco Housing Commission
Monte Cardwell, San Francisco Council of Churches
Jeff Mori, Japanese Comm. Youth Council
Michael Davidow, author
Kevin Barnes, Education for the Handicapped

Sue Bierman, San Francisco Planning Commission
Rev. Melvin Suddereth, Trinity United Methodist Church
John Pairman Brown, Exec. Direc., No. Cal. Ecum. Council
Joe Johnson, former Deputy Mayor of San Francisco
Kerny Cavallari, Chile Democratico
Patrick Hallinan
Mary Rodgers, San Francisco Housing Authority
Charlene Grogan-Bealle, attorney
Alice S. Hamburg, Women for Peace
Geraldine Johnson, Pres., No. Cal. Coalition of Black Trade Unions
John Massen, No. Calif. Div. of U.N. Assoc. of USA
Tony Kilroy
Phil Martin, attorney
Mr. & Mrs. Fred Hirsch
Rev. J. Austell Hall, S.F. Police Commission
Archie Brown, I.L.W.U. (ret.)
Ken Orduna, Special Ass't. to Lt. Governor
Monsignor James Flynn, St. Peters Church
Rev. Walter Grumm, S.F. Council of Churches Board of Direc.
Jean S. Mellor, President, North of Market Senior Organization
Oliver Newson, North of Market Senior Organization
David Fishlow, Exec. Direc., No. Calif. ACLU
Ruth Jacobs, attorney
John Garb
Sylvia Yee, Chinese Friendship Assn.
Percy Steele, Bay Area Urban League Director
Michael Shaw, President, S.F. Urban League
Rev. Joe Masse
Mahlan Harmon, Director-Youth for Services
Father Eugene Boyle
Charles R. Garry
Dr. A. Hunter, West Side Lodge Rehabilitation Center
Bill Maher, Board of Education
Newton Hudson, Religion in American Life
Rev. Dennis Savage, 1st Christian Church, Whittier, Ca.
Rev. Ivan Ball, SFCC Board of Directors
Bill McCarthy, Unity Foundation
Rev. Dennis Short, Chaplain, Chapman College

[Note: Because of space limitations and our press deadline, the list of supporters is by no means exaustive. The organizations listed above are for identification purposes only."]

Only a few days before the New West exposé appeared, Jim published a list of prominent names that he claimed supported him and commended him for "setting a high standard of ethics and morality in the community...."

In 1975, Al accompanied Jim and some staffers on a trip to Jonestown, Guyana. Jim wanted Al to take some photos to use as propaganda. Since there was no fruit—because nothing would grow properly in Jim's paradise—they bought groceries in Georgetown and flew them out for the photos. Unfortunately, they forgot to get rid of the grocery sack. (Photo by Al Mills)

Deanna and Al Mertle, November 1968. A photo taken on our wedding day.

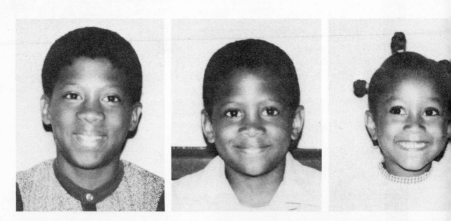

ABOVE *From the membership cards of Searcy, Ollie, and Najah, the three little children who lived with us in Redwood Valley and in Berkeley until we left the church. None survived Jonestown.*

Lillie May Victor—a teenager who lived with us in Redwood Valley. She died in Jonestown.

Al shot this photo of me and four of the five kids during the summer of 1969. Linda and Diane are the big ones; Daphene and Eddie, the smaller.

My mother, "Grandma." She was our "guardian angel" during the six years in the Temple. We wouldn't have made it through the struggle without her. (Photo by Al Mills)

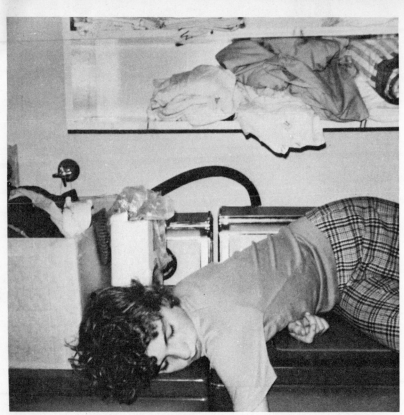

OPPOSITE *Sleep deprivation was a major factor in Jim's brainwashing program. In these photographs, two of our kids are seen "sleeping on the job." Daphene was doing laundry; Eddie was attending a service at the temple. Exhaustion simply got to them. Many former members describe similar incidents. When caught, the "offender" received a public beating. (Photos by Al Mills)*

Jeannie and Al Mills. After ten years of marriage and six years with God.

Jim Jones with some of the hundreds of children who accompanied him on the Temple's nationwide tour, covering 22 states and 10,000 miles, the summer of 1976.

Some of the 750 young and old Temple travelers at the Capitol in Washington, D.C.

Jim Jones delivering the keynote address to 20,000 people at the Muslims' Spiritual Jubilee in Los Angeles in May 1976. This joint rally was held at the Los Angeles Convention Center.

Jim Jones dining with famous private investigator, Hal Lipset.

Jim Jones claimed that he was the special guest of attorney E. Robert Wallach (past president of the San Francisco Bar Association) at a dinner. The claim was made in the Peoples Forum and dated November 1976. He later quoted Bob Wallach as saying: "I deeply respect Reverend Jim Jones and the work which he does and all of you who assist him in these noble goals."

TOP *Jim Jones and attorney Frederick P. Furth. Our daughter, Linda, told us that she and many of the other members of Peoples Temple were assigned to work for attorney Furth in his campaign for the Democratic nomination for the state Senate out of San Francisco, when he was running against Robert Mendelssohn. (Mendelssohn won that campaign, then ran against Senator Milton Marks and lost.) After the New West article in August 1977, prominent San Francisco Chronicle columnist Herb Caen said that Jim Jones had hired two of the "fiercest libel attorneys," Fred Furth and Charles Garry.*

CENTER *Jim Jones with American Indian Movement (AIM) leader Dennis Banks, his wife, and children.*

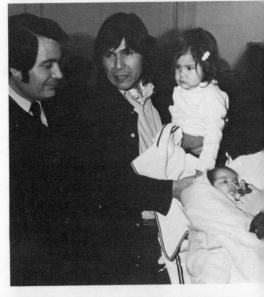

BOTTOM *Carlton B. Goodlett, M.D., Ph.D., and editor of the Sun Reporter, a San Francisco newspaper, poses here with Jim Jones. Carlton Goodlett was quoted by Jim as stating: "I have known Jim for several years and have worked with him in the movement for liberation and self-determination of all peoples. Jim is a highly sensitive man, one who is completely dedicated to the cause of social justice. I have seen him under fire from reactionary elements, and he has never wavered in his commitment. He is undoubtedly one of the most articulate and effective leaders in the United States today."*

Senator Milton Marks of California, speaking at the San Francisco temple, sharing the platform with Mike Prokes and Jim Jones. Milton Marks is quoted by Jim Jones as follows: "I am grateful that Peoples Temple is located in the fifth Senatorial district which I represent. . . . It is heartwarming to have among us human beings who are willing to get involved."

At a September 1976 testimonial dinner for Jim Jones, the speaker in this photograph, Rev. Gerald B. McHarg, assistant to the executive pastor, Christian Church (Disciples of Christ) of Southern California said: "One gets the impression of being in the midst of the human race at its best: a community of people whose primary concern is to love and to share. Peoples Temple is led by a man of deep integrity and sensitivity."

Also seated at the speakers' table, from left to right, are: San Francisco District Attorney Joseph Freitas and California State Assemblyman Willie L. Brown, Jr., who is credited with the following statement: "I have had the great pleasure of knowing a leader with tremendous character and integrity. . . . Rev. Jones is regarded among government officials, civic and religious leaders, and particularly the black community and working class people, with utter respect for what he has done to upgrade the quality of life in our area and to bring greater health and well-being to thousands of poor, minority, and disadvantaged people."

To the right of Rev. McHarg are Jim Jones and Mervyn M. Dymally, then the lieutenant governor of California. To the far right is Marcelline Jones, wife of Jim Jones.

At an outside gathering, surrounded by members of the Peoples Temple church, Jim Jones stopped to allow a cameraman to take a photograph of him with San Francisco Police Chief Charles Gain (center) and Rev. Cecil Williams (left). Cecil Williams made the following statement about Jim Jones: "What I appreciate about you is that you extend yourself beyond specific situations and provide the experience of sharing in the cause to which we are committed."

Jim Jones standing with a group of people in Mayor Moscone's office, while the Mayor reads a document. Mayor George Moscone of San Francisco supported Jim Jones publicly up until the day of the ambush of Leo Ryan, one week before his own murder in San Francisco, November 25, 1978. His praise for Jim Jones was widely quoted by the members of the church: "Your contributions to the spiritual health and well-being of our community have been truly inestimable . . . you have demonstrated that the unique powers of spiritual energy and civic commitment are virtually boundless, and that our lives would be sadly diminished without your continuing contributions."

Jim Jones entertains Guyana's honorary consul in the United States, Claude Worrell, at the Los Angeles Peoples Temple church.

Jim Jones accompanies Mrs. Rosalyn Carter, wife of United States President Jimmy Carter. They dined together, and Jones later said he talked about such issues as the First Amendment rights that concern all freedom-loving Americans. Jim Jones's comment about her reaction was that she "appeared to be very sympathetic."

At the same rally, Mrs. Carter is walking toward the platform. Standing behind Jim Jones is Jim McElvane, the head of Peoples Temple security team.

Attorney Ralph Nader (left), consumer rights advocate, meets Jim Jones and is introduced by attorney Bob Wallach (center). It was this photograph that prompted me to send Ralph Nader a letter describing the beatings and harassment that Peoples Temple members were subjected to. Somehow my letter got back into the hands of Jim Jones, and I later received a middle-of-the-night call from Mark Duffy threatening me.

Mervyn M. Dymally shaking hands with Marcelline Jones, wife of Jim Jones. Dymally was a staunch supporter of Jim Jones throughout his term in office, and even when the unfavorable publicity came out he still didn't speak against Jim Jones.

California Governor Jerry Brown seen here with Jim Jones. Governor Brown spoke at the Peoples Temple church when they held a public celebration January 15, 1977.

Jim Jones was invited, along with San Francisco Mayor George Moscone, to speak with Vice-Presidential candidate Walter Mondale in his airplane suite and then accompany him to another meeting.

A church service in the San Francisco Peoples Temple. Note the guard posted at the side of the podium. Counsellors are seated at the rear of the stage and Jim Jones at the speakers' platform.

*

1973

Father is God,
In every atom and cell of his bodily frame,
Father is God,
He is the Word made flesh.

Father is God,
And we are blessed,
I know you're God, I know you're God,
I know you're God, God, God, God, God.
  —from a Peoples Temple song

Our Los Angeles congregation was growing rapidly and the services there were netting a great deal of money. Jim was pleased with his decision to start a congregation there. One Saturday evening in Los Angeles Jim made a strange announcement. "I have had a revelation that something strange might happen tonight. No matter what happens, I don't want anyone to call an ambulance." After this announcement he went on with his sermon.

Suddenly Pinky, one of the older members, passed out in the rear of the building. It looked as if she was dying and Marcie quickly called an ambulance. She hadn't heard Jim's order. A few minutes later Jim heard the siren and asked the guards what was happening. A guard looked outside the door just in time to see the ambulance drivers carrying Pinky on a stretcher. He quickly reported it to Jim.

Jim shouted over the microphone, "I said no ambulance was to be used tonight. Get outside and see that it isn't!" The guards ran outside.

The men carrying the stretcher were ready to put Pinky inside the ambulance, but the guards quickly stood in front of the doorway. Johnny Brown, one of the guards, said in a tone of authority, "She is all right and is not to be put in that ambulance." The other attendant, sensing trouble, called the police on his C.B.

radio. Within moments, several police cars were gathering. The policemen tried to help the attendants get Pinky into the ambulance. Marcie appeared on the scene. Jim's guards began to fight with the policemen.

One policeman got a broken nose when Johnny hit him. In the midst of the scuffle another of the guards grabbed Pinky's limp body and carried her inside the church building. The policemen subdued the guards and took two of them, Clay and Johnny, downtown to be booked in jail. Marcie tried to prevent them from taking the guards and she was thrown into the paddy wagon, too.

Inside the church the ushers were running up and down the aisles shouting, "Remain calm, everything is all right. Father will take care of everything." None of us had any idea what was happening outside.

After the police and the ambulance left, Jim came back to the service for a few minutes. "Early this morning I had a revelation," he began somberly. "I told everyone in this building that there was to be no ambulance called because I knew this type of trouble would happen. Someone didn't hear my instruction and called an ambulance anyway. Our sister, Pinky, had collapsed, but I knew that my power could take care of her. She is fine now, in an adjoining room. Through my power, she disappeared off the stretcher as the policemen and guards were arguing about her."

Jim asked one of the counsellors to take over the remainder of the service while he went to the jail to see if he could get Marcie and the guards released. He took Mark and a few of the staff members with him.

Jim didn't return until late that night. Later he told us that he had gone to the jail and said something that made the policemen there so angry that they put him in jail, too. It took hours of negotiations before Jim and Marcie were allowed to go, but Johnny and Clay stayed in jail for several days. We were never told what happened, but when the guards returned they testified that Jim's "amazing power" had gotten them off scot-free.

Al and I talked about Pinky's strange collapse and I asked him why he thought it was so important that she couldn't get into the ambulance. In the back of my mind I suspected that Pinky might have been given some drug by Jim or one of the nurses to make her collapse so that later he could revive her. And, for the thousandth time, I rationalized my doubts. "If Jim feels it's necessary for the Cause, who am I to question his wisdom?"

*   *   *

One of the elderly members brought her little foster child, Anthony, to the Los Angeles church services. Nine-year-old Anthony was a ringleader in a street gang of city urchins, and his foster mother was at her wit's end. She asked Jim if he could help her teach this child that stealing was a sin. Jim agreed to try.

He called Anthony to the front of the church at the beginning of a Saturday-night discipline session and sternly asked Anthony, "Is it true that you have been going from store to store stealing things with a gang of boys?"

This tough little guy stood up straight, looked Jim directly into his eyes, and proudly answered, "That's true. I'm the leader of the gang."

"Haven't you heard my teachings that stealing is wrong?"

"Yes, I have." Anthony answered belligerently.

"Do you know that people who steal get sent to prison?" Jim was half smiling in this exchange with a little boy who was totally unafraid of him.

"Only if they get caught," Anthony answered.

Jim became serious. He knew that it would undermine his authority if he allowed this to continue. He made motions with his hand as if he were casting a spell on Anthony and shouted, "You've seen me cause the dead to come back to life, but I can also take life. Do you want me to strike you dead, Anthony?"

Little Anthony crossed his arms defiantly in front of his chest and said, "Go ahead!"

Jim answered, "If it weren't for the fact that you're so young, that's just what I would do. But because you are only nine years old I'm going to refer this case to council."

Anthony became even cockier as Jim began to back down on his threat. "Why, can't you strike me dead?"

Jim quietly motioned for Jack to come over to him and whispered something into his ear. Jack immediately left the room and returned a few minutes later with a glass of water. He took the water over to Anthony and told him to drink it.

As soon as the water was gone Jim asked again, "Do you still want me to strike you dead?"

Again, Anthony, who was now enjoying the game, responded, "Yeah, go ahead."

Once again Jim made motions with his hands and then walked over to Anthony and said, "In a few moments you will fall dead. Are you sure that's what you want?"

Anthony was beginning to be a little unsteady on his feet but he still answered, "Yes, go ahead." Jack handed him another glass of water and Anthony naively drank it. Jim and Jack stood quietly by as Anthony began reeling back and forth on his feet.

Jim asked again, "Are you sure you want me to strike you dead?" This time Anthony could hardly talk. His eyes were becoming glazed and he could barely stand.

He weakly answered, "Yeah, go ahead," just as his little body crumpled on the floor. Several guards carried him out.

Jim calmly announced to the congregation, "Anthony will not remain dead. It is important, though, that he learns he cannot mock this Prophet of God. He will be all right tomorrow."

That night the Planning Commission members gathered for the Saturday night meeting. Jim was sitting on a big chair in one corner of the room and beside him, on a blanket on the floor, was Anthony, completely passed out. He explained, "Because of Anthony's defiance it was necessary that I use more energy than he could deal with so I want to observe him as he awakens." Suddenly I realized that Anthony had been drugged.

A few hours later one of the nurses put cold water on his face and tried to bring him back to consciousness. Anthony began to stir. Jim quietly ordered, "Turn off the lights." In a low voice he said, "Anthony, you are waking up in hell and I am the Devil. This is where little boys who steal are sent." Anthony dropped back into unconsciousness again and Jim had the lights turned back on. He explained, "This little child has lived on the streets so long that it is going to take a big lesson to teach him to follow the rules here. The next time he awakens I want you all to make nosies as though you are suffering in hell. Perhaps if we do this while he is in a half-conscious state it will seep into his subconscious and he will learn his lesson."

Throughout the long night, every hour on the hour, the nurse would again attempt to awaken him, and each time the lights would be turned off and we made noises as if we were suffering. By morning Anthony was fully awake and mentioned that he'd had some strange dreams but that he was all right now. Jim asked him, "Anthony, are you ever going to steal again?"

With his big brown eyes opened in terror Anthony replied, "No way. I learned my lesson." Although I was frightened at the thought that Jim had drugged this little boy, I justified Jim's actions when I realized that Anthony's whole life had been changed that night.

*　　*　　*

One evening Al and I started recalling the way things had been when we first joined the church. "Remember the atomic bomb and the cave?" Al asked.

I suddenly realized that I had almost forgotten about Jim's

bomb prophecy. "He hasn't said anything about his cave for months now. I wonder why?"

"Maybe he made up that whole story to scare people into joining the church," Al said.

"I'm so confused. Sometimes I don't understand Jim's strategy. It seems he tries to make people afraid so they'll stay in the church." We talked about how cruel Jim was sometimes.

We were quiet for a few minutes, vividly remembering the sadness we had felt as we drove away from Cy and his family that morning. Suddenly, I added, "And the offerings! They're about to drive me crazy. Do they bother you, too?"

"Not as much as they seem to be affecting you," Al answered. "Now that I am a bus driver I just tell the guards I need to check something on my bus and I get out of the meetings. I suppose if I had to stay there and listen it would get to me too."

The offerings were, indeed, getting out of hand. Jim had said that no person should have a checking or a savings account. Then every person was told to turn in his or her jewelry, antiques, and heirlooms so they could be sold and the money given to the church. In addition to this, the young people were being encouraged to move into houses that were owned by the church and were being operated as communes. The young people were supposed to "set an example for the rest of the members of how to live apostolically."

We talked long into the night. We didn't often spend much time criticizing Jim and the church, but tonight it just felt so good to be able to vent our anger and hostility. We didn't know what we could do to change things, but the knowledge that we both disliked the direction in which the church was going gave us comfort.

"I guess the offerings are necessary, though," I added apologetically.

"Well, I'm just thankful that I can go out to the buses when things get rough," Al responded.

"Lucky you," I said in mock jealousy as we turned over and went to sleep.

The next day was Wednesday and neither of us mentioned our conversation of the night before as we prepared to leave for the Wednesday-night meeting with our family.

Again there were too many offerings and the sermon was too long. We just smiled at each other, knowing that we were sharing our secret rebellion. Somehow, in the act of sharing it, the hostility we had felt was diluted.

Confrontation time again. Tonight a young man named Fred was on the floor for getting drunk. He had been sent home from work drunk and his wife often complained that he got drunk on weekends.

Jim seemed angry as he shouted, "Your father was an alcoholic and you're getting to be just like him."

Fred was apologetic and in his defense mentioned the name of another man who had been drinking with him. The name he mentioned was one of the church counsellors and now it was Jim's turn to be on the defensive.

In an effort to redeem the reputation of his counsellor Jim asked every person in the congregation who ever drank alcoholic beverages to raise their hands. Up to that time I hadn't heard about any rule against social drinking. Jim said he wanted every person who'd had even one drink to raise his or her hand. So Al and I raised ours, too, because we occasionally had a glass of wine before we went to sleep.

"Do you think it was fair for all of you to sit here quietly while this young man was being confronted for drinking?" he asked accusingly. No one responded to his question, so he continued, "I think that every person in this room who has been drinking, and yet sat quietly in their seats while Fred was being accused of the same thing you are doing, should get the same punishment that I was going to give Fred."

Since Jim hadn't mentioned any punishment yet, this statement was perplexing. Jim said again, "Every person in this room that raised his hand should come forward now and be punished."

This was the first time many of us had ever heard Jim talk about physically punishing people, and we all sat in our seats, dumbfounded. "I want each of you to come forward now and get a whipping!" he shouted.

A few people stood and came forward. Slowly, the rest of us who had raised our hands began to stand and form a line. The line was so long it went around two walls of the church.

Jim called two of his ministers forward, Jack Beam and Vinnie. Jack was white and Vinnie was black. Even in his punishments Jim wanted to be sure he practiced integration. He asked the men to take off their belts and give every person standing in line three whacks—"Hard."

The two ministers gave each person three hard whacks. Some of the people cried in surprise and pain as they were hit.

I hadn't been whipped since I was a young child and I was filled with fear as I watched these two men whipping everyone. It was obvious from the screams of the victims that Vinnie was hitting twice as hard as Jack.

I was standing in front of Al in the line and with a quick

calculation Al realized that I would be hit by Vinnie and he would be hit by Jack. He suggested that we exchange places. "I'm much tougher than you and Jack's whipping won't hurt so much," he said.

Finally our turns came and we each bent over to receive our whippings. I was astonished by the pain I felt when the belt hit me. Instead of flinching or cying, though, all my emotions erupted as pure raw hate. We had just been publicly humiliated and painfully hurt for extremely moderate drinking! The more I thought about it the angrier I became.

As we walked out of the church that night I was seething inside. Al knew that I was angry and stood with his arm around my waist as we walked toward the car. Neither of us dared speak because the children would hear us. We didn't want our feelings repeated to Jim or to the council.

As soon as we got into our bedroom I started to cry from the humiliation.

Al and I discussed the whippings. They were absurd but we tried to come up with a rationalization—anything to defend our commitment to the ideals of the church.

"I guess it's not worth quitting the church over, so I'd better stop feeling sorry for myself!" I decided.

*   *   *

Many of the new church members coming in from Los Angeles and San Francisco areas were still caught up in their need for religious trappings—the theological niceties such as baptism. Jim had often joked about people who thought baptism—the act of being dunked or sprinkled—could earn them salvation; but now he changed his message and altered it to suit the hundreds of religion-oriented members he was gaining.

One Friday night he announced that there would be a mass baptism service the following Sunday. "Every person that considers himself a devoted member should sign the list to be baptized." The line of people formed immediately, almost 300 people waiting to put their names down requesting baptism from the "Prophet."

The following Sunday, after the morning service, three of Jim's assistant ministers went into the swimming pool with him. He made a joking reference to the water's being blessed. "Now that I've stepped in here, this is holy water," he said, but his words were taken seriously by most of the members. Children, teenagers, adults, and even the elderly made a three-hour parade into and out of the water with the three ministers assisting but with every person being dunked by Jim Jones personally. Several of our children joined the rest of the members in the baptism ceremony, but somehow I couldn't bring myself to go down into that cold water.

As the baptism was drawing to a close Jim again mentioned the fact that the water in the swimming pool was blessed but this time he was completely serious. "Many of you here didn't choose to be baptized but every person in this room should get into the water now to receive a blessing. A few of the members protested that they hadn't brought swimming suits or a change of clothes, but things like that never stopped Jim when he had decided on something.

"I said that everyone in this room should get into the pool for a blessing. If you feel you need special clothes to be blessed, you obviously don't regard the blessings very highly." Within the hour every member of the church was in the pool fully dressed— even me. No one wanted to be accused of rejecting Jim's blessing.

*   *   *

Besides the youth communes, Jim purchased three apartments in Santa Rosa for the college students to stay in while they attended the Santa Rosa Junior College. Each of these apartments housed nearly twenty young people, so they were logically called dormitories. In the crowded conditions and with the heavy meeting and study schedules the young people were expected to keep, it was inevitable that some personal conflicts and problems would crop up among them from time to time.

In the church service on Saturday Jim was dealing with the fourth dormitory-related confrontation for the evening and suddenly said in exasperation, "There isn't enough time in my meetings to take care of these matters that involve one small group of people." Impulsively he formed a "college commission" and appointed people who would act as counsellors in dealing with the problems in the dormitories. "The following people will make arrangements to go to Santa Rosa every Tuesday night to discuss the students' problems with them in their living rooms."

The last name on the list was mine. "Each of you will be counsellors for these students only," Jim stated. I did not want to be a counsellor of any sort. I hated the confrontations and the disciplinarian role the counsellors were forced to play. I hurriedly scribbled a note and gave it to Linda Amos to be passed to Jim: "Because of the large family we have and the amount of work I have to do, I will not have time to be on the college commission. Sincerely, Jeannie."

A few minutes later Linda came over and whispered in my ear, "Jim says that you will do a good job for him and it is important that you keep this position. The college students need a person with your sense of fairness." No one was allowed to refuse a direct order from Jim, so I reluctantly accepted my new role.

The following Tuesday night six of us got into my car and headed for Santa Rosa. I had never been to the dormitories before and as I stepped inside I was impressed. The apartment we were going to use for the counselling was immaculate. Lovely furniture was tastefully arranged in the living room, and the three bedrooms had been converted into study quarters with seven desks in each bedroom. The large double garage was the only room that didn't look good. Here were ten sets of bunk beds where the twenty students slept. None of the young people complained, though, so I guessed it must be more pleasant than it looked.

We talked with a few of the students and then it was Kathy Stahl's turn. She had been accused of getting bad grades.

"You can sit here," one of the counsellors said, indicating a chair in the front of the room facing the six of us who had come together.

"Okay, Kathy." Edith Roller was the first counsellor to speak. "Why did you get those bad grades?"

"I don't know. I was so tired when I was taking the tests and I just didn't do well."

"That's no excuse. You know Jim never sleeps, but he got top grades when he went to college."

Kathy was beginning to recover from the nervousness she had felt when she first came in, and she began to get defensive. "I know that. I've heard it before, but I have never done well without enough sleep. We have to go to all those meetings in Redwood Valley and still keep up with our studies. I just can't function that way."

Jack Beam stopped her. "All the students living here have the same schedule that you do, and yet they aren't getting warnings. I wonder if maybe you've got another problem? Do you want to tell us about it?"

Kathy looked blank. "I don't know about any other problem. I'm really trying to get my grades up."

"Maybe you have sex on your mind."

"No, I'm not even dating anyone."

All the counsellors began firing questions at her. Sometimes before she was able to answer one question, another counsellor would interrupt with another question. "You're jealous of your sister because she's married, aren't you?"

"No."

"Yes, you are. You think she's got a good life. You don't know what hell she has gone through with her husband. He's always flirting with other women."

"I don't think that's true, he loves her."

"Now we're getting to the real problem, aren't we?" Jack asked her with a knowing nod.

"What's that?" Kathy asked.

"You're in love with Judy, aren't you?"

"No."

"Yes, you are, and you won't admit it to yourself. I'll bet you think of making love with your sister and that's what is making your grades go down."

"No, that's not true."

Jack was directing all the questions now. "Come on, Kathy, admit it. You've always been jealous of her and it's because you really want to make love with her, isn't that true?"

"No, I've never even thought of it."

This grilling and harassment went on for another half-hour before Kathy finally quit fighting it. "If you want me to say it's true, I will. It's true. Now can I go back and finish my homework?"

"No. Now that you've finally admitted the truth I want to make sure that you really believe it yourself," Jack said taunting her. "Describe what you want to do with Judy."

"I don't want to do anything with Judy."

One of the counsellors was Kathy's stepmother Carol Stahl. She knew Jack well, and once he started out to get a confession from someone, it was impossible to stop him until he got it. She tried to help Kathy out. "Kathy, you've already admitted to Jack that you want to make love with her. Why don't you just say what he wants you to say?"

Jack continued, "You admit that you want to make love to her. Now describe how you want to do it. I just want to help you face your problem so you will be able to do better in your studies."

"What do you want me to say?" Kathy asked facetiously.

"Tell us exactly what you want to do with her breasts."

"Okay, I want to touch her breasts."

"Now tell us what else you want to do. Don't you want to suck on them?"

"Okay, I want to suck on her breasts." Tears of frustration and anger were welling in Kathy's eyes, but Jack wouldn't stop.

"Now, what do you want to do to her vagina?"

"I want to suck on her vagina, too."

"And do you want her to suck on your vagina?"

"Yes."

Finally, Jack was satisfied. Carol and I were looking at him in disgust. Linda Amos said "Okay, Kathy, now you know you are a lesbian, just like all the other women. You have always acted as if you were someone special, and that's why you still flirt with men. From now on, we all know that you're a lesbian, and we'll be watching to make sure you don't try flirting with men anymore."

"Can I go to my room now?" All the color had drained from Kathy's face, and her eyes were downcast.

"Yes, Kathy," Linda answered with a loving tone. "We are pleased that you have finally faced what you really are." Her tone became a little sterner as she added, "You'd better not forget it either, because we're all going to be watching you."

It was so obvious to me that Kathy didn't believe any of the things she had been forced to say that I was sure no one else in the room believed that she actually thought of herself as a lesbian. Somehow, though, every one there had allowed this to happen. I was disgusted and angry, as much with myself as with anyone else. I wondered what would have happened if I had sided with Kathy against Jack, but even as I wondered, I already knew the answer. Jack was Jim's assistant minister, and I knew that Jim would defend Jack's actions.

After Kathy walked out of the room, Jack said proudly, "Well I guess she won't think she's special anymore."

I decided that I did not want to be a counsellor and the following week I stayed home. About half an hour after the dormitory counselling was to begin Jack called me on the phone. "What are you doing at home? You're supposed to be here helping us."

"I'm writing some letters tonight and I can't come," I lied.

"Jeannie, you were assigned by Father to be here." Jack paused and Linda took the telephone from him.

"Jack said you are doing the church's letters," she said. "You can do your letters later tonight after we finish up here. You should have planned your schedule better. Counsellors can't excuse themselves from their duty. If you don't get here right away you will be called into council yourself!"

I had planned to spend the evening with our children, but I knew I would be in real trouble if I didn't go. As I kissed our children good-bye Daphene looked up and begged, "Mommy, please stay home with us tonight."

"I have to go, honey," I answered sadly. "Father wants me to work for him tonight." Daphene's eyes filled with tears because I had promised that I would spend the evening at home. The disappointed faces of the children who had been looking forward to a fun evening made my heart heavy. "What a shame," I thought. "Here is such a beautiful family and I'd love to be able to enjoy them, but I have to go out and make people miserable."

That was to be the last counselling session I would attend for many months. The following day I sent a long letter to Jim begging him to allow me to stop counselling because of my heavy schedule. He must have sensed the desperation in my request because he gave his permission for me to be excused.

As soon as space was available, Meri and Len both moved out of our house and into the commune across the street from the church. They had become so involved in church work that we seldom saw them, and I knew that this would save them travel time each day.

Communal life was difficult, at best. The communards carried a full eight-hours-a-day job, and anywhere from four to eight additional hours of church work each day. Every commune also had a weekly "house meeting" where they discussed the business of running the household or any personal problems that they might need to solve.

There were only twelve beds in each house, but the household population was usually between twenty and twenty-four. At night there was a scramble for the beds. The commune members who worked at the church office or in the publishing house usually ended up sleeping on the floor where they had been working. Since they only got a few hours of sleep each night it didn't matter that much where they slept. Sleep felt wonderful wherever and whenever they could get it.

There were a few young people who weren't able to survive the rigors of communal life and this was to be expected. It only served to make those who stayed feel stronger and more dedicated. They had endured where another person had failed.

One of these "failures" was Inga. She was one of the newer church members, and since she didn't have any family or friends in the group she was assigned to live in a commune. Inga was seriously underweight and, since communal members were the "examples of apostolic living" to the rest of the members, the other household members decided that she should gain weight. As soon as they found out that Inga was a vegetarian they insisted she begin eating meat. She refused, saying that she didn't believe in eating any type of animal flesh, so the counsellors turned her name in to Jim to be dealt with at the next public meeting.

"Inga," Jim said, asking her to come to the front of the room, "I understand that you refuse to eat any meat."

"Yes, Father," she answered humbly. "I have been a vegetarian for many years and I really don't want to start eating meat now."

"You will learn to eat meat tonight. I will not have someone living in one of my communes who is trying to get sympathy and attention from the rest of the household members. You will either eat meat or you will leave this group. Look at you, you're a disgrace to us." He called Eva in the kitchen, "Bring me some chicken." The chicken was quickly brought and Jim made Inga sit on a chair in front of the entire audience. "Now eat!" he commanded her.

Inga shrank back from eating the chicken, but Jim persisted. Finally, he had several of the counsellors forcibly feed her the meat, and when she had swallowed it he was satisfied.

Inga moved away from Redwood Valley later that week. Jim's only comment was, "Good, I couldn't stand that bitch anyway. I hope she starves to death." As soon as Inga moved out another young person moved in, so life went on.

*   *   *

There was an unwritten but perfectly understood law in the church that was very important: "No one is to criticize Father, his wife, or his children." This was a difficult rule for me to keep, because his wife and children didn't keep any of the rules that the rest of us were expected to adhere to. She wore her wedding rings, and beautiful shoes and stylish dresses. She didn't have to attend the meetings because she had to go to work the next day. She would take her family to expensive department stores and spend hundreds of dollars on clothes for them, while the rest of us were expected to wear clothes from thrift shops. Although everyone saw these inequities, no one was allowed to question the activities of the "mother" of the church.

Jim's children were worse. They had an unending supply of money to treat their friends with. Other children were only allowed two dollars a week, but Jim's sons were often seen with rolls of money.

Andre, who was friendly with the Jones boys, would come home and tell me that Steve Jones had paid him a dollar to run to the store and get a ten-cent candy bar for him. None of our children were allowed to participate in school sports, but Jim's children were the stars of the local school basketball team.

I tried to keep quiet about this double standard, but apparently I had said something to the wrong person because my name was read on a list of people to be counselled Tuesday night. There were only two counsellors waiting for me this time, Carolyn Layton and Jack Beam.

Carolyn angrily asked, "Don't you realize that Father's children have to live with the daily fear that their dad might get killed? They have to share him with the rest of the church members. Father tries to do the best he can for them, but it's people like you, who criticize the way he raises his children, that cause so much trouble. Can't you just leave his children alone?"

It was a quick and humiliating lesson. I promised myself that I would never again let anyone hear me criticizing Jim's kids. As I went to work the next day I was sure all the counsellors in the office knew of my "treason" and were secretly condemning me. Although no one mentioned it, I still felt that they were looking at me in disgust. "How is it," I wondered, "that I keep getting into trouble even when I'm trying to keep all the rules?"

*   *   *

Jim's requests for offerings were escalating. He introduced the "church commitment," which meant that all members who wanted his protection should begin giving 25 percent of their income to the church.

"Most of the people who have been with me since we were in Indiana are already giving this amount. Now it is time for the rest of you to carry your share of the financial burden," he said.

Since most of us had never heard of the 25 percent rule, the edict hit many of the new followers, including us, like a ton of bricks. Jim explained, "When you come into the services from now on you will be given an offering envelope. You are to write your monthly earnings on the envelope and tell what percent of these earnings you are pledging for your commitment. If it isn't 25 percent, we will have counsellors ask you to explain your reasons." When he asked who in the audience would refuse, only a few raised their hands. Most of the people were afraid to disagree with him.

The following day a long line of people waited at the door while their "commitment envelopes" were checked. As we walked through the door we were handed a church bulletin with an ominous message printed inside: "The offering envelopes will be gone over by the Prophet and if people have given honestly, as they have prospered, they will be put on the *Special Notification List*... This is vital! Never has such a warning pertaining to offerings come. Please weigh this procedure seriously!" We all understood that Jim was telling us that if we didn't tell the truth on the envelope, a terrible evil would befall us.

As the meeting began Jim announced, "Some of you did not turn in any envelopes and some have lied on the envelope. You tried to lie to this Prophet! I'm going to pass out the envelopes again and this time I want each of you to tell the truth. Write the honest amount that you make every month and this time tell the truth about how much you are going to give." Once again every person did as he was told.

As the envelopes were collected for the second time he went over each in front of the whole audience dramatically passing his hand over several of them, as though feeling whether the person has told the truth or not.

As soon as he had checked them he stood in front of the congregation to show off his used clothes. "I never buy new clothes for myself because I don't want to spend any of your money." He raised the bottom of his shoe for everyone to see the hole he was so proud of. I silently wondered why he went to the trouble of wearing old clothes while his wife and children were dressing better than most of the other members could afford to.

Apparently he had thoughts along this line, too, because he went on to say that he couldn't continue to show these old clothes because the "image" of the leader was suffering. "Since I only wear used clothes and it is important that I appear presentable, I am going to begin wearing a robe to cover these clothes. If anyone has a used choir robe, please turn it in to me so I can wear it." Almost twenty people raised their hands with robes they were anxious to have him wear.

Jim continued to wear old clothes under his newly acquired robes but still showed off the old clothes by raising the robe in front of everyone and proudly displaying the hole in his shoe. Now with his beautiful robes he was beginning to take on the godlike image he wanted to portray.

When the edict about the 25 percent commitment came out, many of the fringe members stopped coming to services. Jim told those of us who were still faithful members: "These people who left weren't dedicated to the Cause anyway. They will all be burned with their money when the atomic war comes, but you who are willing to stay and give as you should will have my protection. I promise that you will all be saved with me."

This was the reference that Al and I had been waiting for, and I smiled to myself as I realized that he needed to use this type of promise to make the less dedicated people willing to give to the Cause.

The offerings became even more intense. "Who in this room still has a checking or savings account?" Nearly fifty people stood up. "Counsellors, please write down the names of the people standing and call them in to discuss it with them." A few of the people tried to sneak back into their seats before their names got on the list, but Jim saw them. He announced the names of each one who had tried to sit back down with the admonition, "These people should get *special* attention when you talk with them."

The following week he asked, "Who still has a life insurance policy?" I began to get a little fidgety because Al had a small policy and I silently hoped he wouldn't raise his hand. As I looked toward him, though, I saw that his hand was up in the air. Jim commanded, "Well, sell those policies and give the proceeds to the church. If you still feel that you need life insurance, then obviously you don't believe in the Cause." Jim was also putting pressure on people to turn their property over to the church. Al and I decided that we would hold on to our property in case we decided to quit. Since Jim never directly asked us if we had property, we thought we wouldn't be placed in the embarrassing position of refusing to give it up.

As the congregation dwindled to the "faithful" who were willing to give at least 25 percent of their income to the Cause, Jim trusted them to learn what his Cause was. *"I have the answers to the problems of society. Someday I will be the ruler of the United States. I will eliminate racism, political oppression, ecological imbalances, and the problem of the superrich and the superpoor. I will make the whole country become like our community. I call this 'Apostolic Socialism.'"*

Jim recited these words as though he had said them a thousand times before. Somehow, when he said it, it sounded wonderful.

*   *   *

Although Jim publicly bragged that every man and woman wanted sex with him I often heard people whisper that they didn't find him especially attractive. Apparently Jim heard some of these whispers because he handed out a printed questionnaire which every church member was to answer. He explained as he gave us the page of questions, "I want to know how each of you personally relates to this Cause."

Nestled in the middle of the page was the question I thought he really wanted to know about, "Do you want to have sex with Father?" I was happy to have the chance to write no, even if he would later use my answer to embarrass me. I found out, though, that many other people had said no to that question, too.

I also found out later that all the people who said they were interested in having sex with Jim Jones were contacted by Patty Cartmell. Patty assured them that "your name has been given to Father and if he feels that you could be helped by relating to him more closely you will be contacted."

As he had the ushers gather the completed questionnaires he asked everyone to find their seats so he could go into a healing service. The boys working on the taping equipment were instructed to be sure that it was functioning in good order. The soft organ music filled the room and everyone was sitting quietly.

A small noise interrupted the organ music and Jim said, "Shhh," as he strained to hear the high-pitched voice.

It came again but louder this time. It sounded like a voice coming from the ceiling. The words were unintelligible but the voice got louder. The words seemed to be in a foreign language. Jim lovingly said, "Speak English, my dear, if you can."

The high-pitched, shrill voice said, "Help me, help me, I'm so cold."

"Who are you?" Jim asked in a commanding voice.

"I was with you on the shores of Galilee and again in Russia. Each time, I betrayed you. I'm sorry. I'm between two worlds now and I'm so cold!"

The audience gasped. We wondered if we were witnessing firsthand evidence that Jim was able to contact dead spirits. He continued speaking to the voice. "What do you want me to do?" His voice was filled with compassion and love.

"I want a body. I want to come back now and be with you. Please forgive me for the times I betrayed you." The voice was easy to understand now and the audience was silent in rapt attention.

"Yes, my love," Jim responded. "I will give you a body." Jim asked us to close our eyes while he allowed this spirit to enter the body of one of the members. "There will be a gasp as the spirit enters a body in this room but everyone must keep their eyes closed." A few moments later there was a loud sigh and a gasp, and Jim announced, "You can open your eyes now. The spirit is with us."

I was consumed with curiosity. I had kept my eyes open hoping to see who the spirit entered but the sound had come from the other side of the room. I asked several others if they saw what happened and one man said that he had.

Vinnie told me, "I was standing next to Georgia when it happened and I heard her gasp. I'm sure she's the one."

I watched Georgia carefully from that day forward to see if she changed in any way. A few months later, when she became one of the first people to leave the group, I was sure that Vinnie had been right.

I realize now that Jim's strategy with the voice from beyond was to complete his circle of fear. Since he couldn't justify beating the older members, he would terrorize them psychologically and play on their many superstitions. After all, who would want to be stuck between two worlds for betraying Jim?

He replayed the tape of the voice from beyond so often that we were able to memorize every word.

*   *   *

Our Publications Staff had been working on the Temple's first newspaper for several months. Every word in the newspaper had to be perfect, with positive overtures being made to the leaders of many of the different factions of the small Ukiah community. The *Temple Reporter* was ready for distribution late in the summer of 1973. After thousands of papers had been printed and folded, Jim found a sentence that had to be deleted. We destroyed thousands of papers because of that one sentence. In an article about "Mr. Muggs," the chimpanzee that our church had adopted, the newspaper stated that Muggs had been saved from scientific experimentation. Jim was afraid that sentence might offend the scientific community, so we had to reprint the entire paper saying that Muggs had been "grossly mistreated."

                              *   *   *

One day Jim walked over to the counter where Al and I were selling his "anointed pictures" and whispered to us, "I've been observing you both and your work and commitment to the Cause. I want to talk with you in our special staff counselling session that I call the Planning Commission, this coming Monday night at 8:30 in the San Francisco temple."

Monday evening we drove to San Francisco. At 8:45, we were ushered into a large room in the new church building. We were surprised by the sight that greeted us as the door was opened. The meeting had apparently been in progress for a long time. There were people lining the walls, sitting all over the floor and on every piece of furniture in the room—more than a hundred people. Jim was in the corner of the room reclining comfortably on an easy chair with a large platter of fruits, meats, and cheeses beside him, along with several glasses filled with various juices and drinks. Every person in the room was positioned to face him.

I noticed that this was the only food visible in the room and I assumed that he would pass it around for everyone to share. This was only the first of my wrong assumptions about the Planning Commission. Jim ate all the food and drank all the drinks himself, while we watched. We were ushered to spots on the floor where space had been made for us to squeeze in.

As soon as we were settled Jim said, "We have been discussing you two tonight and I feel that you would be the best people for us to send as missionaries for our church." Ignoring the startled looks on our faces he continued, "We realize that we will not always be able to exist as an organization in this country, because one day fascism will take over and we will be persecuted for our beliefs. We need to look for some land, in another country, where we will be able to live in peace until this country goes through its period of upheaval. Then we will be able to return. I have been watching the creative things you both have done, and the amount of money you have been able to produce, and have decided that you would be the best people for us to send."

Al was the first to respond. "I realize this is an honor, but as you know, we have children in our home. They mean a lot to us and we are very happy living here."

Archie answered him. "I'm sure we're all happy living here, but we have to be willing to do some things for the Cause even if it means giving up a little comfort for a while."

Al tried again. "We can't leave a houseful of children and go off to some other country."

Jim answered this time. "You know that we will take care of those children. I realize that you care for them, but they will be well provided for until you return or until our group comes to join you." Jim was using his most loving and convincing tone.

I risked the possible label of treason as I said, "It sounds like an interesting assignment and I'm sure it would be a lot of fun to travel, but we can't leave our three youngest children. They're still too small to be separated from their parents." I knew this was contrary to Jim's teachings about families being willing to separate for the Cause, but I didn't want to leave the children I loved so much.

"Your three youngest will be sent with you." The amazed looks of the counsellors made it apparent that they hadn't expected Jim to give in to this demand. Now that Jim had accepted our terms we couldn't think of any reason to refuse.

"Okay, we'll go," Al agreed.

"You will be leaving in a couple of months. You can stop all your other church projects and start studying about Kenya because that's the first country we're going to consider." Then Jim excused us. He made it clear that he did not want us to stay but I couldn't understand why.

"If we're going to be your missionaries and represent this group in another country, don't you think we should join in this meeting to learn more about the Cause's mission?"

"There are things that go on in this room that neither of you would understand. I'm not sure that you would want to be involved in the secret things, the inner workings of this organization."

As I remembered the counselling session I had sat in on with Kathy I began to change my mind. "You're probably right. We can study as you first suggested, and you can let us know what you want."

But he decided to allow us to join. "In this room you will learn all the secret workings of our organization," he said. "First we need to clear the air about some of the things both of you have been saying."

Linda Amos asked, "Did you say that the punishments are unfair, Al?" She was glaring at him as she waited for his answer.

"Yes," he answered belligerently. "Sometimes I think there are inequities in the punishments." I nodded my head in agreement.

Jim admonished him, "Now, Al, surely you don't think I am unfair in my judgments, do you?"

"No, Jim," he answered diplomatically, "but sometimes you haven't been given all the facts."

"You are the one that doesn't have all the facts!" Jim shouted. "I know what I am doing when I punish people. I know their histories and I know, metaphysically, what is the most appropriate punishment for each person. As a counsellor you will not be able to talk like this anymore. You must uphold the office of the leader to every person you talk with. Do you agree to this?"

"Yes, Jim," Al answered humbly. "I apologize for judging things without having all the facts."

Meri, who had been my close friend when she had lived in our home, now glared at me as she asked, "Did you say you never wanted to have a child by Jim because you can't stand his natural son, Steve?"

"Yes, I did," I answered arrogantly. I was angry that Meri had broken our confidence.

Carolyn quickly jumped in, "We've had this trouble with you before, and it's disgusting. You don't realize the strain that Father's children live under. They can't be expected to be perfect, you know. Everyone watches his family and judges them. When people like you say this kind of thing about his son, it puts pressure on Father." Carolyn had the personality of a pickle, and after her last statement my dislike for her turned to hatred. I began to wish with all my heart that I had never said anything about staying in this meeting.

Jim seemed to sense my hostility toward Carolyn and said, "It's a relief to know that you are the one person I won't ever be asked to have sex with. There are so many women in this church begging to have a child by me, I find it refreshing to know that you will never make that demand. However, it was an unwise statement to make to someone as new in the group as Meri was when you had the discussion." I was amused to get the impression that Jim was threatening never to have sex with me.

Meri then asked me, "Did you say that Jim's children got better lunches than you could afford for your children?"

"Yes," I admitted. I was beginning to hate her now. I began to realize that she had probably reported everything she and I talked about privately. "I was upset because the council said no one could buy lunches from the school because Jim's children took sack lunches. Since we qualified for free lunches it made more sense to let the kids have the hot lunches."

Carolyn Layton answered again. "You should never compare Jim's children and what they have to any other children. They live under the constant threat that he will be killed, so they do receive some extra privileges. When you say things like this you put a lot of pressure on Father. He knows that things are not always equal but he tries to be fair to everyone." Carolyn was being too defensive of Jim's children and I began to wonder why.

As if Jim knew the question in my mind he gave an explanation. "Carolyn has been chosen by me, and by Marcie, to be the guardian of our children in the event that something should happen to us. If Marcie were to be killed Carolyn would become my wife. Carolyn has always been dedicated to the Cause and she loves my children. This takes a lot of worry off me because now I know they will always be loved."

Jack pointed an accusing finger at Al. "Did you say that you and your wife have a good sexual relationship?"

"Yes, we do have a good relationship and we intend to keep it that way." Al was never able to stay cool when he was angry. As Al glared at Jack, Jim realized he had better drop the subject.

"We don't want to get into their relationship now. I think we've cleared up some of the ugly rumors that had been floating around. I believe that Jeannie and Al will be good P.C. members. Welcome to our group. In this room are the people who will one day change the world."

On this cue Linda Amos stood up and said, "Jim is the fairest man in the world. He knows how to help people in their time of need. I was a tramp before I met him. I confess that I asked him to have sex with me and he did. But more than that, he made me feel that I was loved for the first time in my life and now I know that I don't ever need another man." Turning to Jim she said, "Thank you for making my life worthwhile."

About a dozen other counsellors, both men and women, stood up to tell how they had had sex with Jim, and each told how it had made him or her a productive and dedicated member of the group.

Al told me later that he'd thought he was going to be sick. All the talk about "screwing in the ass" and "sucking people off" had turned his stomach.

Jim asked Patty Cartmell and Jack Beam to stand up.

"You two seem to be having some problems. Do you want to talk about it?" Jim explained that Patty and Jack had been having a sexual relationship (even though we knew they were both married to other people), and now that their relationship was ending they were inordinately hostile toward each other. It surprised us that Jim seemed to accept this sexual relationship at all when he repeatedly forbade sexual relationships either in or out of marriage. Apparently, there was a different law for the P.C. members than for the other church members. After these two spent an hour screaming at one another, Jim asked Mark to tell how his relationship with Christine Lucientis was progressing and how he was doing in his affair with Katherine.

"Christine and I are having some difficulties. She demands too much of my time and I can't spend hours talking to her as she expects." He was talking as if she weren't there when she was actually only a few feet away from him. Apparently she knew that she was his "assignment" but was willing to keep up the relationship anyway. Mark continued, "Katherine is a bigger problem. You said I should have a relationship with her but not actually fuck her. How far should I go? I keep saying no but she can't understand why."

Jim seemed to be enjoying Mark's predicament with the two women he had been assigned to "keep happy." "You know how far I have told you to go and don't go any further than that. You can sleep with her but do not fuck her. Tell her that you don't believe in it, or that you are homosexual or something, but do not fuck her." His tone changed as he said, "Some people in here are wondering why I trust you with these sex assignments so I think you should tell about the time you asked me to fuck you."

Mark's answer was not exactly what Jim wanted him to say and he worded it cautiously. "I know that your teachings are that I am a homosexual. I appreciated your fucking me because I knew I needed it. I found the experience to be both physically and mentally painful. I know that the pain was an indication of how much I needed to be fucked. I am taking your advice and using a vibrator up my ass so that I can learn to enjoy it. Thank you for helping me realize what I really am." Mark had said all the right words but he hadn't conveyed the idea Jim wanted. By carefully choosing the words, he had been able to say that he didn't enjoy having Jim use him sexually.

The meeting lasted all night and into the morning. Although Jim enjoyed delicious food and fruit juices all evening, no one else had anything to eat. At six in the morning he began to doze off. When he awoke with a start he called the meeting to a close. He went upstairs to his bedroom and the rest of the counsellors got on a bus to travel the 120 miles home. Al and I got into our car. We were tired, hungry, and disgusted. This was the great P.C.? Where was all the planning? Jim hadn't even discussed the missionary venture we were about to go on. But still, we had to admit it was going to be a lot easier studying about Kenya than working the long hours on church projects.

As we crawled into bed at 8:30 in the morning we realized how lucky we were to have been relieved of our church duties. That evening we told our children that we had been chosen by Jim to be missionaries and that Diana, Eddie, and Daphene would be going with us. The other children were disappointed but they had been trained not to question Jim's decisions. I reminded them, "We won't be gone that long, you know. And, if it works well in Kenya, the rest of you will be joining us and the whole church will be together again."

The more we talked about the P.C. meeting the more thankful we were that we were going to be leaving. "Maybe when we move the church to a peaceful place Jim will settle down and be the man he was when we first joined the church," I said.

There was a lot of planning to take care of in the few weeks before we were to leave. Our passports had to be obtained, and we had to get shots. Camping equipment and clothes suitable for a tropical climate had to be bought.

We asked the council to find a couple who could stay in our home and take care of our children, as well as manage our farm and provide transportation for my parents if they needed to go into town. A couple was recommended that we thought was ideal. They had four children of their own, and since we would be taking three children with us there would be plenty of bed space for them. Carol, the wife, wanted to get acquainted with our family right away, so we traded houses several weeks before we were going to leave.

*   *   *

The time moved rapidly along. Three days before we were supposed to leave, Gene Chaikin, the attorney, called and asked to speak to Al. "In order for us to take care of your property and affairs while you are gone, we will need to have you sign a power of attorney statement. Otherwise, we won't be able to do anything in case of an emergency." He told Al that he had the papers already prepared and he would bring them right over. He added, "Since our whole church will probably be joining you within a few months we might need to sell your property. I have also prepared quitclaim deeds for you to sign."

It was a difficult decision. We had seen enough questionable things to make us hesitant but still we had to admit that we couldn't take care of the property from so far away. "If we are going to leave this country and possibly spend the rest of our lives in a mission field, I guess we don't have much alternative but to sign those papers," Al said.

Gene arrived with all the legal papers drawn up. We signed three times and it was all over. When Gene asked us about the house we were living in, we told him that Grandma's name was on that deed so we couldn't sign it over.

He also handed us a letter signed by Tim Stoen and addressed "To Whom It May Concern," introducing us as "representatives of the Peoples Temple of the Disciples of Christ Church." The letter went on to say, "These persons are authorized, commissioned and delegated as missionaries for the purpose of locating and investigating a permanent missionary location to be developed and supported by this church."

As we read this letter, we became even more enthusiastic over the prospect of starting a mission. We felt we had been honored to be chosen for this important task.

The day of our departure was drawing near. We had already purchased the tickets and our bags were packed. The three children were euphoric. We were to leave the next morning at six o'clock and had made every last-minute preparation. That night at midnight Gene called us. "Father just realized that you folks are planning to go tomorrow. He asked me to tell you that he has learned of political problems in Kenya right now. He feels it would be unwise for you to leave now. He knows you and the children will be disappointed, but he asked me to convey his message that it is better to be disappointed now than to wind up in the middle of a revolution."

Our three children cried when Al broke the news, but he assured them that it would be only a few more weeks before we would be leaving to go to some other country.

During the rush of preparations we had not attended P.C. meetings, and no one had said anything about it. It was Monday again. We smiled at the thought of the hundred people cramped together in a secret room somewhere, listening to a lot of people screaming at each other. We went to bed at 10:00 P.M. and prepared for a good night's sleep. At eleven, the telephone rang. It was Gene Chaikin.

"Why aren't you here?" he asked.

"No one told us where it was, and we haven't gone for several weeks because we were getting ready to go to Kenya. We are too

PEOPLES TEMPLE of the Disciples of Christ

P. O. Box 214, Redwood Valley CA 95470 --- Phone: (707) 485-7219

James W. Jones, Pastor

TO WHOM IT MAY CONCERN:

    This letter shall introduce Elmer J. Mertle and
Deanna M. Mertle who, together with or separate from Donald
Beck, are representatives of the Peoples Temple of the
Disciples of Christ, a member of the denomination of the
Disciples of Christ, Christian Churches. As representatives
of this church those persons are authorized, commissioned
and delegated as missionaries for the purpose of locating
and investigating a permanent missionary location to be
developed and supported by this church.

    It is our wish that all persons who receive this
letter aid and assist them in their journey, understanding
that their purposes are charitable and humanitarian, and
that their goal is to create a facility that will educate,
care for, and relieve the suffering of many persons.

Respectfully yours,

TIMOTHY O. STOEN
Chairman, Board of Trustees
Peoples Temple of the Disciples
    of Christ

busy preparing for the missionary trip to go to those meetings," I answered.

"Now, Jeannie," Gene was talking to me as if I were a child. "You know that once you're a member of the P.C., you can't quit. Dick Tropp is on his way over right now to pick you up. He should arrive in a few minutes and Father expects you to be ready when he gets there." We quickly threw our clothes on and within a few minutes Dick was knocking at our door ready to escort us to the meeting.

Jim looked up nonchalantly as we walked in. "What made you think you didn't have to come to P.C. anymore? I told you that you were members."

"We didn't know where the meeting was to be held," I answered truthfully.

"You should have asked one of the other members," he said without expression.

"I'm sorry, Father," I stammered. "I thought maybe you had changed your mind and didn't think it was necessary for us to come anymore." I was lying, but I knew the truth would sound even worse. I hoped he would let me get away with a lie just this once, and he did. He smiled and indicated that we should sit down. Several people had to crowd together to make room for two more bodies on the already crowded floor.

This meeting was like the first one we had attended—a lot of people praising Jim and many discussions about sex. Only the names and faces of the people who were on the floor for confrontation were different. Once again Jim was discussing sex. One of the counsellors had been reprimanded for asking Phyllis Houston to spend the night with him. "You men don't have anything to offer these women," Jim sneered. "The only thing the women in here want is to be treated as equals. The only reason sex would ever become necessary would be to produce children, and of course at this time in history, when we are concerned about an impending nuclear disaster, we don't need any babies in our group."

As he thoughtfully mulled over the words he had just spoken, Jim had an interesting idea. "Perhaps a lot of problems in our church could be averted if all the male church members were to have vasectomies. I know that some of the more dedicated men have already had this operation. If I were to ask the rest of the men to take this precaution, then we wouldn't need to fear any unwanted pregnancies."

Patty Cartmell was the first person to respond. "Father, I think that it would be a very appropriate thing for all our men to have vasectomies. Any man who refuses is only concerned with his own male ego. After all, any person who wants a child should be willing to adopt an unwanted baby, instead of adding to the world's population."

Al objected even though he had already had a vasectomy twelve years before. "After all, there might come a time in the future when our women should have babies," he said reasonably. "And then all our men would be sterile."

Linda Amos sneered at him, "You just don't want to give up your own masculinity."

Al answered, "I've already had a vasectomy, Linda, and I'm not the least bit worried about my masculinity. I'm concerned that the time might come in the future when we will want to produce children."

Carolyn Layton volunteered, "If we ever try to produce a super-race, then Father should be the person to impregnate the women."

Al's anger had been aroused, and he wasn't going to give up until he made his point. After all, our son Steve would be one of the members who would be included in this plan. "What if something happens to Father? Then there won't be anyone left who is capable of performing this duty."

Linda Amos answered, "What we should probably do in that case, Father," she said almost reverently, "is to have a sperm bank with your sperm in it. I've read that it's possible to keep sperm alive for many years under the proper refrigeration. This way even if something were to happen to you, we could still produce your children."

Somehow the thought of a hundred little Steven Joneses came to my mind, and I was horrified. Then I remembered that Jim had boasted he could only have male children. Smugly I raised my hand and commented, "Since Father says he can only produce boys, we'd really have a problem with the next generation. There wouldn't be any girls for them to marry, and the whole race would be doomed to extinction."

Jim realized the pointlessness of continuing this debate, so he closed the subject by saying, "Well, this isn't the time in history for us to make these decisions. However, in the future if it becomes necessary, I will indeed save my sperm for posterity. There is a unique factor in my heredity which can produce very special children."

The discussion ended, and I was grateful that no final decision had been reached.

*   *   *

A couple of days later, Jim told us to prepare for another missionary trip, this time to the Andes Mountains in Peru. We were told to purchase equipment for the cold mountains. A date was once again set for departure. Jim told us, "We want you to find a place where our church can eventually find refuge from the fascist dictatorship which will one day overtake this country." He explained that if we ever returned to America, our property would all be returned to us. We obtained our tickets, our visas, and letters of introduction and waited. A few nights before we were to leave, Gene phoned. "Jim wants to talk to you right away," he said. In the middle of the night, we headed for Jim's house.

"The leader of Peru is having some medical problems and we don't know if the government will remain under his control. This leader has always shown himself to be friendly to our beliefs, but we don't know what another leader would be like. We'd better hold off on your trip for a while. I'm sorry, because I know you and the children are ready to leave. We wouldn't want to send you over there and have you killed."

We smiled, trying to hide our disappointment. Next morning when we told the children, they were silent. The bitter disappointment on their faces was the same bitterness we felt in our own hearts. How could Jim do this to us twice, we wondered. And after a day of cogitating we realized that the real plan had been to abscond with our real estate—as politely as possible.

When we said we were ready to take care of our property again, Gene informed us that it would be managed by another member. "You're both too valuable as church workers to be burdened with the maintenance of these houses," he said. "Father wants to use all your talents to help the Cause." Within six months the Willits tract with nineteen homes became so run down from lack of essential maintenance that the former owner went through foreclosure and took the property back. The church hadn't even recorded the deed that they had made us sign, so the foreclosure was done against our names. Al asked Jim if we could at least go to the court to fight the foreclosure, but he assured us that his legal staff would take care of everything. A week later the notice of foreclosure arrived in our mailbox. We looked at the legal papers and realized that the church had thrown away nearly $50,000 in equity.

We had to face painful reality. Our life savings were gone. Jim had demanded that we sell the life insurance policy and turn the equity over to the church, so that was gone. Our property had all been taken from us. Our dream of going to an overseas mission was gone. We thought we had alienated our parents when we told them we were leaving the country. Even the children whom we had left in the care of Carol and Bill were openly hostile toward us. Jim had accomplished all this in such a short time! All we had left now was Jim and the Cause, so we decided to buckle under and give our energies to these two.

It took several weeks before the kids trusted us again. Even Grandma and Grandpa were aloof. When we'd moved away, Grandma told us she felt we were abandoning her to a church hostile to her. It was a painful reunion. And, as it turned out, within a few weeks, things did return to normal and we got down to the business of working for the Cause.

One afternoon the P.C. counsellors received an emergency

message. "Come to the church immediately for a special meeting." We dropped what we were doing and left as instructed. When we arrived it was obvious that Jim was very upset.

He began, "Eight people left the church last night. They cut the telephone wires so Tom couldn't call to warn us." He was speaking in a low voice as though he were afraid the walls might hear what he was saying. "No one knows why they left, but Jim and Terry Cobb, Wayne Pietila, Micki Touchette, and four others all disappeared. Don't worry, though, I'll find them." Jim tried to sound confident, but then he shook his head in despair. "These eight people might cause our church to go down. They could say things that would discredit our group. This might be the time for all of us to make our translation together." He had mentioned the idea of a "translation" a few times before, but no one had ever taken it seriously. His idea was that all the counsellors would take poison or kill themselves at the same time, and then he promised we would all be translated to a distant planet to live with him for eternity. The few who believed this fairytale said they'd be happy to do it anytime. Now, however, faced with death, it became obvious that there were many who didn't want to.

"What about the other church members, and our children?" Linda Amos asked.

"Oh, yes, that's the problem. Those who would be left behind." Jim was speaking slowly and deliberately now, and it seemed that he was trying to formulate his ideas as he spoke. "Perhaps we could devise a plan where the children would be sent to another country first." I relaxed as I realized that his plan wasn't as well thought out as I had feared. Since he hadn't worked out these important details, I was sure he couldn't insist that we all kill ourselves right now.

"I want to take a vote today to find out how dedicated you all are," Jim said. "Life is a bore. Surely no one here is enamored with his existence. You've seen too much reality in all the hours of counselling at the P.C. meetings. How many of you here today would be willing to take your own lives now to keep the church from being discredited? Perhaps this way we will go down in history as revolutionaries. We could leave a note saying that we were doing this as a sign that we want peace on earth, or that we couldn't exist as an apostolic socialist group, or something like that."

Jack Beam was the first to speak. "I don't want to die. I don't know about the rest of you people, and, Father, I'm sorry to have to tell you this, but I don't want to kill myself." As he finished speaking, Jack walked away. Jim couldn't believe his ears. He was shocked that Jack would take this so seriously, and now Jack had set a dangerous precedent for the rest of the counsellors. A few others bravely said they weren't ready to kill themselves either, but many of the people stood up and offered to die for the Cause.

Jim wrote down the names of those who had said they weren't ready to die yet. He read this list slowly and with emphasis, and then he said, "The names I have just read are people who can't be trusted yet. A person is not trustworthy until he is fully ready to lay down his life for this Cause."

Mike Cartmell, Jim's son-in-law, stood up. "Father, I'm ready to die for this Cause, but I think I need to point something out to you. We could all take our lives, and it certainly would be newsworthy. But if you look at it objectively, you will see that there is a possibility the public might think of us as the biggest fools of all time, instead of as courageous revolutionaries."

Jim thought about Mike's statement, and he seemed to agree. More than 100 bodies lying dead in his church might indeed make him look insane. He dropped the subject for the time being and settled for a debate on how to chase the defectors.

*   *   *

The youth communes were producing a lot of money for the church treasury, and Jim was beginning to encourage all the church members to go communal. This meant that two or more families would share the same home or that a group of people would share expenses and turn all savings over to the church. Fortunately, our home fell under the category of commune, so we didn't have to make any changes. The church was supporting our household already. Our finances weren't questioned.

The communal setup was very profitable for the church. Each person who lived in a commune had to give his entire paycheck to the house treasurer, who would in turn pay the bills, purchase food, and give each person the money needed for clothes and expenses. Every person was given an additional two dollars as a weekly allowance. Each commune was expected to function under the same rules, but some of the house treasurers were liberal, while others were strict. It became evident that some communal members were dressing better, eating more, and sleeping longer than the members of other communes.

The young people began to complain about these inequities. When Jim heard the grumbling, he decided that he would determine equality for all. He appointed Ellen, who was known to be very frugal with money, to be the head treasurer for all the communes. Every penny that was spent would have to be cleared by her. Things changed radically from that day forward. Since

Ellen received praise from Jim for every extra dollar she squeezed from the communes' budgets, she saved with a vengeance. Instead of the food they requested, each commune was given an identical box of staples to live on for a week. The few pieces of fruit or sweets would be gone the first day. For the remainder of the week, these young people would live on peanut butter sandwiches, soybeans, and other staples.

I began to notice that the people in the communes were learning to find happiness in pathetically small events. Mike Rozynko found a dime in a telephone booth and talked about it for a week. Bob Houston was overjoyed when I shared a chocolate candy bar with him. Grace Stoen baked a loaf of bread and put it on the table for everyone to share. It disappeared within minutes. People had lost all sense of morality and took whatever they could get. Food became an obsession.

One day I put six ice-cream bars into the tiny freezer compartment of the Publications Office's refrigerator. Then minutes later I walked in and saw Mike, again, finishing the last bit of the sixth bar.

"How could you steal my ice cream?" I asked him, disgusted that he would be so brazen.

He looked like a rabbit that had been caught in a trap as he tried to apologize. "I know they didn't belong to me, but I am so hungry for something sweet that I couldn't stop myself," he said humbly.

"Those were for my children when they come by after school. You know, Mike, we're communal, too, and I don't have much money. I can't afford to feed my kids and you, too." I was angry, but suddenly the impact of what Mike had said hit me. I added, "Mike, I know you guys don't get the kind of food you'd like to have. Would you like to come home with me for dinner tonight?"

He didn't hesitate. "I'd love to," he said. Mike enjoyed spending a couple of hours with our family. He looked at the children in our home, enjoying life in the friendly atmosphere of our house, and casually mentioned that he wished he had been as fortunate. "I don't like living in the commune," he said wistfully. "They're so strict about everything, and the food is terrible."

It sounded as if he was hinting for an invitation to come live with us. But Mike seemed emotionally unstable, and I knew it would be impossible to spend the necessary hours with him, and he was already nineteen. As he threw out yet another hint I answered, "Mike, we have so many kids, there just isn't any room."

Mike seemed embarrassed as well as disappointed. "You can't imagine what it's like living in the commune," he said. "Besides the rotten food, we have no privacy. I'm supposed to sleep in a room with eight other men but most of the time I don't get home in time to get one of the beds. I usually sleep on the floor in the darkroom."

Since Mike was in charge of our photographic darkroom, I never had any reason to go in there after I thought he had gone home. The next morning, at 2:30, when the work was finished, I decided to tour the building. I looked into the darkroom, and sure enough, Mike was readying his sleeping bag. In the composition room I saw Nancy Sines, already asleep on the table that was used for layouts. In the bindery, just off the press room, I saw Tim Clancey in his sleeping bag, leaning against large sacks of mail, sound asleep. Upstairs, where the files clerks had been busily sorting names and addresses, there was a long row of sleeping bags filled with the communal people who hadn't been able to get home in time to get a bed. Although I'd known that some people occasionally slept there, I hadn't realized that this office had become sleeping quarters for almost twenty communards. It was 3:30 A.M. by the time I got home and into our king-size bed beside my sleeping husband.

I had a hard time falling asleep, even though my body ached with fatigue. I couldn't forget the sight of rows of those sleeping bags. These kids had forgotten their natural desires for love, for companionship, and even for sex, as they longed for an extra half-hour of sleep or for an extra piece of chicken on Sunday when the church furnished food for everyone.

Soon Jim raised the required commitment to 30 percent of every member's income, and more people were forced to go communal or go broke. Within a few months, all the people in the church were told to go communal or leave. By now, most of the people were too frightened or so completely controlled that they gave in, sold every possession, and turned the money lock, stock, and barrel over to Jim Jones's People's Temple.

* * *

A frequent guest at the San Francisco temple was San Francisco's assistant mayor, Joe Johnson. Jim hadn't been able to make any alliances with Mayor Alioto, so he decided he would have to settle for his assistant.

Johnson seemed totally taken in by the friendly members of Peoples Temple and the wonderful minister who always encouraged him to "give us a few words." As Jim continued to praise and encourage him, Joe became more and more excessive in his praise of our church.

He started reciting poetry to us. As Joe would read a poem, Jim would stand behind him making funny faces. One time when Al was taking pictures, Jim walked over and hugged Joe, whose back was to the camera. Just as Al clicked the shutter, Jim extended his middle finger in a lewd gesture toward Joe's back.

As Al showed him the picture later, Jim laughingly remarked, "Joe and his stupid poems. I'm so sick of them that I could throw up when he stands up to recite, but that's just one of the sacrifices I have to make for the Cause." Jim kept the photograph and put it in his file—the expanding file of important people Jim was compromising by their association with him.

*   *   *

Another little girl started visiting our home regularly, Daphene's girlfriend, Stephanie. This was Marceline Jones's favorite grandchild.

Stephanie told me that her stepfather was being cruel to her and asked if she could please move in with Daphene and Janet. Her parents agreed to a temporary move, so we did, too.

Stephanie was a very pleasant addition to our family. She could carry on intelligent conversations with adults as well as with children. Her deep sense of justice helped smooth out ruffled feathers in our household from time to time. It was hard for us to believe that she could actually be a product of the Jones upbringing.

It was summertime again, and all the members were getting ready for a church "vacation," with Jim preaching in major cities across the country. I was becoming so resentful of the long hours I had to spend away from our home that I tried to find a reason to stay home. Fortunately, our goats, which had to be milked twice a day, provided me with the necessary excuse and, amazingly, Jim said okay. I had thought he might try to find someone else to stay in our home to take care of our animals, but he didn't.

Three weeks later, when everyone had returned, Jim told us about some of the people he had picked up during the trip and brought back to Redwood Valley. I was especially intrigued by his story about three little boys from Philadelphia who had been rummaging through garbage cans to get their meals. "These three boys asked me to take them back to California because they didn't have any parents, so we packed them into my bus and brought them back with us," he said with a triumphant smile.

The three boys were assigned to a home in Ukiah with Judy Ijames, but after two days she realized she couldn't take care of all of them. They were wise beyond their years, and Judy was too young to keep up with all their mischief. Judy called Linda Amos to ask for another home for one of them. Linda called me and asked if we could make room for the oldest one, nine-year-old Joey. "He really needs a strong father figure like Al," she said. We were thrilled to be able to take care of this little homeless child who had been forced to eat from garbage cans.

Joey was a heart-warmer. He had lived on the streets of Philadelphia where he had learned to manipulate people for his own survival. Since he had arrived with only the clothes on his back and thongs on his feet, the first thing I did was take him into town to buy him a brand-new outfit. Instead of being shy and embarrassed, as I had expected him to be in this new situation, Joey strode confidently into the store and immediately won the hearts of most of the clerks there. I was amused as he talked to the girl helping to fit him into a new pair of shoes. "Hey, baby, how about a date tonight?" he asked with a flirtatious smile. "I'm getting all new clothes today, and you and me could go somewhere and have a ball."

Jim had told us so many times that everyone outside of the church was racist that I braced myself for the woman's reaction to this comment from little Joey, who was very, very black. She bent over and kissed his kinky hair! "That's really nice, kid," she said with a grin, "but I already have a date for tonight. You come back in a few years and we'll talk about it again." She smiled at me and I was amazed.

Two more black children arrived at our home the following week. Beth and Lillie were in their late teens. They both lived in Los Angeles and had asked the counsellors if they could spend their last year of high school in Redwood Valley where they would be closer to Jim and the church family. Since we needed some older girls to help our ever-growing family as big sister figures, we were delighted when they said they wanted to live in our home.

The work at Publications was getting so intense that Jim began to assign a few of the newer members to work with me. One of these "volunteers" was Ann. She was a young woman who had moved from Los Angeles to Redwood Valley to help the Cause. She had come into the church with a legal problem because she had heard that the church might be able to help her. Jim readily agreed to solve her problem.

She was a tall, beautiful young woman with big brown eyes and pretty freckles on her face. Her auburn hair completed a picture that was lovely enough to frame. She had a childlike trust in Jim, and she offered to do whatever she could in repayment for his help. Ann had an exceptional writing talent, and I asked her to write some articles for a magazine we were publishing. Although she had every good intention, her work habits were erratic and undependable. One day I asked her why she couldn't arrive at work on time and she burst into tears. "It's my children," she cried. "I love them so much, but I just can't take care of them and go to work, too." She said that one of the order women in the church, Edith Cordell, had been kind enough to take care of her eighteen-month-old baby, Candy, but that Candy now needed to go to a doctor because she was running a fever.

I realized that Ann was little more than a child herself. She didn't look more than nineteen years old, and my heart went out to her. "Would you like me to take Candy to the doctor?" I asked. Ann said yes and kissed my cheek in gratitude.

I had only ever seen Candy from a distance. I drove quickly up to Edith's trailer house and knocked on the door. Edith was an immaculate housekeeper, and although she had four babies with her at the time, her trailer was in perfect order. As she handed Candy to me I thought I was looking at the most beautiful baby in the world. She was half Negro and half Caucasian and had the finest characteristics of both races. Her complexion was warm tan, and yet her hair was formed in little finger curls haloing her head. She had a white fuzzy coat on and she looked up at me like a frightened rabbit.

When I held her close I realized that her body was very hot and her hair was soaking wet. Edith had wet it to make those beautiful little curls. As I placed her beside me in the car I knew that this was the baby I had been longing for since the first time I had looked at a mixed-race baby. I took her warm coat off, tousled and dried her hair, and held her close. Candy clung to me and sobbed and sobbed.

Acting on intuition, I took her to my house rather than to a doctor's office. As only a mother can understand, I knew that Candy wasn't really sick; she only needed attention and security. As soon as her hair was dry and she had cooler clothes on, her overheated body cooled and she began to smile at me. It was several hours before Al would get home, so I called the Publications Office and told Tim Clancey, our pressman, that I wouldn't be able to return until evening. I spent the next few hours hugging and playing with Candy.

By the time Al and the other children got home, I knew in my heart that Candy belonged to me. She seemed to sense it, too. I had been dreaming and longing for this baby for almost four years, and now I had her in my arms. I didn't even consider the fact that Al might not want to take on the additional responsibility as I proudly showed her to him. He reached out to touch her and Candy drew back and began to scream as though she had been beaten.

"What's the matter with her, Jeannie?" he asked, but I didn't know. I reached my own hand out and touched Al and again Candy screamed, louder and louder, until finally I had to take her into another room.

"Candy," I quietly begged, "please don't act like you hate him. I want him to love you. I want you to be our baby." As soon as we were alone again, Candy began to smile and caress my shoulder. I put her on the bed and started to walk out to talk with Al, and Candy started to scream again. As soon as I picked her up, she stopped crying.

I was beginning to realize that it wasn't going to be as easy as I had thought to keep Candy, but deep inside of me, I knew that she wasn't spoiled. Something was wrong.

As long as I held her Candy was fine, but Al didn't try to get close to her for the rest of the day. "Can we please keep her, please, Al?" I begged.

"She is one of the most beautiful babies I have every seen," he said "If you think Ann would let us have her, we'll try to keep her. I'm sure that in time she'll stop being so afraid of me."

I phoned Ann and told her that we had kept Candy at our house instead of taking her back to Edith's. I told her I wanted to talk to her before I returned Candy. Ann agreed that we could keep her for the night and that she and I would talk the next day.

The next day, I went to see Ann. I saw three little boys running around the outside of the house, screaming and yelling, hitting each other with sticks, and throwing sticks all over the yard. I cautiously walked past the boys and knocked on the door. Ann was sitting inside and invited me to join her on the couch. I had purposely left Candy at home with Grandma to reinforce the request I was about to make. "I came over to talk about Candy," I began. "Al and I really love her, and she seems to be happy in our home. We were wondering if you would let us keep her."

Ann looked exhausted. She had been taking care of her four-year-old son, Carl, and the two other boys, for several days. I could see that she was on the verge of tears. "Everyone loves Candy because she's a baby, but I want my two children to be raised together. I'll let you keep Candy, but I want you to keep Carl with her," she said with determination.

I looked outside at Carl, who was perched on a tree branch, throwing small branches down at the two boys beneath him, and took a deep breath. "Okay, Ann," I said. "I'm not sure we'll be able to handle Carl, but we'll try." She agreed to sign papers for us to get legal guardianship so that we could take care of their medical or other needs without getting her signature each time. She quickly gathered up Carl's clothes, along with the rest of Candy's belongings, and handed them to me. "I'm just so thankful that they will have a father," she said through tears. "I love my children but I just don't have time to take care of them and do church work. Maybe now I'll be able to help more at Publications."

She walked outside and called, "Carl, get down here right now." Carl scrambled out of the tree and obediently ran to her side. "Jeannie and Al are taking care of Candy and they are going to take you to their home, too," she said. He seemed puzzled and I quietly added, "You know we have goats, ducks, chickens, and even a rabbit at our house. We have a big swimming hole where everybody swims in the afternoon." That's all it took to persuade him to go. It was a hot summer, and most of the afternoons the temperature was over 100 degrees in Ukiah. The thought of a cool swim convinced him that he wanted to live with us.

Every day and every night for the next three weeks, Carl begged to go back to live with Ann. "I just wish I could still be with my mommy." When we tucked him into bed at night he would cry, "Why can't I go back home to my mommy?" When we would go to church he would run to Ann and jump on her lap, begging to be allowed to return. Soon both Ann and I realized that it was unfair to take Carl away from her. They had been through so much together. He was the man of the family. He had been born when Ann was barely sixteen years old, and they were actually growing up together. Ann took Carl back, but she had already signed the guardianship papers, and we never got around to changing the papers that had given both of her children to me.

Candy quickly learned to talk and to relate well to other people. She came to love and accept Al as her father and our home as her home. Since neither of us was able to have more children, we decided that Candy was the baby we couldn't have. Often in the years to come when we would think about leaving the church, the thought that we would lose Candy made us change our minds.

As I sat in the church services now, I always held Candy on my lap, with her arms wrapped tightly around me. We realized that it would still be months before Candy would feel safe enough to let go of me and believe that I would still be there when she came back. I realized that I needed Candy as much as she needed me, and I enjoyed every minute with her. The long offerings didn't seem so long anymore. In fact, nothing seemed as bad as it had seemed before Candy came into my life.

Joey was beginning to really enjoy life on our farm, and the big family he had been assigned to. One day, as I was sitting alone in the living room, he snuggled up beside me. "There's something I've been wondering about, Mom," he said.

"Yes, Joey, what is it?"

"Well, when I was in Philadelphia, all my friends were black. The white people were always mean to us, but you're white, and you're really nice to me. How come?"

"Because of Father's love," I answered him dutifully. We had all been instructed to give the credit to Jim if we were praised for something. "Father has taught us to show love to everyone."

"Oh, I see," said Joey thoughtfully. "But you don't have to be nice to me when he's not watching, do you?"

"No, Joey," I said. "I'm nice to you because you're so sweet and because I love you," and I tickled him on his stomach.

"I love you, too," he said solemnly. It was the first time he had shown any appreciation or love, and I treasured the moment. As we sat there in this quiet mother-and-son time, Joey began to open his heart to me. He told me about his mother who had beat him when she was "shooting up" (drugs). He explained what it was like to be hungry day after day and always running from the "fuzz" (policemen). "Lots of times, I had to lie to people so they'd give me some money to buy food. Sometimes I stole money to feed me and my cousins." I closed my eyes in horror.

"Here's another indication that Jim is really helping people," I thought. "I shouldn't be so critical of him. I have living proof, here in my home, of a truly humanitarian thing Jim has done."

Our home was like a slice of what I believed heaven should be—lots and lots of beautiful children. And every one of them was special to me. As the kids began to beg me to spend more time at home, I realized that I was resenting my time at work. Simultaneously, though, our work load was increasing and we were getting more volunteers. My work as manager had taken on tremendous additional responsibility. One day Al asked me if I could arrange my work schedule so I could help him more at home with our growing family.

All the inner frustrations I had been feeling suddenly gushed forth in uncontrollable sobs. "I want to stay home, I love it here," I said crying. "When I drive across the bridge and see our dogs, and the goats and ducks, and our beautiful kids, I wish I could stay here forever, and never again go out the gate. Then when I go to work, and all the young people there need me to help them with the work, I realize that I've just been selfish in wanting to stay home. I asked Linda Amos if I could get more help at the office, someone to help me manage the work, and she got angry. She said I'm being selfish with my children, and that most of the mothers in the church don't even get to have their own kids live with them. She said I should be grateful that I can see them once in a while. I feel like I'm being torn apart. Part of me wants to help Jim and the Cause, but inside, all I really want is to be home to enjoy the children, and spend time with you and my parents."

Al hadn't realized that I was so sensitive on the subject, that I missed him as much as he missed me, but now he understood some of the pressure I was under. "Don't forget, Jeannie, we can leave any time you want. The most important thing is our marriage and our family, and if you can't take the pressure, we'll just quit going to church," he said, holding me tenderly in his arms.

For a moment I wanted to do just that. Then I thought about Eddie's healing, Joey who was so happy in our home, Candy who had brought joy into our lives. "Never mind, Al, we can make it here. Jim needs us and we need the church. We'll make it, honey!" I didn't want to think about losing those terrific kids.

And I would stoically remind myself that every great cause is built by sacrifice. I had to sacrifice many of the joys of motherhood so that I could help Jim change the world.

Another Thanksgiving was coming, and Al's mother had invited us to her house for a family reunion Thanksgiving feast. I sent a note to council asking permission to take our family to Berkeley for the holiday. The answer came back directly from Jim. "It's time for you to cut your family ties. This church is your family now. Blood ties are dangerous because they prevent people from being totally dedicated to the Cause." Al called his mother and made an excuse. We reluctantly made our plans to spend Thanksgiving day at the church.

I was very disappointed. I had been looking forward to showing off Candy to her new grandma. She had become an outgoing and pleasant child, and we wanted Al's family to be able to enjoy her, too.

Jim asked Jack Beam and Linda Amos to teach us his rules about family relationships. Thanksgiving was already over, and I didn't see why we should have to be counselled about this now that we couldn't change our plans.

As usual, Jack was the first one to speak. "Families are a part of the enemy system. They do not love you. If you were in trouble, only Jim and his church family would be there to help you. Your family would turn their backs on you if you needed something that might cause them inconvenience. They don't understand this Cause and therefore you cannot trust them." We knew better than to argue with Jack, so we nodded our heads in agreement.

"When you do have to see your families, you are to go for just one purpose," Linda explained. "You should make up some sad story to get them to give you money or valuables. Ask them for presents or clothes, or anything you think you can get."

"That sounds so cold," I argued. "I don't think we could do that to our parents."

Carolyn Layton had walked into the room and listened to part of the conversation. She said with a sneer, "If you can't do that, then you don't understand the Cause. Don't you realize that when the atomic bomb comes, all your families will be burned up and their money will be burned with them? It's better for you to get it now, so we can use it to help make a better world today and a just society for the future."

Al decided to say what they wanted to hear so we could return home. "We understand what you are saying, and we will follow your advice whenever we visit our parents," he lied.

They seemed to be satisfied with his answer, and we were allowed to leave. Al's strategy was successful, because from that time forward we were able to visit his mother or other relatives whenever we came to the Bay Area, without counsellor interference.

It was Monday night and P.C. meeting again, another dreary twelve hours of listening to people's personal and sex problems and listening to Jim ramble and ramble. This night, though, something interesting happened to liven up our evening. It had been a practice of long standing that Jim would walk outside to urinate in the bushes when he held our P.C. meetings at Helen's house on the mountaintop near the church. Each time Jim would step outside, guards would stand at the door to make certain no one else went out. Since there was a bathroom right around the corner from the room we were meeting in, I had often wondered why he went outside. I whispered my question to Karen Layton, who was sitting beside me. "Jim wants privacy when he urinates," she explained. "People are always trying to walk in on him because they want to see his penis."

I believed her, and since Jim had told us many times that his organ was extremely large, I guessed that sight of it would cause others some embarrassment. As Jim stepped back in, the meeting continued. Maria Katsaris, a new P.C. member, was on the floor. She had been talking a lot about her family, and Jim wanted to explain the rule about family relationships to her, but with a few revisions. Maria's father was very influential in the community, and their verbal support of our group could be helpful.

"In your case, Maria, we are going to make an exception. Usually we try to avoid contact with our families who are not in the group, but your father has always seemed very friendly to our church, and we hope that you will do everything you can to keep him positive about us." Maria was young and anxious to please

Jim, but it was obvious that she also cared very much for her family. She promised that she would be able to keep her family alliances without hindering her deep devotion to the church.

As Maria sat down, Jim walked outside again, for the fourth time. He came in a few minutes later looking startled. "As I was out there I heard a neighbor's dog barking. I am certain someone was sneaking around in the bushes trying to take an infrared photograph of me urinating. People will do anything to try to discredit me. It was probably one of the eight people who defected last spring, trying to hurt our Cause by getting a picture they could use to accuse me of indecent exposure." The guards looked at one another in confusion. They had been instructed not to follow him outside because he was afraid that they, too, might look, and now it sounded as if they had shirked their duty.

"Well, don't just stand there," he shouted condescendingly. "Go out and see if you can find someone snooping around." Seven guards jumped up and ran outside, several with loaded guns. They looked around the grounds for half an hour but didn't find any indication of prowlers, so they returned.

It was Wednesday, "family meeting" night, when the members came together to discuss personal matters. Tonight Jim began talking about his marriage and about the many things he was forced to do for the Cause.

"It all began several years ago in Brazil," he began solemnly. "Marcie and I were down there, trying to run an orphanage, and we ran out of money. Here we were with over a hundred children that had to be fed, and the church in Indiana wasn't sending us any money, and we were down to our last few dollars.

"Several of the politicians' wives had offered to pay me to make love with them, but of course I had always refused. One night, Marcie and I watched the children go to bed, knowing that the following day we would be out of food and with no money to replenish our supplies.

"I talked it over with my wife, and she agreed that it was important to get money. I called up one man's wife, a woman who had been trying to get me into bed for several months, and I told her, 'I'm interested in that proposition you've been making. If you can give me five thousand dollars, I'll come over and spend the night with you.'"

"She asked me to come over, and I did. I gave her her money's worth that night. The following morning when she tried to pay me, I was so sickened by the fact that I had prostituted myself with her that I decided she should see exactly where her money was going. She had on a beautiful white dress and fancy shoes, and I took her right down into the heart of the poor area, where my orphanage was, and made her talk to my children so she would know that she was giving money to them, and not to me."

Marcie was in our P.C. meeting the night he told us the story, and it was apparent from her pained expression that she was going through some conflict about Jim's disclosure. Suddenly she stood up and walked to the front beside Jim. "Honey, I don't understand why you want to share something that was so personal this way."

Jim answered her, "Because this is our family. I want them to know how much I trust each person in this room. Also I want people to understand what is sometimes required of me for the Cause."

Marcie smiled at him sadly and said, "I'd like to make an announcement, then, if it's a good time to do it."

Jim replied, "Go ahead. I don't know what you're going to say, but if you feel it's important, then go ahead and make your announcement."

Marcie took a deep breath before she began. "It's true that I have had to share my husband in the past, for the Cause. It was always painful for me because I love him very much, and just like everyone else, it's painful for me to see the person I love with someone else. Several years ago Jim asked me for a divorce because I just couldn't make the adjustment to being married to a man who was also married to a Cause. At that time I had to do some serious introspection and decide on my priorities.

"I knew that I didn't want to lose Jim, so I agreed that I would share him with people who needed to relate to the Cause on a more personal level. This has been a very difficult thing for me to live with, and it's caused me a lot of heartache. However, tonight, as I heard him pour out his heart to you, explaining the suffering he goes through when he has to use his body to serve the Cause, I realized that I have been very selfish.

"I want to make a public statement tonight that I am willing to share my husband for the Cause, and that I won't resent it any longer." With that Marcie walked out of the church building, leaving the audience silent.

Jim, too, seemed stunned. He said, "I hope Marcie's unexpected offer doesn't cause a lot of you to begin making demands upon me. I am already overworked in this area."

Even though Jim said he was already "overworked," he told us in the Planning Commission meetings that Patty Cartmell was assigned to make up his appointments for sexual encounters with the different members who expressed a need to "learn to relate to the Cause" on a more personal level. He laughingly called her his "fucking secretary," saying that, "if you feel you need this service you'll have to talk to her."

*   *   *

It was almost Halloween, and Jim announced that there would be a hobo bazaar for the church children.

Roz and Joanne both had a flair for drama, and between them, our children were the best hobos we had ever seen. Roz charcoaled their faces as Joanne put the final touches on their tattered clothes. The children were bubbling with excitement as I handed each ten dimes to spend. We got to the church early to be sure the kids didn't miss any of the fun.

Since there were so few fun times, the children made the most of this evening. They ran from booth to booth, throwing dimes for goldfish, going through the haunted house, and shrieking with delight as mock vampires came over to suck blood out of their necks. One of the booths that always had a crowd of observers around it was the jail. There was a small fenced area where the victims of children who paid their dime were kept for five minutes in prison.

One little girl, Mabel Cordell, paid her dime and looked around for a victim the jailkeeper could arrest. Her eyes fell on Jim, and she got an excited gleam in her eyes and pointed to him. The jailkeeper, one of the counsellors, thought that it would add fun to the booth to have him in there for a few minutes, and ran over and brought him back. Jim good-naturedly went into the jail area and smiled at the children and at the crowd that had gathered to watch. After a couple of minutes, though, Jim began to look a little restless, and he asked someone to have Linda Amos come over. She stepped up to the fence and Jim whispered something in her ear.

Linda went to the jailkeeper and demanded that he let Father out immediately. Jim was released, but that was not the last we were to hear about the incident. Later, after the bazaar was over, the members gathered for a church service. Jim began the evening meeting by announcing, "I want to deal with the people who saw any humor in my being placed in jail. Surely you all know that I will probably be locked in a real jail one day, and it isn't funny." Silence filled the auditorium. Seven-year-old Mabel slowly raised her hand. Jim spent the rest of the evening telling her, and the rest of the congregation, how terrible jails are and impresssing upon them that "There is no humor in any game that involves jails." All the joy of the evening had been destroyed by his sermon. Mabel cried and apologized to Jim and to the church members. Jim, in his great love, forgave her.

His first words of revelation as he began the healing service were "Someone is going to try to shoot at my church tonight at midnight. We will hear two shots fired. No one will be hurt as long as you all stay near my aura of protection." Then he proceeded with the healing service, calling some people out by revelation to heal them or tell them a warning prophecy that would save them from future disaster. Midnight was drawing closer. Few people were paying attention to the healing service that night. All eyes were glued to the clock. Several of the older women asked if they might be excused to go home, but Jim reassured them that he would protect every person from harm. "The only harm will come to people who try to leave early," he said ominously.

At twelve o'clock, just as he had prophesied, two shots rang out. The bullets came through a window and went zinging through the back of the building. Jim clutched his hand to his forehead even though the bullets had been heard far from where he was sitting. He announced, "Those bullets would have hit one of the members in the back of the room but, by my power, I drew them here to the front and took them into my own head so that none of you would be hurt." Throughout the next hour, he continued to rub his forehead with his red prayer cloth.

Marvin Swinney later confided to Al that he had been in his bus at the time of the shooting and had seen one of the counsellors run behind Jim's house with a gun shortly after the shots were fired. Marvin took Al to the window where this counsellor had stood and they saw bullet holes. Al realized that Jim had deceived his members—again, for the Cause. He decided to keep all this a secret from me.

The effect of this episode upon the members was better than Jim could have hoped for. Members testified that they had seen "Father show infinite compassion" when he took the bullets into his own head that should have hit someone else. One lady shrieked, "I was a firsthand witness to his God Power when he didn't die after I saw two bullets penetrate his skull!"

* * *

A few days before Christmas day, Jim handed me a note. "Andre is causing our church some real embarrassment because of his medical problems. He is going to be a pathological killer when he grows up, so I want you to call the placement agency right away and send him back to his welfare department."

Andre had been having some problems that required hospital-ization in the local medical clinic; we felt he was our son, not an embarrassment. I showed the note to Al and together we wept. The church had brought Andre into our lives, and now Jim was going to take him away from us. "I hope he can find another home with people that love him as much as we do," Al said without much hope in his voice.

Jim told us to destroy the note as soon as we had read it and not to tell anyone why we were returning him. I called the social worker the following morning, the day before Christmas, and told her that she would need to find another placement for Andre. "Why? What has he done wrong?" she asked in amazement. Andre had been so happy in our home and he related to us as if we were his own parents.

"There are just unresolvable conflicts in our household, and we feel that it would be better for Andre to be placed somewhere else." We were saying the words that Carolyn had instructed us to use.

As the social worker arrived to take him away, Andre pleaded with us. "What have I done?" he asked again and again.

Al tried to explain. "Andre, you need more medical help than the local clinic has been able to give you. Maybe in the Bay Area you will be able to find a doctor who can cure you."

We kissed our son good-bye. "How heartless to boot him out at Christmastime," I said angrily.

"Who knows," Al answered, trying to be optimistic. "Maybe he'll have a better Christmas with another family. You know, Christmas in this church isn't much for a kid to brag about."

1974

Deep in my heart
I do believe,
I know,
I know you're God.
                    —from a Peoples Temple song

Chris Lewis, a fierce Temple guard, got himself into trouble with the law—big trouble this time. When he had first joined the church, he brought an expensive drug habit with him. Through the positive reinforcement of the church he had kicked this habit and dedicated his life to Jim and to the Cause. Although Chris tried to follow Jim's many rules, he had errant tendencies and so a significant part of his life was spent on the streets of San Francisco. Jim knew about this side of Chris's life but for some reason never confronted Chris or asked him to give the total life commitment the rest of us were expected to give.

But now, witnesses had seen Chris murdering someone in San Francisco. Jim had a long, serious discussion with the P.C. about the incident. "I have always allowed Chris certain latitude in his actions and in his living situation, because he has contacts that are very helpful in some areas of my work, areas that few of you are aware of. I cannot allow him to go to jail. We need to maintain his contacts. And, more important, I do not fully trust Chris. If he were left in jail it is very probable that he would tell everything he knows about our group. His testimony could be harmful to our welfare. It is imperative that we keep him out of jail at all costs."

"At all costs" came to $36,000, Jim told us. Chris was released—free of all charges.

Now, however, Jim faced another problem and discussed it at

the P.C. In the course of Chris's business dealings on the streets, he had made several very powerful enemies, and one of these enemies put out a contract on Chris's life. It was necessary to hide Chris for a while where no one could find him. With our trailer recently vacated by Roz, Jim decided to move Chris and his wife into it for a month. By the end of the month, Chris was acting like a lion in a tiny cage. He told Jim he couldn't stand living there any longer. "The country life may be okay for some folks, but for a city dude like me it's worse than prison." So Jim sent Chris to another state where he could live in a different big city. Anything to keep him happy and quiet. Eventually he went to Jonestown.

*   *   *

A rumor began to circulate among the black members of the church. "If Jim isn't racist, why is it he only brags about having sex with white people, never black?" Jim heard the rumor, and the following Sunday he was ready with an answer which he thought would clear up the question. "Black people have suffered so much at the hands of the white people," he explained, "that I wouldn't want to ask a black woman to go through something that would remind her of the pain her grandparents suffered at the hands of slave masters." His answer sounded sincere enough until one night the next week, in a fit of anger, he lashed out, "You people tell me how to dress, how to love, and now you even try to tell me who I can fuck. I think since I am the leader, I should have the right to choose my own sexual companions. I have preferences just like you all do. Let me choose my own types and my own complexion, and leave my sex life alone!" No one again questioned his choice of partners—at least, not openly. Many people, however, now understood that his love for minorities stopped at his bedroom door.

Everyone had noticed by this time that Jim had a strong preference not only for fair complexions but also for small breasts and slender bodies—Marcie...Carolyn Layton...Meri. Occasionally, he would spend a night with a different type, but this was apparently little more than the spice of life.

But best of all, Jim liked compulsive workers, and he was talking about developing a mission field again. He had studied several areas and he decided the mission field would be in Guyana, South America. "I have been there before," he told the congregation, "and in the evening the trade winds blow, and the weather is always pleasant." He had sent several of his trusted staff workers to check out the political situation in the country and received an encouraging report. They told him there was a border dispute between Guyana and Venezuela and that Guyana was encouraging people to develop the jungle areas, near the border, to prevent Venezuela from trying to make a claim on the territory.

Jim realized that a group effort of reclaiming the jungle land for agricultural purposes would be much appreciated by the government. He began to give reports to the church members about the "Promised Land" he was beginning to prepare for.

"This is the land that I have been promising you. When fascism takes over in this country, we will have a place where we will all be safe." The church members cheered his words.

The prospect of a jungle paradise was exciting. The counsellors began to speculate about who would be chosen to help develop the land and prepare for the housing for the rest of the members. Al and I assumed that our family would be among the first to go. However, there was no mention of our names as the first list was read. Instead, to everyone's amazement, he read the names of the rebellious and troublemaking members who had been up for discipline in the past.

When one of the counsellors asked Jim why he wasn't sending the people who were skilled in construction or who had been working with public relations, he responded by saying, "Are you questioning my decisions?" Obviously no one wanted to be accused of treason, so the subject was closed.

There were two radically different reports about this mission field. One report was the description being sent to Jim. This was very different from the paradise Jim was promising the members. The church members weren't told about the heat, the bugs, the diarrhea, the deadly poisonous snakes, or the extreme poverty of the people in Guyana. They were never informed of the problems encountered in trying to grow food in the tropical climate. Instead, the people were told about a land flowing with milk and honey, where miracles were happening every day. "All you have to do is reach your hand up wherever you are and pick delicious fruit from the wild jungle trees," Jim boasted. "Every time you drop a seed in the ground it grows. The people there are friendly and they love us. There is no stealing in this jungle paradise." To listen to Jim's reports the members had every reason to believe that he had discovered heaven on earth.

The poor members in the congregation, who had never been able to look forward to a time of plenty and prosperity, suddenly envisioned themselves walking the roads lined with tropical fruit trees. They were assured their jungle paradise would provide them with food and happiness for the rest of their lives. Now that they knew the Promised Land actually existed, members began to turn in money at an even faster pace. They willingly sold everything they owned and gladly begged on the streets for more money, because they believed that every dollar they turned in was being used for their future happiness.

As Jim explained week after week about the Promised Land, he also began to talk more about the oppression of black people in our country. Movies graphically portraying the horrors of the Nazi concentration camps were shown to the church members. Several movies that had been smuggled out of Chile also made their way to our church services, horrifying us with pictures of tortures that had been used to try to force the Chilean revolutionaries to give information to the fascist regime.

After one particularly gruesome movie, Jim told everyone he was going to give them a "test" to see if they fully understood the implications of the movie. He wanted to be sure that the members were sufficiently afraid of government oppression. One of the young black members wrote the following letter: "This was about the lady you wanted us to tell you about. She went down to stand against fascist oppressors. She had to deny knowing her companion. When those S.O.B.'s tortured him they asked her if she knew him. She said no. Then those fascists pigs cut his erection off and they made her look at him go through hell, but she would not sell out her freedom as you would say, Father. I think, Father, the more they did to him it made her stand for justice more. And the mother fuckers pulled her baby out of her body and put rags and splinters up in her, those fascist S.O.B.'s, but she had to be silent. If not, then that movement would not succeed. Though she loved him she could not sell out and they did not look at her like they wanted her to help them. We should know if you sell out socialism you have sold out your plan of salvation and you cannot find socialism until you have found Father Jim Jones.... Christianity has brainwashed people of captivity. Some Christianity has murdered innocent people...."

As Jim read her letter, he praised her for understanding the message he had tried to help people understand.

*   *   *

The Planning Commission meetings began to include some real planning, as Jim asked for advice about the Promised Land. Each counsellor was instructed to find out anything he or she could about Guyana. Some were assigned to study agriculture, while others were to investigate the problems of raising livestock in the tropics. Few of us talked about anything else, and every person secretly wished that he or she could be the next person assigned to leave.

One Monday night, in the midst of some animated discussion about the mission field, Clifford began to drop off to sleep. Bill punched him in the arm to wake him up, and Clifford, startled, punched him back. Jim saw this exchange and asked, "What's happening over there?"

Bill responded, "Clifford was falling asleep and I was trying to wake him up."

"Bill punched me in the arm and I punched him back," Clifford retorted.

Jim asked Clarese, Clifford's wife, to stand up. "Does he act like this at home?"

"Yes, sometimes he acts like a real baby." Clarese was saying what any wife would be expected to say in this type of confrontation.

Jim continued to question Clarese, "Well, how do you think we could teach him a lesson?"

Linda leaned over and whispered into her ear, and Clarese answered, "I'll tell you one thing. Clifford is a prude. He has never been willing to have oral sex with me. He thinks it's vulgar."

This was an astonishing admission for Clarese to make. She was usually shy and reserved, and I was shocked by her words. Jim continued, "He doesn't like pussy? Well, I wonder how he'd like some black pussy." Jim had suggested some disgusting things in the past, but this was by far the most bizarre thing I had ever heard him say. Jim looked around the room and his eyes fell on Alice. Motioning to her, he said, "Alice, Clifford doesn't like pussy. Take off your pants and give him some of yours and we'll see how he likes it."

"Right here?" Alice was stunned.

"Yes, my love, you're among friends." Jim pointed to a long table in the room and asked Alice to get on it. Alice was paralyzed. If someone had taken a vote on the ten shyest people in the church, Alice would have headed the list. She sat there, unable to speak. Jim looked at her and encouraged her, "Come on, Alice, you can do this for the Cause." Alice didn't move.

Tami came to her rescue. She would do this for the Cause. "I'm on my period, Jim. I'll give Clifford a little bloody black pussy."

Jim looked relieved at not having to make an issue of this with Alice. It was obvious that she couldn't go through with it. "Okay, Tami, thank you for your dedication to the Cause. I know this is a big sacrifice for you to make."

Tami lay on top of the table. She pulled down her underpants and sanitary pad and spread her legs. Jim looked at Clifford in disgust and said, "Come on, you think you're so pure. Go over there and have some."

"I'm not going to do it." Few people dared refuse what Jim demanded, but Clifford was desperate.

Johnny Brown, one of Jim's most powerful boxers, jumped up and stood in front of Clifford. "What's the matter? Are you prejudiced?"

"No, I just don't want to do it."

"Come on Clifford," Johnny taunted him. "Do you think you're too good to lick Tami's pussy? You're insulting my black sister."

Clifford looked pleadingly at Jim. "I'm sorry, Father, I just can't. I'll do anything else you ask, but I can't."

Clarese spoke up. "See what I mean? He's a prude!"

"Clifford," Jim was speaking very calmly but with determination, "I insist that you do this right now."

"No."

"If you refuse to do as I have requested, you will have to leave the group."

"Fine, I'll leave today."

"Do you mean you are so prudish, and so racist, that you would leave your family, your job, and this group, just to save yourself the embarrassment of licking Tami's pussy?"

Tami was still lying spread-eagled on the table and beginning to feel utterly foolish. "Oh, come on, Clifford," she called to him, "let's get it over with."

"You racist, you racist pig!" The counsellors were shouting now, and Clifford's anger overcame his aversion to Tami. He strode over to Tami, put his mouth between her legs and licked, not gently, but with hostility and rage. Tami was startled at his roughness, but she did nothing. He continued to lick until Jim realized that Clifford had lost control of himself and commanded him to stop.

Clifford stormed out of the room and Jim allowed him to leave. Jim knew Clifford didn't want to leave his wife and children and was sure he'd be back. Tami was trembling. She stood up, grabbed her underwear, and ran downstairs to the restroom.

"Are you all right, Tami?" Jim called to her.

"Yes, thank you, Father," she shouted from the foot of the stairs.

Intense fear flooded my mind. If Jim could make Clifford do this, there was a real possibility that others might be forced into similar actions, and I was at least as shy as Alice. By that time, though, I had become so mind-controlled, so dedicated to the Cause, that I didn't even consider leaving the church. My major concern was a fear of personal embarrassment. I hoped that Jim was going through some weird emotional cycle and that before my turn came he would be more normal.

As Jim's sadism increased in the P.C., it was also becoming more apparent in the church services. In his effort to "help people grow," he was using more physical punishments. Spankings had become a regular part of nearly every church service. One young, very overweight girl named Carla was confronted for breaking a rule. Jim sentenced her to receive ten hits with the belt, and she pleaded with him to punish her some other way.

"Please, Father," she cried. "I can't stand beatings. I get so many beatings at home. Please give me some other punishment."

"Obviously you don't get enough of them at home, or you wouldn't be up here for more," Jim said with a bit of a smile. He turned to Jack and asked, "Do you have a belt on?"

Jack got his belt ready while the guards told Carla to bend over. Jack's first whack was hard and Carla jumped, screaming in pain. "Please, Father," she begged again. The guards were trying to hold her still, but she was thrashing around in pain. Jim started to laugh at her contortions.

"Carla, can't you just take your spanking without making such a fool of yourself?" he asked condescendingly.

She bent down again, and Jack hit her the second time. We all watched as her fat flesh went in two inches under the impact of his belt. Again, Carla screamed and jumped. Jim was laughing now and couldn't stop. Between giggles, he told Jack, "Just finish this whipping, will you please?"

The guards held Carla tightly while Jack hit her eight more times. She was sobbing, hurt, and angry. She glared at Jim with hatred in her eyes. "My mother gets drunk and beats me with an electric cord, and I can't stand the pain. I don't understand why you laugh while I am being beaten. I never thought I'd get a beating here in my church."

The audience was shocked. They waited in fear to see how Jim was going to react to Carla's criticism. We hadn't heard Jim laugh during a whipping before, and there was a lot of sympathy in the audience for Carla.

Jim realized that everyone knew he had lost control of his emotions. "I'm sorry, Carla. I wasn't laughing at the pain you were going through. It's just the contortions and jumping around that you were doing that seemed funny. Please forgive me, though, I shouldn't have laughed." Jim had regained his composure and once again sounded like a loving father. Carla had calmed down, too.

"Father, I'm sorry, too. I know I shouldn't have broken that rule, and I certainly did learn my lesson. I'm sure it looked funny watching me jump all around the stage." She had redeemed herself and had helped Jim save face.

The next person to be called forward for confrontation was Amy. She made the mistake of telling one of her friends that she and her husband were still having sex. The friend had turned her name into council as Jim instructed everyone to do.

"Hank and Amy, please come to the front," Jim announced. "I understand that you two are still having sex, even after all the honesty I have given you in these past months. Amy, can't you see that you're hurting Hank? I try to help him grow stronger, but every time I try to help, you tear it down by allowing him to fuck you. Now, I'm going to ask you a question, and I want you to remember that the Cause is the most important thing in the world before you answer." He paused to allow his last sentence to sink in, hoping she would say what he had earlier instructed her to. "Do you really enjoy fucking him or are you just putting on a good show for his benefit?"

Amy answered dutifully, "I'm just pretending that I enjoy it."

"Do you ever have orgasm?"

"No."

Jim turned to Hank. "Do you still think you are the great lover? Are you going to continue to make Amy do something she finds so distasteful? Can't you just appreciate the fact that she is a good mother to your children, and a great help in many of our church's projects, and leave her alone in the bedroom?"

Hank hung his head and promised never again to make Amy have sex with him. They both had been with Jim for many years, and they knew they had said what Jim expected. They also knew that they would continue to do what they wanted in their home. Amy told me later that she swore that night never to confide in anyone again about their sex life.

Jim's continual haranguing about sex had led to a voluntary commitment from each member to ban sex from his or her life. I am certain that many couples like Hank and Amy, and Al and myself, verbally agreed to what Jim asked in order to escape the confrontations. But many of the young people, who had committed their lives totally to Jim and the Cause, naively gave up all hope of ever having a fulfilling love relationship because Jim said it was counterrevolutionary.

One afternoon, while I was working, the telephone rang. It was Daphene's teacher calling me to speak with me. "Your daughter is a very good girl and a good student, but she has the nastiest mouth I have ever heard in a young child. The jokes she tells are disgusting." I apologized for her and promised to have a long talk with Daphene that evening.

It was inevitable that this would happen. These small children listened to Jim for hours on end, and his speech was filled with crude words. How could I tell Daphene that she couldn't use the same words she heard Father using and still ask her to respect him as our leader? The teacher threatened Daphene with suspension. I knew I had to do something. Al and I decided to let the counsellors handle it. The church had created the problem, let them solve it.

That evening, Daphene went to talk to Don Beck, the children's counsellor. As we watched him talking with her, we could see a bit of a smile on the corners of his mouth. Daphene was tiny for her age, and she looked so innocent. Don did a good job of explaining the situation to her. "Daphene, sometimes Father uses certain words to help people understand a point he is making. When he says these words, it isn't like swearing. But outsiders don't understand these things. If you use the same words or tell the same jokes at school, your teachers will get mad. You have to learn never to use those words at school."

Daphene promised that she wouldn't swear at school again. It had been Daphene's first experience with the council and she was still trembling as she got into our car. "I was so scared, Mommy," she said.

* * *

Jim began dyeing his hair jet black to hide the gray hairs that were showing. He penciled in his long sideburns to make them look fuller. His robes were hiding more than the used clothes he wore. They were hiding a paunch. A close look at him was a shock to a member who had been admiring him from afar, but those who were spending time in bed with him were aware of his potbelly, his thinning hair, and his penciled sideburns.

It didn't matter to them, though, because they would be among the members to get special privileges. In the bedroom, Jim would tell each new person, "I love you more than I love any of the others," but he would later humiliate his newest conquest in the P.C. meetings. In front of the person he would brag, "I tell them all I love them most. Actually, I only love the Cause."

Jim had often told us about the women he was "fucking to keep them in the Cause," but now he was being "forced" to perform the same service for some of the men. He referred to Eric as "The Noxzema Kid." "When Eric asked me to fuck him, he said he always uses Noxzema, and I believed him," he said laughing, in spite of Eric's blushing and mortification. "As soon as we used it, we both knew it was a mistake." Even in this act, though, Jim had to make himself look good. "As Eric was crying in pain from the burning Noxzema on his rectum, I got a cloth and helped him wash it off. I didn't even take the time to clean myself up, although I was also in pain."

*   *   *

The Planning Commission meetings were often used as Jim's testing grounds. If a new idea worked on us, he would try it in the public meetings. Even his homosexual activities were going to be shared with the rest of the church members. In explanation to an attorney, who strongly suggested that he should keep this part of his life quiet, Jim explained, "If people were to find out about this through some other source, they would never forgive me. However, if I tell them myself, and explain that I am doing it for the Cause, then no matter what they hear from anyone else, they won't feel that I have betrayed them."

Sure enough, at the next Sunday service Jim broached the subject of his homosexual acts. "One young man here was having problems relating to the Cause, and he asked me to relate to him in a more personal way. Even though I find homosexuality disgusting, if one of my members needs me to minister to them on any level, I will not refuse them. However, this man was most inconsiderate when he came to me without having first cleansed himself." He was looking directly at Randy, one of the guards, who was standing near the front in full view of the audience. "That person who begged me to do something that I find completely foreign to my own natural desires should have at least taken an enema before he came to me!"

It was apparent to almost everyone there that he had been talking about Randy, both by the blush Randy had just acquired and by the fact that Jim was staring at him. In deep humiliation Randy stood up, raised his head, and said, "That's true, Father, and I apologize for being so thoughtless."

Jim had accomplished what he wanted. He had been the first to tell his members that he was having sex with men, and he had made it sound as if it had been nasty and disgusting to him.

Jim's sermons began to be filled with discussions about sex. He was changing his own sexual practices and seemed to need to justify it in his meetings. "Every man is a homosexual and every woman is a lesbian. I am the only man alive that really knows how to make women happy. Every man wants to have a dick up his ass and every woman wants to suck another woman's pussy." The first time Jim had talked like this, people were shocked, but like everything else he did, after a few times, it ceased to be shocking.

A few brave men tried to disagree with his blanket statements, but when they did Jim humiliated them. "If you think you can fuck women, prove it here, in front of everyone. If you think you know how to make love, then show us. You fuck your wife and I'll fuck mine, and we'll see who's able to do it longer and better." No one was brave enough to take him up on his challenge.

He seemed to be becoming more and more obsessed with his sexuality by the day. It was nauseating to listen to him tell a congregation of a thousand or more adults and children that he had the biggest penis of any man. "I'm called upon to use this organ for the Cause all the time. What a curse it is to be so sexually potent that people continually demand that I fuck them."

He publicly laughed about Patty Cartmell's job as his "fucking secretary." "I have been so beseiged with demands to meet the personal needs of my members that I have had to make appointments. Fortunately, Patty keeps track of these things for me. If you feel the need for this type of relationship with the Cause, you should talk to her.

"However," he warned, "if you do approach her and ask for a specific time to be with me, you'd better keep that appointment. Last week one young woman, who had had difficulty relating to the Cause, made an appointment. She was to meet with me at three o'clock the following afternoon. I had a doctor's appointment at that time, but I canceled it because I knew that she needed to spend the time with me. She kept me waiting for almost an hour, without even the courtesy of a call, after I had given up an appointment with my physician to meet her need.

"This kind of inconsideration is unfair to me and to the office I represent. The woman knows who she is, and she has apologized, but I just want each of you to realize that these appointments are very important. I expect that you will show enough respect to be there on time."

In his sermons, he was beginning to graphically hint about his unusually active sex life. "I get so tired of women begging me to fuck them," he bragged. "The next woman that begs me to fuck her will get a fucking like she's never had before. My organ is so big that she will be sore for a week. I can be very strong when I fuck, or I can be very gentle." Hour after hour we had to listen to him boasting about his diversified talents in the bedroom.

Kathy Stahl was up for discipline, accused of eating extra meals at the college cafeteria in Santa Rosa. Jim looked at her with disgust as he said, "Why do you think you should have better food than the rest of the college students? You are terribly overweight already. The only way you will understand these rules is through embarrassment."

He paused, trying to think of a suitable punishment to teach

Kathy not to get extra food. "Maybe if you have to show everyone how fat you are you will learn your lesson. You're here with your church family, Kathy, so you don't need to worry about being seen by strangers. I want you to take off all your clothes except your underwear, and then go for a cold swim. Maybe then you will learn your lesson."

Kathy looked at Jim in disbelief but, as she waited, realized that he wasn't going to change his mind. This was her punishment, and she knew she was going to have to do it. While the entire audience watched her, Kathy removed her blouse, her skirt, her shoes and nylons, and finally her slip. It was obvious that she hadn't expected this; her panties had a safety pin holding the elastic band together, and her bra was evidently old and worn. There were small rolls of fat on her body and legs, and we looked with pity at her standing there sadly. Jim callously looked at her and said, "See what I told you? You don't need any extra food!"

Kathy was then sent to the back of the room where Don Sly, the swimming instructor, pushed her into the deep end of the pool. Kathy was only a fair swimmer, and it was with a great deal of splashing that she finally made it to the other end of the pool, and walked shivering into the rest room, where Linda Amos was waiting with a towel and her clothes.

Jim's disciplines were becoming more and more violent. "I tried to rule with love, but people took advantage of that. The only thing people understand is fear," he said as he ordered a child to receive ten whacks with a belt. The five-year-old child begged so pitifully for mercy that people in the audience were asking Jim to reduce the number of hits. Jim realized that he had been harsh in his sentence, but he never backed down once he set the prisoner's sentence.

So he tried to redeem himself in another way. "Since this is the little boy's first offense, I will take his discipline for him." Several counsellors started to protest, and a few of the older members in the congregation began to cry.

One elderly woman said, "No, Father, please don't let them hurt you. You healed me of cancer. You saved me from an accident. You haven't done anything wrong!"

But Jim was adamant. Someone had to receive the whipping he had ordered for the child, or he feared that other people might expect to have their sentences reduced. As he bent over to receive his whipping, Jack hit him lightly with the belt. "You know that's not the way you've been hitting these other people," he remonstrated with Jack. "Hit me the same way."

Jack did, and Jim flinched with pain. Even though he was only hit twice with the belt, he complained about pain in his kidneys for the next three meetings. "Jack hit me on my back instead of my butt," he said, "and he injured my kidneys." The next day he was complaining that the whipping had caused him to have blood clots. "I have a special type of blood, and I've suffered from blood clots since Jack hit me." Jack apologized for having been so careless when he whipped Jim.

I commented to Al, "If Jim has suffered this much from two hits, and only one of them was hard, can you imagine what the other people must be suffering? Some of them have had as many as a hundred hits."

Al answered, "Yes, I know, but they're not allowed to complain. Only Jim can complain."

* * *

The attorneys on Jim's staff began to worry about the legal implications of these beatings and they mentioned it to him. Jim answered, "I refuse to lead this group of people without some discipline that will keep them in line! You do what you have to, to make it legal for me to beat people, or I will quit being the leader." The attorneys wrote a release form which each person had to sign before being beaten. When a child under eighteen was sentenced to a beating, their parents had to sign that they requested Jim to discipline the child with the specified number of whacks. The forms were supposed to be notarized later so that Jim could use them as legal evidence if anyone took him to court because of the beating.

Now that Jim felt legally safe, there was no stopping his cruel beatings. He decided that the belt didn't hurt enough, so he had the guards bring in long elm switches. They kept breaking under the force of the hard whacks, though, and Jim realized that he would have to use something much sturdier.

He asked Tom Grubbs, the electrician, to make him a switch, using an electric cord with a triple cord end. Tom was a compassionate and sensitive man who had difficulty watching the punishments at all, but, because Jim insisted, he made the switch according to specifications. It had a thick handle about a foot long and three thick electric cables tied together at the handle. He carried it with him in his electrician's box for a few days, unable to bring himself to give it to Jim.

One day, when Tom and I were talking together, he told me he had finished the switch. "Do you want to see what it looks like?" he asked.

I winced with horror as he brought it out. "God, Tom, can you imagine anyone using a torture instrument like that on children?"

He put it back into the box. "That's why I haven't shown it to Jim," he said. "I'm going to tell him that I couldn't make one and hope he doesn't get too mad." Tom never had to show the switch to Jim, because Jim had something worse in the works.

He'd designed a spanking board, carved from a one-by-four-inch board about two and a half feet long. It had a handle carved into it about eight inches from one end. As he held it up to show it to the church members, he bragged, "I've finally found something to use for discipline that should work. This board won't break, and it really hurts. Maybe now you people will learn to obey the rules."

He assigned Ruby Carroll to do the beatings. She was a tall black woman who weighed at least 250 pounds. She was strong and knew how to whip hard. The first few people who were beaten with this board screamed in agony. Horror filled the faces of the people sitting in the audience. To be sure that everyone knew how painful it was, Jim had the microphone held to the mouth of each person being beaten. Screams filled the room and fear filled every heart. To prevent the person being beaten from wildly thrashing about, two strong guards were assigned to hold the victim. They found that the only way to immobilize these hysterical people was to stretch their bodies in midair, one holding the arms and the other the legs, and let Ruby beat them as many times as Jim had determined.

At the next P.C. meeting, Jim was on the rampage again about people who were "forcing" him to have sex with them. "When Oscar made me fuck him, he didn't tell me he had a rash, and now I've caught it from him. He was so filthy he smelled like he hadn't bathed for a week." Jim told Oscar to pull his shorts down and spread his buttocks so the counsellors assembled in the room could inspect the area and see if it was clean. Obediently, in front of nearly 100 people, Oscar did as he was told. Most of the women in the room didn't raise their eyes from the floor, but several men were ordered to inspect Oscar. The men commented that they didn't see any indication of a rash. Jim still swore that the rash had been there and made Oscar promise to go to a doctor. "When you get your medication, bring me some of it so I can clear mine up, too. It would never do for me to go to a doctor with this type of rash," he explained.

He continued to complain about the trials and tribulations of being forced into sex with so many people. "Meri and her goddamned venereal warts," he said disgustedly. "I've had to live with these damnable things ever since I fucked her. No one knows what kind of pain they can cause, do they Meri?" Her face turned beet red, but she quickly said, "That's right, Father."

I remember Meri's warts. Her backside had resembled a head of cauliflower with warts extending from the anus and covering a part of her buttocks. She'd suffered terrible agonies with them, and, even though she'd had them cut out, they had promptly started to grow back.

Jim was continuing to complain, "These women that I have to fuck all think they're special to me. Suzy thinks she's sexy when she whispers love poems in my ears, but I know she's a treasonous bitch and I fuck her to keep her in the Cause." I was surprised that he would talk about Suzy when she was present, because he usually talked about her only behind her back. I looked around the room, though, and saw that she had left to run an errand for Jim.

After he degraded a few more people, Jim looked around the room to see whom he'd missed. He asked, "How many people in here have had sex with me?"

About twenty people, both men and women, stood. Jim looked at a man named Harry, who was sitting quietly, looking out the window, and said, "Someone in here is ashamed to admit that he asked me to have sex with him. But you sure weren't ashamed when you were squealing with delight as we were fucking the other night, were you, Harry?"

Harry jumped up quickly and apologized. "I thought you didn't want me to mention that, so I didn't stand. I'm not ashamed of what we did."

Jim smiled at Harry. "Well, I just don't want anyone thinking they're special to me. You are all special whether I fuck you or not." He tried to give people a loving look, but he wasn't successful this time.

*   *   *

Summertime was approaching, and the church members were told to prepare for another evangelistic tour across the country. Jim didn't try to call it a vacation anymore, and the only excuse for not going was a full-time job. Most of the young people were launching an all-out effort to get a job, any job, to avoid the grueling trip.

I remembered the previous summer when I had stayed back and our children had come home with bladder infections from not being allowed to go to the bathroom for long periods of time. I also remembered the overpowering loneliness I had felt, so, without any argument, I prepared for the trip. Our oldest daughter, Linda, volunteered to stay home and take care of the animals. At sixteen, she was certainly old enough to handle the responsibility.

In order to avoid the disgusting bus ride, we decided to take our Dodge Maxi-Van and 13 kids in it with us. To get permission to use our own vehicle we promised to haul the musical instruments. The

instruments were put into large square boxes, and by carefully
arranging them, we made room for each of the children to have
sitting space on and between the boxes. It was worth the crowding
just to avoid the unending offerings. Al had to drive one of the
buses, so Tim Clancey, the pressman, helped me drive the van.

We had some last-minute work at Publications and left several
hours after the buses. We drove all night and the next day but
arrived in Houston, Texas, late for our first meeting. The band
members were waiting for their instruments and complained
bitterly about our tardiness. They got their instruments in time for
the song service, but without any time to practice. We were elated
as they said, "We'll have to take these instruments on our bus
since you can't seem to get to meetings on time."

Al and I slept under his bus, and the children slept in the van.
Somehow, the fact that we had our own car made the trip more
bearable. As we were preparing to get on the road, though, we ran
into a problem. The council had agreed to reimburse us for gas and
oil. I gathered our receipts and took the bill to Rose Shelton. She
coldly looked at the bill and said, "Since you aren't able to get here
on time and you aren't carrying the instruments anymore, we
aren't going to pay for your gas." I ran to Al and asked him what
we should do.

Jane came over to straighten out the situation. "Jim has
decided that this van could be put to better use if someone else
drove it and your family rode in the buses." I wasn't about to let
Jane destroy our only hope of a reasonably nice trip. "This is our
car, and I have permission to drive it," I said.

"Well, we have decided that Tim has to go in one of the other
vehicles. If you want to drive your car, you'll have to drive all by
yourself," Jane said, sounding more immature than a nine-year-
old child.

Al was getting angry. "The council promised to cover expenses
for this trip," he said, almost shouting. "Jeannie and Tim have
thirteen children in that car, and the buses are too crowded to take
even one more person. Either you folks come up with the money, or
we'll drive our van home right now."

"You make me sick, Al," Jane said with a sneer in her voice.
"You don't have any understanding of the Cause. All you care
about is your family. With that type of attitude, you're a real
traitor." Al and I were eating ice-cream cones that had been
distributed as dessert at lunch. As Jane shouted at Al, her face
close to his, he took his ice-cream cone, smeared it on her face, and
popped it into her mouth. Jane stepped away shocked but silent
for the first time that we could ever remember. Without another
word, she turned and walked away.

Al and I had enjoyed the little triumph, but we were angry. We were still faced with the prospect of being without money for the rest of the trip. With our tight budget, we had brought just enough cash to get us to Houston. We weren't even sure we could make it back to California without getting more money first.

We walked away from the parking lot and sat behind a grassy knoll. "Let's quit this stupid church," Al said angrily.

"Are you sure that's what you want?" I asked him. "We tried that before and came back. I don't want to quit and come back again. You know, if we quit, we lose Joey and Candy."

"Yes, but why should we beg and grovel to get the money for a trip we didn't want to make in the first place?" Al said convincingly. As we continued talking, weighing the pros and cons of quitting the church, Jane was reporting her side of the conflict. Mark Duffy came over to us.

"Is something bothering you?" he asked innocently.

Mark was one of the few staff members I felt comfortable with. "We're really disgusted, Mark," I said, hoping that he could straighten out the situation. "We were promised reimbursement for our gas and oil. Now they're refusing, and they expect us to give up the van."

"What's wrong with that?" Mark asked casually. "That's the way most of the other members are traveling."

Al broke in, "A promise is a promise. If Jim won't see to it that the church reimburses Jeannie for the gas and oil, we're going back home."

"Jeannie, let's go talk to Rose. I'm sure we can get the money," Mark said.

I went with Mark, but instead of going to the bus where Rose was, we walked into the building. We entered a small room where Jim was obviously waiting for me. "Well, Jeannie, what seems to be the problem, dear?" He sounded so loving that I was certain he would understand how upset I was.

"The church promised to reimburse my expenses for this trip. Now Rose is saying that because we were late someone else is going to take over our van and we're going to squeeze into the buses. You know, Father, that there isn't enough room for us on those buses." He didn't look sympathetic with my plight so I decided to use Al's threat. "If we don't get the money that was promised us we're going to take our kids home right now."

It worked! Jim said, "Things aren't as bad as they seem, Jeannie. Sometimes Rose gets carried away with her position of power and makes irrational decisions. Mark, you tell Rose that I said to give Jeannie her money."

"Yes, Father," Mark answered respectfully. As we walked back down the long corridor I was gloating inside. I had learned that Jim could be made to back down! In my moment of victory, I forgot our discussion about leaving the church.

As we were getting into the van, the other members were piling into the buses. Children were stuffed in the luggage racks and on the floors. Some of the adults and children were getting in the baggage compartments under the buses, where there was no light and very little air but where a person could lie down without fear of being stepped on.

Jim was riding in the lead bus, which was air-conditioned and bulletproofed. He had a comfortable compartment that the church mechanics had built for him, with a soft bed, a refrigerator, and small table with chairs around it. I had seen his compartment because this was where Rose sat to dole out money to drivers during the stops. Jim justified his conveniences by saying, "Most leaders would take an airplane while their members rode in buses. I don't consider myself to be special, so I am riding in the buses with the people."

There were other differences, though, between Jim's bus and the other buses. Jim's bus was never crowded. In fact, there were usually several empty seats on it because only a chosen few were allowed to ride with him. "People won't leave me alone," he complained. "I have to choose people I feel comfortable around to ride with me." No one complained, out loud, about this double standard, but a few grumbled about the empty seats on Father's bus as they sat squeezed together.

We stayed with the buses, traveling day and night, stopping only for meals or meetings and occasionally for a rest stop. At these stops, the older people would take a brisk walk or jog, trying to get their systems working. Constipation, one of the most frequent topics of conversation, was an ever-present evil during these trips. Between swollen legs, infected bladders, and constipation, the trip was miserable for most of the people, but especially for the senior citizens who had been told they had to go if they wanted Father's protection.

The meetings were all nearly identical as we traveled from city to city. Someone would collapse and "die" at the beginning of the service. He or she would be carried to the front of the church and lie in full view of the audience until Jim was ready to "ressurect" him or her at the close of the service. There would be a testimony service with counsellors telling about Jim's amazing miracles, and then the offering plates would be passed. Jim delivered the same fiery sermon in each city, and as the meeting drew to a close, there were several amazing healings. Local people would be called out for revelations and given warnings of impending doom. Before the meeting ended, Jim would go over to the "dead" person and, in a loud voice, command him to awaken. Sometimes the "dead" person would be so groggy he had to be "awakened" several times. A few even had to be helped off the stage.

Jim assured the congregation that he would minister to this person after the meeting, and that the person would return to the next day's meeting in good health. A few returned, but many did not.

During the last meeting in each city, Jim would invite everyone to join our group in Redwood Valley. At least one would come along.

As we got close to Philadelphia, the city Joey had come from a year before, he began to seem very upset. Finally he said, "Mommy, do I have to go to the meeting in Philadelphia?"

"Why, Joey," I asked him, "are you afraid?"

"Yes, I'm afraid my real mother might make me come back home with her. If she heard about our meeting, I'm sure she'll be there." I didn't want Joey to be taken from us, so I asked Tim to leave Joey and me at a nearby park while he drove the rest of the children to the service. Joey and I had a marvelous two days, swimming and camping together, while everyone else went to the services. His gratitude was deep and sincere. "My real mother never loved me like you do. I just couldn't go back to live with her," he said solemnly.

An unusual situation arose at the meeting in Philadelphia. A man came in armed with a gun and a knife. Somehow one of the security guards spotted him fingering something in his jacket and discovered that he had a holster strapped around his body, with a gun in it.

A couple of guards grabbed the man and took him to a side room where, Jim was later to tell us, they beat the man until he was unconscious. Unexpectedly the man died, and the guards were faced with the problem of disposing of the body.

One of the young guards later confided to me, "They took the body, wrapped it in a blanket, put it into a car, and then drove it to the edge of the city and dumped it there." Although Jim bragged for weeks about his guards beating this man until he lost consciousness, he never mentioned the fact that his body had been dumped into a river at the edge of Philadelphia. Later he showed us a newspaper clipping that reported the recovery of a body from the river, and Jim claimed it was the same person.

After Philadelphia, we stopped in New York, Chicago, and Indianapolis. We arrived home still smiling. The trip was pleasant because we were all able to stay together. "Being able to use the van was worth all the arguments with Jane and Mark," I told Al as we were driving home. "We had a wonderful trip."

*   *   *

Joanne was becoming increasingly hostile toward the church as the disciplines continued to escalate. One day she decided to leave quietly. She packed up Julie's clothes in a separate suitcase because she knew she wouldn't be able to keep her. On her way out of town, she dropped Julie off at her mother's house late in the night, so that no one would know that she was leaving. Julie cried as she kissed her good-bye, and Joanne and Gwen vanished into the night, never to be heard from again.

*   *   *

Our sixteen-year-old daughter Linda was called up for confrontation. She had hugged a girlfriend whom Jim considered to be a traitor. Linda stood before Jim and admitted that she was guilty.

Jim looked at her sternly. "You have been unwise, in the past, in your choice of friends, and it is important that we teach you a lesson you won't forget. Your only friends are to be the people who come to our services. Outsiders, or people who come when they feel like it, are not friends. In order to help you learn this lesson, you will get seventy-five whacks with the board." He looked at me sternly and asked, "Do you think Linda deserves to be punished?"

I knew there was only one answer I could give. "Yes, Father," I said. Then I bowed my head and squeezed my eyelids together until they hurt, wishing I could shut out the horrible scene, as well as my guilt over being helpless. Linda had always been stoic, and I prayed that the pain of this beating wouldn't be more than she could handle. The guards stretched her body in midair, and I was powerless to stop them.

Ruby got the board and began to hit. On the first whack, Linda screamed. It seemed that no one else even realized she was screaming. Ruby continued to hit, two whacks, three, four, five, six, seven, eight, nine, ten. Jim was counting the whacks. At the count of ten he told Ruby to pause, giving Linda a few seconds to prepare for the next ten.

Count to twenty, pause. It seemed an eternity was passing. I looked across the room at Al and saw the agony on his face as he watched his daughter screaming hysterically while Ruby methodically gave her seventy-five whacks. Count to thirty, pause. Linda continued screaming, sobbing, struggling to be free. Count to forty, pause. I looked at Diana and Nichol, who were standing nearby, tears flowing down their cheeks. Count to fifty, pause. I looked at Candy, who was biting on her fist, her eyes tightly closed. Steve was sitting at the public address system, his knuckles white as he clutched the sides of his chair. His younger sister was being brutally beaten and he could do nothing. Count to sixty, pause. I thought I was going to throw up as I watched Linda, her body writhing under the tremendous impact of that board. Count to seventy, pause. "Oh God," my thoughts were racing. "Just let it be over, please, and I'll leave this place and never return."

"Seventy-one, seventy-two, seventy-three, seventy-four, seventy-five." In a monotone, Jim said, "That's all. Hand her the microphone."

A young man pushed the microphone into her hand so everyone could hear her gasp, "Thank you, Father." One of the guards let her lean on him as she walked back to the restroom.

Linda Amos walked over to me. "Could you come to the kitchen, please," she asked sweetly. As I walked with her, I noticed that Al was being escorted back, too. Gene Chaikin, the attorney, was sitting there with a stack of papers in front of him. "Each of you is to copy this release form, now, saying that you asked Father to have Linda whipped."

I felt that we were living a nightmare. Refusal to sign the form would be insanity—there were six guards, including Johnny Brown and Chris Lewis, in the small area, and all eyes were fixed on us. My hands were trembling so that I could barely sign my name. Obediently, we signed a statement that said we had asked Jim to have our daughter whipped seventy-five times as discipline for disobeying a church rule.

As we drove home, everyone in the car was silent. We were all afraid that our words would be considered treasonous. The only sounds came from Linda, sobbing quietly in the back seat. When we got into our house, Al and I sat down to talk with Linda. She was in too much pain to sit. She stood quietly while we talked with her. "How do you feel about what happened tonight?" Al asked her.

"Father was right to have me whipped," Linda answered. "I've been so rebellious lately, and I've done a lot of things that were wrong. While you were on vacation I was smoking pot and doing other things I wasn't supposed to do. I'm sure Father knew about those things, and that's why he had me hit so many times."

As we kissed our daughter good night, our heads were spinning. It was hard to think clearly when everything was so confusing. Linda had been the victim, and yet we were the only people angry about it. She should have been hostile and angry. Instead, she said that Jim had actually helped her. We knew Jim had done a cruel thing, and yet everyone acted as if he were doing a loving thing in whipping our disobedient child. Unlike a cruel person hurting a child, Jim had seemed calm, almost loving, as he observed the beating and counted off the whacks. Our minds were not able to comprehend the atrocity of the situation because none of the feedback we were receiving was accurate.

Another meeting, another confrontation time, and tonight Peter Wotherspoon was called to the front. One day earlier in '74, a young couple, Peter and Mary Wotherspoon, came to our farm to see Grandma's garden. Al and I noticed that Peter had an unusual softness in his smile and a gentleness in his manner. As we talked with Peter and Mary, they said they were lonely. They didn't know anyone in town and were looking for friends. Naturally, we invited them to our church and, without asking any questions about our beliefs, they accepted our invitation.

The following Sunday they attended their first service and told us they'd decided to join. "Everyone here is so friendly," Mary said. "Little Mary even got to ride one of the ponies this afternoon. We're so glad you invited us."

The following Wednesday night I saw Peter in the hallway, talking to one of the young boys. As they spoke, I noticed Peter stroking the boy's hair and smiling sweetly at him. Later, during the meeting, I was sitting next to Peter when Jim asked us to hold hands to begin the healing service. Peter began stroking my arm. I wasn't sure whether Peter was calling out for love or whether he had an emotional problem, but I didn't stay long enough to find out. I excused myself and spent the remainder of the service on the other side of the room.

Although we saw Peter and Mary several more times during the summer, I didn't notice Peter behaving strangely again, so I assumed that he had just misunderstood the friendliness of our church members. They spent many long hours with Grandma in her garden, learning her methods of organic gardening.

And now, six months later, a young boy complained that Peter had fondled him sexually during the vacation trip.

"Peter, is there any truth to his charge?" Jim asked.

"Father, I'm sorry to have to say this, but, yes, it is true," Peter answered humbly. "I've had a problem for several years now with young boys, and I don't seem to be able to help myself. I've gone to a psychiatrist to get help, but so far nothing has helped."

Jim asked the young boy to come forward and demanded that Peter apologize to him. Then Jim said, "Perhaps where the psychiatrists have failed, a switch will succeed." He asked Jim McElvane to bring in several long switches from a nearby tree, and while Peter obediently bent over, Jim McElvane broke switch after switch on Peter's backside while he sobbed in pain. It was a pathetic sight, watching the young boy standing helplessly by, his young eyes filled with guilt as he watched Peter suffering.

When it was over, Peter took the microphone and said, "Father, thank you for caring about my problem. I really believe I have learned my lesson now. You're the first person that ever cared enough about me to punish me for hurting others." Turning to the boy, he added, "And believe me, this won't happen again."

Jim lovingly said, "My son, I believe that you have indeed learned your lesson."

As Peter and Jim looked at each other, Peter suddenly blurted out, "I think this whole problem started when I was in prison in Chile. I was subjected to unbelievable tortures there and I think something in my mind must have snapped. Maybe the whipping tonight has stopped whatever problem started in Chile. I really believe it has."

Jim was astonished to find out that Peter had been in prison during the revolution. As they continued to talk, Peter also revealed that he had been close friends with Victor Jara, a Chilean hero. Jim then told us the pathetic story of Victor Jara, a revolutionary, who bravely sang songs of freedom in a prison camp where he was confined for his condemnation of the fascist regime at that time. As Victor sang, the prison guards tried to shut him up. They finally got so disgusted that they chopped off his arms so he couldn't play his guitar. He continued singing the song until he died. It was an inspiring story, and we felt honored to know Peter, who had been Jara's personal friend.

The sermon that night was a chilling tale of the future Jim saw, by revelation, for the black people in America. He spoke of concentration camps, torture, rape, and murder. He saw the cities fenced with barbed wire and black people imprisoned inside. He saw black people who had left our group hanging by their necks ("eyes bulging out") from the trees in the Golden Gate Park. Then he reminded the white people in the audience that "Since you have been in this church, you too will have these persecutions, because you are now identified as being sympathetic with blacks."

The following night he announced, "I want every white person in this group to be legally identified with black people so that he can never leave or betray black brothers and sisters." He said he wanted every white family to get legal custody of a black child. Young white people were instructed to look for blacks they could legally marry. "This will be a paper marriage only," he reminded them. "I just want you to prove that you will never betray this

Cause. The only way you can do that is to become legally a part of the sufferings of black people."

I breathed a sigh of relief because none of our children were old enough to get married yet. Deep in my heart, I hoped that some day they would be allowed to marry partners they loved and cared for and have the happiness I had found with Al. I never voiced these treasonous thoughts, but I never forgot them either.

Most of the white members were anxious to prove their loyalty to their black brothers and sisters. Many of them unhesitatingly entered into mixed marriages and adopted children of minority races as Jim had requested. After hearing about the horrors that faced black people, we all wanted to be indentified with them. The Cause was becoming very real. We could even condone Jim's violent disciplines and rigid regulations because we were working together to keep black people free.

Jim's stories about his sex life were becoming so bizarre that it was difficult to continue to believe them. In one church service he bragged, "When I fuck a woman, I go for eight or nine hours." Another time he boasted, "I have so much sperm that I have to ejaculate at least twenty-five times a day." In order to prove the veracity of these spectacular claims he often said, "Jack can testify that I am a powerful lover because he slept in the room next to Marcie and me in Brazil." Jack would dutifully stand up and swear that Jim was a superb bed partner. He had heard proof from the next room.

His favorite story "proving" his insatiable sex needs was about the time he had sex with Karen Layton. When he told the story publicly, he never mentioned her name, but all the P.C. members knew to whom he was referring, and Karen would always blush. "This certain young woman kept begging me to fuck her. She thought she was great and she kept telling me that she enjoyed the sex act. I had to teach her a lesson before she could relate to the Cause. I took her out into the thorns and fucked her for eight hours before she decided she'd had enough. She spent the next two days pulling thorns out of her ass." The story sounded so ridiculous that I wondered why he kept telling it. After a while, though, I realized he continued to tell it publicly only because of the embarrassment it caused Karen.

I thought back to the time when Jim had told us, "Whenever a man starts bragging about his performance in the bedroom, you can be sure it's because he's having trouble keeping it up! Those who are able to make love, do it, and those who can't, talk about it." Each time he would tell an exaggerated story about his great sexual prowess, I would wonder if he might be covering up tremendous sexual insecurity. The most perplexing thing to me, though, was why so many people continued to have sex with Jim, when every one of them was humiliated afterward. Even when Jim didn't say the person's name, he would give us so many hints that we knew exactly whom he was talking about.

When rational, Jim would admit to the members of the P.C. that he was having trouble keeping his emotions under control. He explained that he had a sugar imbalance which caused people to go crazy. "People who have this problem usually become murderers," he said, "but I am able to stay in control." He explained to his bodyguards that there might be times when he would be unable to control his "righteous indignation" because of this sugar imbalance. His instructions to them were "Watch me if I should begin to lunge toward someone. Pull we away from them so I don't harm an innocent person in my anger."

It wasn't long after this talk that the guards had to follow these instructions. It was another confrontation meeting. Pauline Groot had been called to the front to face charges that she had made a racist comment to an older black woman. Jim seemed to be almost insane that night. He jumped down from his pulpit and began to choke her.

The guards looked dumbfounded and we sat on the edges of our chairs. For a moment no one had the courage or presence of mind to rush to Pauline's rescue, because it would discredit his image. One quick-thinking guard then grabbed Pauline away from Jim and started hitting her, thus removing her from Jim's grasp and still proving that Jim's punishment was warranted. Jim nodded his thanks to the guard and sat down again at his podium. Pauline was carried out, almost unconscious.

After the meeting ended, the counsellors were called together. Jim confided to us, "I lost control of myself tonight, and I could have killed Pauline. Fortunately, the guards came to her rescue. I want each of you to watch her closely for the next few weeks and give her special attention. If she were to decide to leave our church right now, she could cause us some legal problems." Pauline responded well to the unexpected "strokes" that the counsellors gave her during the following weeks. She didn't even mention leaving the group, and Jim was relieved. A crisis had been averted.

*   *   *

Jim's paranoia was becoming increasingly apparent. He was certain that someone was trying to poison him. The guards were instructed to take extraordinary precautions with Jim's food and drink. One guard stood by while his food was being prepared and didn't take his eyes off it until it was served directly to Jim. His drinking glasses were covered with aluminum foil as soon as they had been filled, and only a few trusted counsellors were allowed to touch either his drinking glass or plate.

The following Wednesday night, as the discipline portion of the meeting began, Jim announced, "I don't want to see any beatings tonight. When we threw Kathy into the pool, she told us that it really cured her of needing to overeat. I think that we'll use our pool for discipline for a while and get away from the whippings."

The first person whose name was called was Chris Lewis. "I understand that you were picked up by a policeman for speeding, and you later bragged to Gene that you used a phony name on the ticket. What are you trying to do to this church, Chris?"

Chris came to the front of the room and answered, "It's true that I used a phony name. In some of the work I do in San Francisco, it's necessary for me to use different names, but they're all legal. I go to the Driver's License Bureau and make a statement that my real name is Chris Lewis but I am using a different name, and they issue me a driver's license with the name I choose. It's very legitimate, and it can't get me or the church into difficulty."

Jim didn't dare let Chris off this easily, though, so he said, "Well, Chris, in view of the fact that you were speeding and got a ticket, I think you should be disciplined. What do you think?"

Chris answered, "Whatever you say, Father." Jim asked him to take off his clothes and keep his shorts on. Chris replied, "I don't wear any shorts, Father."

Jim was having a hard time maintaining the upper hand in this situation, but he refused to back down. "Somebody bring him a towel!" he commanded. Linda Amos was at his side in a few moments with the towel. Chris put it around his waist and removed all the clothes he was wearing. When he got to the pool he dropped the towel, exposing himself to the crowd, and jumped into the pool.

Next, Jim called Jann Gurvich forward She was a young white woman from Berkeley who had recently joined the church. Since Jann was an excellent swimmer, Jim thought up something new. "As your discipline, I want you to strip down to your underwear, but, before we throw you into the pool, we're going to tie your hands behind your back so that your punishment will be equal to the punishment of people who aren't able to swim well."

Jann smilingly agreed, and after she had removed her clothes except for her underwear, her hands were tied behind her back. As we watched her walking toward the rear of the room, to be pushed into the swimming pool, we were frightened. It seemed impossible for her to swim the entire length of the pool with her hands tied behind her, but Jann was a good swimmer—better than Jim knew. Within a few moments, she had made it, and the people in the audience clapped for her.

Jim realized that his punishment wasn't working as well as he had hoped. When Kathy had taken off her clothes, her intense embarrassment proved that the discipline had been effective, but neither Chris nor Jann had shown the least bit of shyness about being disrobed. It was the end of the "swimming pool" punishments. He knew he'd have to go back to the beatings with the board.

*   *   *

Three more children were about to come into our home. Searcy Darnes was first. He was Eddie's closest friend and had come to our home to visit several times. One evening he asked Al if there was enough room in our house for him to stay. "My mother lives in a little apartment, and we don't have any yard. I'd like to live here, where I could play in the mountains and swim in the river." Eddie's pleading added pathos to Searcy's story, and Al said yes. Within a few hours, Searcy had bicycled to his house, packed his few belongings in a backpack, and rode back up the hill to our house. As soon as he arrived, he and Eddie took off on their bicycles and spent several hours traveling the mountain trails together, enjoying their new-found companionship as brothers.

The very next day, Searcy asked if his little brother Ollie could come and visit him. "He's just five years old, and he's really lonely for me," Searcy added. Searcy bicycled back to his mother's apartment and brought Ollie and another full backpack to our house. I didn't realize that the backpack was filled with Ollie's clothes, "just in case."

I couldn't help falling in love with Ollie as he followed me around that day. Whenever I sat down, he was beside me. When the table was set, he pulled up his chair to the corner of the table so he could sit beside me. When I started to do the dishes, Ollie grabbed a dish towel to help. Finally, I became suspicious. "Ollie, do you want something?" I asked him. Ollie's little brown face bobbed up and down and his brown eyes got a mischievous twinkle in them. "What do you want?" I asked him with a grin.

"Please, can I come to live with you, too? I promise I won't get into any trouble."

Al looked across the long table at me with a little smile. We already had so many children in the house, one more precious little boy wouldn't make that much difference. We nodded our heads, and we both gave him a big hug and a kiss. I said, "Well, Ollie, if you're going to be our son, we'd better get your clothes."

With a mischievous little smile, Ollie ran into the bedroom where he had stashed his clothes. He brought them out to the kitchen proudly. "I just knew you'd say yes, so I already brought them with me!" he boasted. We called up their mother and asked her how she felt about Ollie's living with us.

"I'm just so thankful that they've found a home where they're happy," she said. "The boys get a Social Security check from their late father's account, so I'll send money each month to help with their expenses," she added. It was an extra bonus we hadn't expected, but we knew that it would come in handy.

The boys still had a little sister, though, and I began to hear whispers that sounded like a conspiracy to get her into our home. This time, Candy was the negotiator. She was becoming quite precocious, and Najah, their little sister, was just her age. "Mommy," she asked me, "can't Najah move in with us, too?"

"Does Najah want to?" I asked her.

"Yes, Mommy."

"Well, we'll talk to her tonight during the meeting."

That night Candy ran over to get Najah. The two little girls came running toward me giggling. Candy whispered something to Najah and she giggled again. "Jeannie, can I please come to live with you and Candy?" she asked as Candy snuggled on my lap.

"Please, Mommy, say yes," Candy pleaded.

"Well, come on," I said, making room on my lap for another little girl, and Najah immediately climbed up. "Now are you happy, Candy?" I asked, and Candy gave me a big kiss for an answer.

Searcy, Ollie, and Najah added a new dimension to our home and our lives. Their gratitude and love for us knew no bounds. Ollie didn't want to leave my side, and Najah joined Candy on my lap every time I sat down. Searcy solemnly told us again and again that he wouldn't ever go any place else to live. "You are the best mommy and daddy anybody ever had," he told us devotedly. His actions and attitude were daily proof that he meant every word he said.

*   *   *

Carolyn Layton had been away from the church for several months, and whenever anyone would ask about her, Jim would simply say she was "on a mission." One evening in Planning Commission meeting, though, Jim finally took us into his confidence. "Carolyn has been in a jail in Mexico all this time. She was caught transporting something, after I had warned her to be extremely careful. While she was in the jail, one of the jailkeepers raped her and she became pregnant. Since there was no way she could get an abortion in prison, she is about to have the baby. When she returns, she will bring the baby with her, and we are all going to say it belongs to her cousin. The story will be that her cousin isn't able to take care of it right now for health reasons." It was an astonishing story, but absolutely believable.

As we anxiously waited for Carolyn to return, we speculated about the terrible ordeal she had been through. And what a terrible place to have a baby. Even though I had never really liked Carolyn, suddenly I felt compassion for her. I could imagine what it was like spending the last months of pregnancy in a miserable Mexican jail. I determined that I would stop my petty dislike of her and make overtures of friendship.

The next morning I went to work, filled with resolve to stop being so critical of the people Jim had chosen as staff workers. I realized that they faced dangers and hardships I knew nothing about. As Linda Amos walked in, I smiled broadly at her. Here was another staff worker of whom I had been overly critical. Linda returned my smile and walked toward the dining area where Mary and her baby, little Mary, were visiting with some of the workers. When Linda walked in, everyone immediately returned to his or her job. Linda commanded fear and respect because of her close association with Jim and her strict adherence to church rules. Mary started talking with her, asking questions about a letter-writing assignment she was working on, and as they spoke, little Mary kept trying to get her mother's attention.

Linda asked impatiently, "Does she always try to get your attention like that?"

Mary reached down and picked up the two-year-old, giving her a kiss on the forehead. "Well, usually she doesn't have to. I spend most of my time at home with her, and we're together constantly."

It was the wrong thing to say to Linda who was probably the strictest disciplinarian in the church, next to Jim. I'd heard counsellors say that she once took a child's dirty diaper and smeared the B.M. all over the child's face, because she felt the child was too old to be messing its diapers. But Mary hadn't heard the tales of Linda's irrational child-rearing methods, so she was casually honest with her.

"Well," Linda responded coldly, "in this church we don't like to see our children spoiled that way. We want our children to be strong and to learn to be independent. Mary won't ever learn that if you keep her tied to your apron strings."

Mary quickly put little Mary back on the floor, and the baby immediately put her little arms up, begging to be picked up again. Linda angrily picked her up and put her into one of the tiny offices in our shop, loudly closing the door behind her.

Little Mary began to scream in fear and anger. Linda quietly started talking to Mary again, as though she didn't hear the screams. Mary, knowing that she didn't dare appear concerned, tried to finish up the conversation she had started. For forty-five minutes little Mary screamed hysterically, while Linda insisted that Mary could not go in to comfort her. Finally, Linda got an emergency message to go to Jim's house, and Mary was free to go to her traumatized child and comfort her.

Less than a week passed before another small child fell prey to Linda's insane discipline. This time it was Dianne Lundquist's four-year-old son, Jamal. Unfortunately, this time there was no one else around, and Linda totally lost control of her temper. As Jamal started to cry for his mother, Linda began whipping him. The more she whipped, the more Jamal cried. By the time she finally stopped, Jamal's body was a mass of welts, and for weeks he had black-and-blue marks on every part of his body. Several counsellors, including me, went to Jim and demanded that she not be allowed to discipline any more children. Jim could see that she had gotten out of control, and he firmly suggested to her to find another home for her two small children and said that she was never again to touch any of the babies in the church. As the word of Jim's decision got around, many of the young mothers breathed a sigh of relief.

Several weeks had passed, and at another P.C. meeting Jim announced that Carolyn had had a baby boy and she was going to return the following day. However, now his story had changed about how the child had been fathered. This time, he said that he had slept with Carolyn just before she went on her mission and that she had become pregnant. "She told me that story about the jailkeeper because she didn't want to embarrass me for having produced a child," he bragged. "Carolyn has been a true socialist throughout her time of trial." He continued, "She could have asked us to help her get out of jail, but she didn't tell anyone where she was so that she wouldn't embarrass the Cause."

Jim told us another big secret that night. "One of the things that Carolyn had been doing was negotiating the purchase of an atomic bomb for us." He was talking almost in a whisper in case the room was bugged. "We have everything but the detonator, and we are trying to get one right now. It is important for our group to have power, and any person with an atomic bomb has power." He began to explain to us how he believed World War III would start. "I believe that someone will probably sneak up from South America and detonate an atom bomb in the United States. Then our country will assume that the bomb was sent from Russia. Our country will retaliate by sending a bomb over there, and within a short time, there will be a nuclear holocaust. Everyone will be destroyed, except the people who are living below the equator."

It was a wild theory, and most of us assumed it was another scare tactic, like the first bomb theory and his cave in Redwood Valley. The part that did impress us, though, was that we were the owners of an atomic bomb. We now felt we had enough power to make people respect and fear our group.

The following day Carolyn did return, and as she stood in front of the congregation, Jim told another story he had contrived. "This is Carolyn's little cousin, and she will take care of it until her cousin's health improves." The continual attention lavished on the baby by all the counsellors, though, belied the story. It was evident to most of the members that this child was very important to Jim.

The meeting was long. It was a beautiful fall day and I wished that we could take our family for a picnic. "I'll bet the beach is warm," I speculated. The sermon went on and on. Offering after offering was taken. Finally, Jim stopped talking, and we knew it was discipline time again. "Oh, God," I thought, "I can't stand to watch another beating." But I knew I wasn't free to leave, so I took a deep breath and hoped Jim wasn't in a bad mood.

The son of one of the counsellors, Chris Cordell, had been caught by another member stealing a purse out of someone's car. "Small wonder," I thought. "These kids get so little spending money. It's enough to make a person resort to stealing." Jim sentenced him to get 100 whacks with the board. He begged Jim to reconsider, but even as he asked, Chris knew that Jim never reduced an amount once he had set it. The beating began. Every ten whacks, Jim would have Ruby pause a few moments to give Chris an opportunity to brace himself for the next ten. Chris was hysterical with the pain. Finally the 100 whacks ended. Chris was handed the microphone and told to say, "Thank you Father." Instead, he fainted.

Jim screamed at him, "Stop faking or you'll get fifty more!"

A nurse rushed up and whispered to Jim that Chris didn't seem to be faking. She ran to his side and confirmed that he was really unconscious. Jim could see that the audience was frightened, so he quietly waited for the young man to revive. Then he demanded that Chris say "Thank you, Father." Somehow, Chris mumbled the words, and as Chris stumbled out, Jim called after him, "You're going to be on two weeks' probation, too." Jim told the rest of the audience, "During these two weeks, no one is to speak to Chris. I want to make sure he learns his lesson."

Kay Rosas was the next person to be called up. She was a resident in a care home who was somewhat retarded. She didn't seem to weigh more than seventy-five pounds. Jim told her to come to the front of the room.

"I understand that you made a racist comment to a black woman in the rest home," he said accusingly.

Kay looked perplexed. "I don't remember making any racist comments," she said honestly. Jim was not in a reasonable mood. He didn't even explain what Kay was supposed to have said. He screamed at her, "You are a racist bitch! I want to see that you learn what it is like to be the victim of racism." He asked for about twenty of the elderly black women sitting in the front rows of the church to come forward and form a line. Not knowing why they were doing it, the women came up as he requested. He had a guard put boxing gloves on the first woman and said, "I want you to beat the shit out of this little racist bitch!"

The woman seemed startled, but she had to do as Jim requested, so she half-heartedly took a couple of swings at Kay. "Harder!" shouted Jim, and the woman hit her harder.

The next woman in line came forward, put on the gloves, and began to hit Kay. By the time the fourth woman had taken her turn, Kay fell down, unable to stand. "Don't let her get off that easy," Jim shouted at the guards. "Hold her up and make her take it."

Two guards rushed over to Kay and held her face toward the next woman with the boxing gloves. As the women continued to hit Kay, her nose started to bleed, and blood was dripping on her clothes, but still the women kept coming, one by one. Finally the disgusting spectacle was over and the guards carried Kay away, collapsed and bleeding. The look of horror on the faces of the black women who had been coerced into doing this cruel thing was unnoticed by Jim, but those faces were to remain in my memory for years to come. Jim had turned sweet women into monsters, attacking a helpless victim, just by his command.

A young child was next. He had thrown a plateful of food away at the church lunch. Jim put him into a boxing ring, pitted against a boy twice his size. As the little boy kept getting knocked down, and standing up again to try to fight, Jim began to laugh. I couldn't stand any more. I went to the restroom where I sat on the closed toilet seat until I could regain my composure.

We hoped that when the mission field was established, Jim wouldn't have to use disciplines on his members. And the mission endeavor was progressing nicely. We were sending regular shipments of supplies to Guyana, for the town that Jim had named "Jonestown." We had a large staff of workers who spent all their time purchasing and shipping the supplies.

Local Guyanese workers were hired to do most of the field work, an arrangement that had been highly recommended by the Guyanese government. They wanted to be sure some foreign money was used to give salaries to their own citizens.

Jim made several trips to cement political friendships there and to check on the progress of the work. Now he decided it was time for the P.C. members to go for a visit.

It was impossible for me to get away from the Publications Office to make the trip, but Al was able to go, and he took all his cameras with him. The trip from California to Georgetown was on a chartered plane and was going to take two days. In an effort to make the long hours go faster, Al was gazing out the window at the scenery. Suddenly, he noticed that there was fuel escaping from one of the motors. As he watched the fuel leaking, he decided to tell Jim about it in case the pilot needed to be alerted. "Father," Al said politely, "maybe you'd better see what's happening over here."

Jim walked over to the window with him and saw the fuel pouring out. "Hmmm, that's really strange. Yes, I'll tell the pilot right away," Jim assured him, sounding concerned.

Al didn't think any more about it until he walked toward the rear of the plane a few minutes later. Jim was lying across several seats, passed out. Several counsellors were fanning his face and putting cold cloths on his forehead. Al went back to his seat, cautiously smiling. He had just found out that Jim was a coward. All Jim's brave words about not being afraid to die had been empty boasting. When this slight danger arose, Jim had passed out in fear!

Jim recovered, though, and the pilot assured him that they would make it to their destination. Al told me that Jim next began to look around for some diversion to pass the long hours. His eyes fell on Maria Katsaris.

She was young, slender, and everything he liked in a woman. He casually walked over and sat beside her, where she was quietly reading a book. Al couldn't hear what they were saying, but he saw Maria shake her head and Jim got up and walked away.

A little while later, Patty Cartmell walked over to Maria and sat down, talking earnestly to her. Maria shook her head again. Al began to wonder what their conversation was about because

Maria seemed to be frightened or apprehensive about it.

Later, Jim came back again, sat down beside Maria, and casually put his arm around the back of her seat. Maria didn't seem to notice him and continued to read her book. Throughout the next few hours Jim continued to sit beside Maria. She seemed to be answering his questions, but was far more interested in the book in her lap.

As night fell, Jim returned to sit beside her, and as he fell asleep, he casually rested his head on her shoulder. He slept in that position through the long night. The next morning Al casually glanced over to where Maria was seated and noticed that Jim wasn't there.

The next day Jim spent an hour beside Maria talking to her, and she always answered his questions. The long day passed, and as evening approached the plane landed in Georgetown, Guyana. The travel-weary counsellors, along with Jim, gratefully rode to the church's house in the center of town.

The next morning, in groups of eight, they boarded several private planes that were to take them to the airstrip near Jonestown, where they would be met by some of the church's work crew in the jungle. Al got into the same plane with Jim because he was the official photographer. Maria was seated next to Jim, and Al sat behind them. He tried to get a good picture of Jim's face, framed by the airplane window, with a view of the jungle beneath. As Al clicked the fifth picture, Maria turned around and crossly scolded him, "Can't you see that Father isn't feeling well? You shouldn't be taking his picture right now."

Jim apologized for Maria's rudeness and said, "Go ahead, Al, and take whatever pictures you need." To Maria he said, "He's just doing his job."

Al stopped clicking the camera and sat back, trying to assess what was happening. He began to realize that the little incidents he'd noticed on the first plane were probably overtures for another sexual conquest for Jim. He decided to watch Jim's technique. He heard snatches of their conversation and realized that Maria was quietly sobbing and Jim was trying to comfort her.

The small planes landed and the travellers were met by one of the landrovers from Jonestown. Al was bitterly disappointed when he first saw the church's mission field. The jungle paradise Jim had been bragging about was nothing but a clearing in a hot sticky jungle. The mosquitoes were insufferable and everyone had to watch for snakes and other predators. The buildings were poorly constructed quarters, inadequate for even the few people that were working there. ·

In this country, where Jim had said there was no stealing, Al was assigned to sit up all night with his old friend, Charlie, to help guard their supplies from the jungle natives. The next day, when Al went to the jungle to photograph the trees laden with fruit, all he found were lumber trees. In order to take photographs that would portray the beauty Jim had bragged about, he and Al traveled to several surrounding compounds and purchased fruit from local stores to spread around Jim.

Another dream about Jonestown was destroyed when Jim announced that there would be an all-night P.C. meeting the first night after their arrival. He had promised that this would be a land of peace and beauty where there would be no long meetings or disciplines. This P.C. meeting was no different from the ones in California. This time, the people called for confrontation were the people who had been working so hard in the jungle. Several of them were accused of not doing enough work. Jim had no mercy for these people who were in a forsaken jungle area, away from their family and loved ones, and intensely lonely and homesick. His judgments were harsh, and the disciplines were cruel.

After a few days' visit, the little planes picked up their passengers and the trip to Georgetown began. Al noticed that Maria looked "like hell." Her eyes were swollen from crying, and she had marks all over her neck. It was hard to imagine a man of Jim's age doing this to a young girl. She seemed to be humiliated and embarrassed and she sat by herself. Jim walked over to talk with her a few times but spent most of his time talking with other counsellors. Al briefly wondered if Jim was going to humiliate her during the upcoming P.C. meetings, as he usually did with the other women after he had spent the night with them. Al felt deeply sorry for Maria; she was too young and sweet to be used as a toy by Jim—played with and then discarded.

At Georgetown everyone was preparing to board the bigger chartered plane when Jim asked all the men to stay outside. The men were astonished to see rows of pallets with large sacks of raw sugar on them. Each sack contained about 200 pounds of sugar, and there were almost fifty of these sacks. The entire luggage compartment of the plane was filled with this sugar which was, Jim bragged, almost a steal. It had only cost him a few cents a pound, and this was when the United States had a serious sugar shortage. The sugar was taken from a large flatbed truck without any markings on it to indicate the name of our benefactor. Jim cryptically said it was from a "good contact" he had made.

The planes returned on Tuesday, and Al was happy to get back home where he could get a hot shower and a good night's sleep. The next night at confrontation time, Chris Cordell was on the floor again. Everyone in the audience groaned when Jim called his name.

"Chris," Jim began sternly. "I wonder what you are thinking about, to be back on the floor again after you passed out from the beating a week and a half ago."

"I don't know, Father," Chris answered humbly. His voice trembled with fear.

Jim gave him a long hard stare and then asked, "What was Kim Fye doing at your house Thursday night?"

Chris's eyes fell. "She came to visit me," he answered quietly.

"Kim, will you come forward right now?" Jim shouted. Kim ran to the front of the room. She, too, looked frightened, and the two young people stood together, waiting to see what punishment Jim was going to mete out to them.

Jim dragged the story out of them.

After Chris had been beaten, Kim had whispered, "I think that beating was too much, you didn't deserve to be hit a hundred times." Chris was so grateful to have someone befriend him, since no one else was even speaking to him, that he asked her to come over to his house on Thursday night when his parents would be gone. Kim was one of the newer members of the church. She didn't have many friends yet, and Chris was considered to be "popular." She had been flattered that he asked her to visit him and accepted, even though she knew it was against Jim's rules.

Jim stood up and took his dark glasses off, staring angrily at Kim. "You bitch!" he screamed. "I'm trying to help this young man who could have been in some legal difficulty because he was actually caught stealing. He has had other problems in the past, and I fairly administered a discipline to help him learn the pain that results from breaking the rules. Then you come along and build up his ego and make him feel like he's something special."

Kim had never been in a confrontation before, and her entire body was quivering. Jim was in a rage and there was nothing that could have stopped him. "I wish I could give you the punishment you deserve," he snarled. "I'd like to put acid up your vagina so you'd never be able to do something like this again." He sentenced her to 100 whacks with the board, but this time he didn't have the guards hold her body still during the beating. Large purple welts covered her back, arms, and body for weeks afterward. She had to wear long sleeves and thick dresses to hide the marks.

*   *   *

As the Planning Commission members gathered for our private meeting the next Monday night Al and I both wondered what Jim

might say to humiliate Maria. As we walked into the room we saw
her sitting up on a table, as close to a corner of the room as she
could get and far away from Jim's easy chair. Her eyes were still
down, and she didn't speak to anyone in the room. Jim was in his
seat, looking angry and sullen. We could tell it was going to be a
rough night.

We had only been seated an hour, discussing the trip the P.C.
members had taken to Jonestown, when Jim had to urinate. "I
can't go outside anymore," he said, as he looked around the room,
trying to think what to do. He was afraid that someone might be
outside with a camera to take a picture of him, he was afraid to go
into the bathroom because someone might walk in on him, and he
didn't want to leave the room, so he devised a foolproof plan. He
had Larry Layton bring him a can, and the nurses held up a
blanket in front of him. This way he could keep his eyes on us and
be sure that no one was sneaking around to try to see his penis.
Each time he felt the urge to go, Larry would again bring the can,
and two nurses would hold up the blanket. As soon as he finished,
Larry would take the can to the toilet to dump it. The long night
progressed, and Jim didn't mention Maria or anything about his
sex life. In fact, he got so involved with bragging about the sugar
he had gotten so cheap, and about the good contacts he had made
in Georgetown, that his mood brightened.

In the early hours of the morning, as we were all becoming
exhausted, Jim again asked Larry to bring him the can. Carol
Stahl accidently dropped her side of the blanket as Jim was
urinating, leaving his penis exposed to those assembled in the
room. Jim frantically grabbed for the end of the blanket, but it was
too late. Everyone in the room now knew that his penis was just
average, and smaller than some. It was far from being the giant
thing he had talked non-stop about through the years. He weakly
made an attempt to excuse his lie. "That should never have
happened," he said to Carol angrily. "This office has to maintain
a certain image for the good of the Cause." None of us ever made
any comments about what we had seen, even to each other. Al and
I just smiled to each other as we realized that this was more
evidence that Jim didn't measure up.

Jim sat back in his seat, obviously upset. Tami realized that he
was very tense and she quietly offered to rub his feet. "I'm trained
in foot massage," she explained. "I can help you relax with just a
few minutes of massage."

"Tami, I don't like the idea of having a black woman rub my
feet," he answered piously. "Black women have had to serve white
men for too many years. But I guess here in this closed room it will

be all right." He smiled at Tami, who was always so anxious to serve him. As she continued to rub the soles of his feet he was surprised at how good it felt. She rubbed them for more than an hour until the meeting was over. Finally he said, "Thank you, Tami, that was very pleasant."

In an effort to reinforce his "voluntary" ban on sex, Jim introduced "women's meetings," where women members were supposed to meet to discuss liberation and sex. Of course, Linda Amos was chosen to be the coordinator of these meetings since she had proven her ability to abstain from sex.

It was to be a testimony-type meeting, with each woman telling the victories she had achieved over her need for men. Linda Amos began the meeting by saying, "I never enjoyed having sex with men, but I felt that it was something I had to do in order to keep a husband. Since Father helped me to become liberated, I know I don't need to have a man in my life. I have become free. No man will ever again be able to rule over me."

Volunteers were called from the audience to say similar things. Linda asked for women who had been hurt or beaten by men to come forward and tell the other women how men abuse women through sex. Several women gave their testimonies bravely, and then a woman stepped forward and said, "My husband doesn't ever beat me or anything. He has always treated me nice, and I treat him nice." She was shouted down with scornful words from the counsellors in the room.

Since the men weren't allowed in these meetings and their wives were instructed not to tell them anything that went on behind the closed doors, many husbands became quite hostile when their wives would come home angry, refusing to make love with them. Those husbands who were angry enough to complain were shamed publicly by Jim. In the public meeting Jim asked how many couples were still having sex. More men raised their hands than women because most of the women were ashamed to admit that they were still weak and allowing their husbands to "use" them.

Jim became angry when he saw so many men raise their hands. "You men are not able to satisfy your wives. I am the only person who can sexually satisfy a woman. Your wives do not like to fuck you, and you are forcing them to do something they hate." He screamed on and on, and then he tried to humiliate them. "If you think you can satisfy a woman, why don't you come up here and prove it. You fuck your wife up here and I'll fuck mine. Any man who can't function with his wife any time, and any place, isn't really a good fucker." No one volunteered, so Jim taunted them even more. "Isn't there any man in this audience who still thinks he can fuck?" When no one answered Jim laughed. "You women shouldn't have any more problems at home, because there isn't a fucker in this crowd."

*   *   *

The long months we had lived working hard for a promised future utopia had passed, and once again it was time to write a Christmas appeal to send to the church's mailing list. This year we decided to ask for money for poor children. Daphene posed in front of garbage cans behind the Los Angeles Temple, and as she sat looking sad, waiting for Al to finish clicking the shutter, I thought sadly, "We didn't even have to change her clothes. She's already wearing the clothes of a ghetto dweller." It was true, her shoes were old and worn and her jeans had been mended several times.

*   *   *

1975 January to August

You'd better be grateful
You'd better be grateful,
For he has brought you
A mighty long way.

You'd better be grateful,
You'd better be grateful,
For he has brought you
To a perfect day.
                    —from a Peoples Temple song

Jim asked Ronny James to give judo and karate lessons to his apostolic guards. He also encouraged several of the guards to practice shooting at a nearby rifle range. "You guards might need to know these things to protect me if anyone should attempt to take my life again," he explained as he issued weapons to his more trusted guards.

When the neighbors around the Redwood Valley temple began to notice the armed guards surrounding the church, a few of them complained. Jim explained, "There are racists and bigots in this valley who would like to see our church destroyed."

One evening, after a particularly grueling confrontation session, Jim collapsed. As he fell from his chair onto the stage floor, Carolyn and several other counsellors rushed forward. A gasp went through the audience. This was the first time most of us had ever seen him collapse and we were frightened. Women began to weep and children whimpered. Carolyn was ineffectively trying to administer artificial respiration on Jim, so Al, who was trained in first aid, rushed forward. He gently but firmly pushed Carolyn away and began to breathe rhythmically into Jim's mouth. He noticed almost immediately that Jim was rejecting the inspirations of air, and it dawned on him that Jim wasn't unconscious at all! He was probably putting on an act. Al noticed something that shocked him even more than his phony collapse.

There was tobacco on Jim's breath. Al couldn't believe that Jim was smoking on the sly and thought, with bitterness, about the many times Jim had sentenced adults and children to brutal beatings because they had been caught smoking.

Al decided not to mention either discovery to me. He felt honor-bound to uphold the sagging image of our leader. After all, he rationalized, Jim was working to help the oppressed.

Most of the church members were rebelling in one way or another by now. The church's rules were so strict that almost any form of pleasure was considered rebellion. Any voice of criticism was called treason. A word against Jim was called blasphemy. Well-intentioned people, trying to obey the rules and regulations, often committed one of these crimes without realizing it.

Treason, blasphemy, and rebellion were all grounds for discipline. Jim would determine how many times each offender was to be beaten. Almost every meeting included a discipline session and Jim was unmerciful in his decisions. One night David Smith was called to the front to answer charges that he had not worked on the church's construction crew for several days.

"Is it true that you haven't been at work for three days?" Jim demanded.

"Yes, Father, that's true. I've been going to the unemployment office trying to find a job."

"You had a job assigned to you and I demand that you be where you are assigned." David had joined the church in 1972 as a result of the publicity Lester Kinsolving had generated. He had come from Colorado with his wife and their eight children. Jim was already angry because David hadn't been able to find a wage-paying job and the church had been obliged to support his family. He didn't believe David was trying to find a job as he claimed. "I think you are lying to me, David, and for that you will receive a hundred whacks with the board."

Most of the church members knew better than to argue with Jim's decisions, but David tried anyway. "Father, I have back trouble," he began.

"I will protect your back with my energy," Jim said interrupting him.

"But Father, I also have a serious problem with hemorrhoids." Jim laughed and the audience knew they had better laugh, too. Jim had no mercy on David. The guards checked him for anything he might be wearing that would soften the impact of the blows. David bent over and Ruby began to beat him. One hundred torturous blows with the board, and the audience watched with horror and amazement as David stood there *without flinching*. Then people realized that Jim had been wrong to laugh. David was not a coward. In all the hundreds of beatings he had witnessed, David was the first person to take the beating without screaming.

More beatings were meted out by Jim. Al began to get sick at the sight of the brutality and rushed out of the room. As he walked downstairs he could hear the microphone loudspeakers. A little boy was accused of buying a piece of candy without sharing it with his friend, and Jim sentenced him to five whacks with the board. Al heard the five-year-old child crying, saying he was sorry, but Jim said, "Five whacks. You must learn to share."

There was silence over the microphone speakers downstairs for a few moments, and then Al heard the impact of the board on the child's body, followed by the terrified scream as the boy felt the agony of having his body jarred by the force of this large woman. Then, from the microphone in front of Jim, Al heard giggling. He realized that Jim was laughing as the child screamed. Inside the auditorium these laughs had been muffled by noise in the audience, but down here, where the only sounds heard were those from the two microphones, Al realized that Jim was enjoying the spectacle of the child's agony. Al walked out of the building and into our car. He held his head between his hands as he sat on a suitcase in the rear of the van unable to formulate any ideas, only knowing that he was shocked beyond thought.

Later that night Al told me what he had heard. "I know," I answered. "I've watched him laugh before. Remember when Carla got beaten and Jim laughed? He's really sadistic. Sometimes I think he just wants to see how much horror we will take before we leave the group." The thought of quitting was always on our minds, but the idea of leaving the children we loved, along with a fear of the unknown outside our group, always forced the thought to recede for a while. Fear, lack of sleep, and continual group pressure had supplanted reasonable thought. We saw things that were horrible but were unable to do anything about it.

Fear became a way of life for all the members. Our children begged to be left home from the meetings, knowing that if Jim was in a bad mood anyone might be beaten. The smaller children would pretend to be sick and often I would use that excuse to stay home with them.

Jim began to notice that a lot of the members were walking out of the service when disciplines began, so he posted guards at every exit. People still left, many going into the restrooms for the duration of the beatings. When Jim realized what was happening he was furious, and forbade anyone else to go to the bathroom. He said, "They have to watch the disciplines. It's the only way I can keep them in line."

One of the counsellors was instructed to buy a portable toilet, and it was set up in the rear of the auditorium in the Los Angeles temple. Two ushers had to hold a large blanket in front of the toilet while a person was using it. Jim announced, "No one is to use the restrooms during the services. You can all go to the rear of the room if you can't wait." The ushers holding the blankets also had the unpleasant task of cleaning the toilet, so they quietly allowed people to leave if they said they were going to have a bowel movement. Unfortunately, Jim saw one of these people walking out to use the toilet downstairs and yelled, "I said no one is to leave these meetings while the services are going on and I mean no one." The ushers stopped opening the doors for anyone.

One of the older black women complained about the lack of privacy. Jim's answer was, "If anyone here doesn't like it, don't come back, but don't expect me to heal you when you are sick and don't expect me to take you to a place of happiness and protection." The superstitious and the fearful didn't want to leave. Those who had given Jim everything, felt they couldn't afford to leave. Those who felt that Jim was the only person powerful enough to help change society didn't want to leave. It is hard to comprehend why people stayed in this unhealthy atmosphere, but most of us did.

Jim was becoming afraid that an enemy would sneak into a church service and try to shoot him, so he instituted body searches at the front door. People were also given membership cards with their photographs on them for positive identification. To get inside the temple, a person had to show his or her membership card and undergo a rather intense frisking by guards. Those who hadn't received their cards were sent to a counselling screening committee where they were questioned before being admitted to services. The search included dumping the contents of women's purses into a plastic tub to be checked. Even pens were opened and checked for hidden microphones. After the search was over each person had to sign his name on the bottom of a blank sheet of paper.

The first time they were handed the paper and told to sign most people balked. "Why should I put my name on a blank sheet?" they would ask. These people were sent to Jack Beam and told, "This is a test of faith to prove that you trust Father. You know he wouldn't do anything to harm his members. When you sign this paper you are proving that you believe in him enough to allow him to write anything above that signature that he wants." A person who still refused to sign the paper was courteously but firmly ushered out and told never to return.

People were compromised even more if they wished to receive a membership card. These had to sign another blank sheet of paper and a release stating that they would never ask for the return of any money or property should they quit. They also signed a letter of resignation stating that they were quitting the church for personal reasons and not because they had any complaints. Again, people who asked *why* were told, "To prove you trust Father. You know he wouldn't use them against you, don't you?" And the devoted members, in an effort to prove their loyalty, would sign their names on each of the papers presented to them.

Hugh was having problems again. As Jim continued to pick on Hugh about his work habits, he decided it was time to discipline Hugh severely. "Maybe this will make him learn that we mean business around here," Jim told us in a P.C. meeting as we discussed the next meeting's agenda.

Hugh was overweight and slow, and Jim was sure that one of the good boxers in the church could make him mend his ways. Hugh was called to the front of the auditorium and confronted for his laziness.

"Tonight we're not going to use the board, Hugh," Jim told him, trying to sound compassionate. "I'm hoping to give you the opportunity to defend yourself in a boxing match." I looked at Hugh, and saw the hint of a smile on his lips.

The gloves were brought in and one of the best boxers in the church came forward to flatten Hugh. Jim said, "There will be three rounds," and laughingly added, "if he lasts that long."

Hugh won the three rounds, rendering the other boxer limp and useless. Jim was stunned. He called another boxer forward and, this time, sentenced Hugh to five rounds. Within a couple of rounds Hugh had this opponent on the floor. Jim found another big man and put him in the ring against Hugh. Once again, the decision was in Hugh's favor. A fourth fighter went in against him. Hugh won. Jim looked the fool. He could not allow Hugh to win again, so he sent Linda Amos to order Hugh to lose the next round "for the Cause."

Hugh did as instructed. When the fifth man came into the ring Hugh went down with the first hit. No one in the audience was fooled, however, and Hugh gained the respect of every member.

*   *   *

With Monday night came another P.C. meeting. As the meeting was beginning, Tami stationed herself next to Jim and removed his shoes. He didn't argue this time and allowed her to rub his feet for several hours.

Jim began to talk about his increasing fears that someone in the P.C. was going to turn against him and the Cause. "Are any of you seated here tonight contemplating leaving the church?" he asked. No one raised a hand. "I want real honesty tonight," he said. "I want every person who has given any thought to leaving the group to raise his hand now!" Seven hands obediently went up. "Okay, I'm glad to see that we have a few honest people. I want each of you who raised your hand to tell me why would consider this treasonous act."

The first person to respond was Clarese. "I got so mad at Clifford the other day that I just wanted to leave him, and I considered taking our children and going back to live with my folks. Of course, it was only a momentary thought, Father, because I would never leave you or the the Cause."

"Thank you, Clarese. Next please."

Another woman confessed, "When a little boy in our home died I was so upset and angry that I thought about leaving. Of course, I wouldn't do it, but for a few moments I did think about it."

Jim looked at her severely. "I didn't think we were going to discuss that in here," he said slowly.

"I wasn't going to discuss it, Father. You asked if we ever thought about leaving and I did think about it then."

"Well, there are certain things better not discussed in this type of meeting," he said. She quietly nodded her head. "Who's next?" Jim asked.

The third person said, "I think about leaving the group often. I see things I don't understand and sometimes they seem unfair to me. I think it would be so easy to run away and never come back."

The remaining four people gave similarly innocuous statements. Another, named Tish, had considered leaving because she didn't think she could stand the discipline if she was beaten, but she added, "This was only an idle thought. I would never leave this group, Father."

After the seven people had confessed their treasonous thoughts Jim said chidingly, "These thoughts disturb me. I know that no dedicated person would want to leave, but some of you have been tempted to leave for unimportant reasons. Because of this it is necessary that our group should have some protection against future treason. A person might become discontent over a small personal problem and leave the group. The way to be certain that he won't is to make each person feel his safety might be in jeopardy if he were to hurt this church."

It sounded confusing but most of us understood that Jim was trying to protect himself in advance from potential traitors. "In order to accomplish this," he went on, "I have had my staff prepare certain statements that would make any person think twice before he tried to harm our family."

He looked around the room slowly and deliberately, his eyes meeting those of a few select people. "Does anyone in this room object to signing statements that could be used against you in the event that you should try to destroy this beautiful organization in a fit of anger?"

We realized that if we objected we were as much as admitting that we planned to leave the church, and we didn't want to admit such a treasonous thing as that.

Meri stepped forward and explained, "The first letter we want each of you to write is about your personal life. Everyone of us has heard Father tell us some of the intimate secrets of his personal life. He tells us these things because he trusts us and wants us to understand and know him completely. But those of us on his staff want to be certain that each of you has the courage to admit things about yourself that are just as personal, and just as compromising as the things he had told about himself. We want you to write a confession that you have had sex with someone that is the same sex as you, that you have had a lesbian or a homosexual experience."

We were handed a piece of paper and a pen, and we began to write our assigned letter. Meri checked each letter and handed some back for corrections. "You must be more graphic about the sex act," she said to one person. "You make it sound like you were forced into the act. Say it was your idea," she commented as she handed the second letter back to be changed. When every person in the room had written a satisfactory "confession," Jim continued with the P.C. meeting.

Tami had stopped rubbing Jim's feet while she wrote her confession and now she returned to continue the foot massage. He looked down at her compassionately and said, "Tami, you shouldn't be the only person to do this. I am enjoying it, but I think perhaps there are others in this room who might be willing to relieve you of that duty." He looked around the room expectantly and Judy Ijames, one of the nurses, stepped forward. Judy rubbed his feet for several more hours until the meeting closed at seven the next morning.

It became a ritual. Each time the P.C. meeting began, one of the women would seat herself in front of Jim and begin to rub his feet. Every hour another woman would take over to relieve her. One night Jim said, "The women have been rubbing my feet for many weeks, but not once have I seen a man volunteer. Is it because you think you're too good?"

Several men obediently raised their hands to volunteer for the "privilege" and they began to take their turns, too, a man doing it for an hour and then a woman. Occasionally two people would rub simultaneously, one on each foot. Al knew that all the men were expected to rub Jim's feet but he didn't want to. He asked me, "Do you suppose I have to volunteer?"

"I don't think so," I answered. "I haven't done it and I don't want to either. It seems degrading to sit at his feet. I sit near the back of the room and no one has noticed that I haven't volunteered. Why don't you do the same thing?" Al and I both sat in the back after that to avoid being called upon for this distasteful duty.

I intensely disliked the power structure that Jim had set up among the members. It was disappointing because I still held on to the dream that everyone should be equal. Although I tried to explain to our children that all members were equal, the inequality was evident in this room.

The top of the power structure was Jim. Second in line were his favorite sexual companions. The P.C. members were third. Apostolic guards were fourth, alongside the counsellors who hadn't advanced to the rank of P.C. yet. The line seemed to stop there. I was never certain where Marcie fit in, because Jim often seemed uncaring toward her. To the general members, Jim spoke of Marcie in glowing terms, as the "mother" of the church. But behind the closed doors of our P.C. meetings, he often talked about her insane rages and jealous tantrums. "My boys hate her," he said one day. I was sure that *if* they did, they had learned their hate from his own cruel statements about her.

The P.C. was predominantly white, although the membership of the church was 80 percent black. Everyone was aware of this, and a few people spoke of it in whispers, but no one dared question Jim's choices. To say anything against the racial structure of the P.C. would be to indicate that Jim was racially prejudiced, and everyone knew that he wasn't. After all, he had adopted a black son and was ministering to black people. He was going to save black people from concentration camps and death; he couldn't possibly be a racist. But the fact remained that his chosen leaders were nearly all white.

One of the young black women in the church also noticed this. She was a counsellor but hadn't been asked to serve on the P.C. She felt it was time for a change to be made. She started a rumor among the black members that Father didn't think black people were qualified for leadership. The rumor got back to Jim that the entire church membership was asking why there weren't more black faces on the Planning Commission. He knew he had to make a major change.

The following week he made a startling announcement. "All the counsellors in Los Angeles and San Francisco will be added to the Planning Commission." Since many of these counsellors were black it meant that the racial balance of the P.C. would be assured.

With the addition of so many new people, Jim became even more afraid that someone would turn against him, so he began to prepare for treason by incriminating the P.C. members even more. It became a weekly ritual for Meri or Jim to think up some new confession or threat for the counsellors to write for him. "Write me a letter saying that you and a friend are conspiring to destroy this country," he instructed one week. Obediently we did as we were told. Within two months Jim had a huge file on P.C. members who had confessed to such illegal or perverted things as blowing up banks, conspiring to start a political revolution, conspiring to kill the president, belonging to the Communist party, having sex with their children and/or parents, having sex with Jim, bombing a train, and on and on. P.C. members were also told to compromise relatives who were not in the church, to put in writing that they were lesbians or homosexuals, and to describe on paper supposed illegal acts they had committed.

Each time we were instructed to write another letter, he would assure us of how much this made him trust us. "You all know I wouldn't use any of these letters against you. It's just that if one person here were to leave this group and threaten us, we could use these statements to convince that person to leave us alone. As long as defectors leave our group alone, we won't try to hurt them in any way." At that time most of us were conditioned to the idea that we'd never want to hurt the group, so we felt reasonably safe in writing the letters. If anyone felt uncomfortable writing the letter, he'd still comply for fear of the discipline that Jim might think of for "potential traitors."

In the regular church services Jim was pressing his members incessantly for more money. Now each person was giving money to assure a place in the Promised Land of Guyana. Each time a person would give a large amount of money, Jim would praise him by saying, "Here's a person who really believes in the mission field. He knows that this money won't do him any good in this country once fascism takes over and now he'll get a place of refuge and safety." Anxious to assure our places in the Promised Land and to be praised by Jim, everyone began to think up even more ways to make money for the Cause.

The church members were instructed to sell their homes, furniture, stocks and bonds, insurance policies, and jewelry, "to put your savings into a land where we will all be free." Soon there was so much money rolling in that it was almost impossible to keep track of it all. Jim told the P.C. members that he was burying a lot of the money, along with jewels and silver or gold coins. "We may have to use these things to bribe the border guards when the time comes for us to pass into another country if the government here should try to stop us from leaving America."

Jim was starting to behave as if he were truly convinced he was divine. Whereas in past years he had allowed a few of his close staff members to advise and help him make decisions about strategy, now he alone was making all the decisions. His staff was no longer allowed to disagree with him, even in private. In past years he had joked with those close to him about calling himself God, but now, I was told, even his most trusted associates were instructed to call him Father, even in private.

His belief in his divinity was further strengthened in April 1975, when he was named one of the 100 Outstanding Clergymen in the Nation by an organization in New York. And in his boasting about the award he said, "This award was given to me, and to our church, for my inspiration in establishing all the humanitarian programs that we have." The Publications Office was assigned to reprint thousands of copies of the Ukiah *Daily Journal* article that reported Jim's winning the award. We mailed it to every contact the church had.

*   *   *

The function of his attorneys was beginning to change. They had previously been consulted before Jim tried anything new, but now he refused to listen to their words of warning. "You just find a way to make it legal," he would say threateningly. Jim was becoming an absolute dictator, and the members of the church were being kept in the group through fear. Gene Chaikin would shake his head sadly as he watched Jim laughing during the unevenly matched boxing or wrestling disciplines. Each time, though, he would dutifully have the victim and the parents of the victim sign releases, saying that the parents had asked Jim to discipline their child.

The work at Publications was becoming an overwhelming job. Tim Clancey, our pressman, had to work until 4:00 A.M. many mornings to keep up with the volume of printing Jim wanted. My work day was ending so late that it often seemed foolish to drive home, just to have to return a few hours later. There was a supply closet in my office, and when I finished with my day's work, if it was after 3:00 A.M., I would just unroll my sleeping bag on the floor of the closet and fall asleep. One evening, Al brought Candy and Najah into the office to visit me for a few minutes because it had been several days since I had been home, and they were missing me. "Is this where you sleep, Mommy?" Najah asked.

"Yes, it's really nice in there," I lied.

"Could we sleep in there with you tonight?" Candy asked. "We never get to see you at home anymore and I really miss you. Please let us sleep with you tonight."

Remorse and guilt overcame my common sense, and I told them they could stay for the night. At 8:30 I put them both into my sleeping bag and kissed them good night. They smiled sweetly at me, enjoying the mommy's kiss that they'd been missing. They were asleep in just a few minutes and I continued my long night's work. At three the next morning I was getting ready to go to sleep and I remembered that my "bed" was occupied by two soundly sleeping children, so I looked around to find another place to lie down.

I walked out into the lobby, thinking that I might find another office with space to sleep on. There, on the slate floor, I saw four young people sleeping, without any sleeping bags or blankets, just wearing their jackets. Two more fortunate young people were sleeping on a long table. There was not an empty spot where I could sleep, so I went back into my closet, put Candy on my chest, and let Najah snuggle in my arm. Candy woke up for a moment, hugged me tight and said, "I love you, Mommy," and fell asleep. It felt so good to have my babies with me that I was able to fall asleep in spite of the squeeze.

*   *   *

People's Temple had been in Redwood Valley for nearly ten years, and the local community was seemed to be becoming increasingly hostile. The armed guards and Jim's continuing complaints about the "local redneck racists" had made him very unpopular with the local residents. He realized that it was time to move his group to "the anonymity of the big city."

The San Francisco temple was again the center of a lot of construction work as the crew prepared it to be the home for a hundred of the church members, including Jim and his children. Dormitories were built on nearly every floor of the building, some of them only six feet by nine feet, and most of the rooms without outside windows or any provisions for fresh air.

Our household was planning to move to San Francisco, too, at Jim's request, and Al and I began to look in the Bay Area for jobs. I secretly hoped that I could find an outside job so I wouldn't have to continue working at Publications. The idea of being able to go home in the evenings was becoming an obsession with me, because now there were days at a time when I didn't even get to see my family.

Al suggested that we might be able to get jobs working for his mother, who owned two rest homes. We had fourteen children living with us, and we knew it would be hard to find a house big enough for them all. We also knew we needed space for my parents to live with us in semiprivacy. It was a lot to ask for. I was afraid that if we didn't find what we needed soon, Al and I might be assigned to live in the Temple building. We knew that the disciplines inflicted on communards were far more severe than on those who lived in their own homes.

We presented our problem to Al's mother. Although we had neglected her for six years, she still wanted to help us get a fresh start. She told him, "I understand what you've been through and I want to help you and your family out. You can run this rest home for six months without paying rent, and keep all the profits to help you get started again. Then when you get back on your feet you can begin to pay rent." Her generosity was much more than we deserved.

We both thanked her profusely, but we couldn't accept the offer without asking Jim's permission, so the next night in P.C. meeting I told Jim and the rest of the counsellors about this opportunity.

Jim asked, "Is she willing to sell the building to you? We don't want to build up a business that someone can take away from us in the event that we should send your family to the mission field."

"Yes," Al answered. "She said that she would sell it to us when we save enough money for the down payment."

Jim motioned for Mike, one of the law students, to come talk to him privately. After a few minutes he looked up at Al and said, "Mike will help you set up the legal papers to make certain that you will be able to turn the property over to the church when you leave the country."

Al and I looked at one another across the room. We were both thinking the same thing. Jim was saying exactly what he had said before he made us turn over our nineteen homes in Willits. Al answered, "We need to talk to my mother a little more before we sign any papers." Jim was anxious to return to the topic he'd been discussing previously, so he dismissed the subject of the rest home.

After the meeting we were in our car driving back to Redwood Valley. "Do you want to let the church get our rest home too?" I asked.

"And let Jim handle it like he handled our Willits property?" Al answered my question with a question.

"That's just what I was thinking," I answered.

We decided that we wouldn't bring the subject up again in the

P.C. meetings, and we also promised each other that we would never allow another piece of our property to be put in the name of the church.

"Do you remember that he used the same line before, that he was going to send us to the mission field? I'm not at all sure I want to go to Guyana," I said honestly. We hadn't discussed the actual possibility of going this time, probably because we hadn't been faced with having to make the decision. But now that Jim had brought the subject up, we decided to talk about it.

"It never seemed important to talk about going before, because I don't think the church members will ever really be moved there. I think Jim is just keeping it for an offering appeal and as a place to send people who get in trouble with the law or who make trouble in the church."

"That's really a sobering thought," I said. "If that's true, then all these people who have sold everything they own are going to be disappointed. They all believe they're going to live in a tropical paradise. What if they find out it's all a big lie?"

"You know, that reminds me," Al said. "During one of the P.C. meetings when we were in Jonestown, Jim said, 'If we ever get the members over here I will be able to keep them in line. While they're in the States they can always make trouble for me if they go out and complain about the discipline. But when they're in the jungle there won't be any place for them to go.'"

"Are you telling me the truth? Did he really say that?" I asked. These words sent a cold chill through my body. If Jim had any worse punishments planned than those we had already seen, I decided I didn't want to be around when he was administering them. As we continued to talk, we decided that we would never take our family to the jungle. "If he ever tells us we have to go, we'll just leave the church," I said solemnly. We both began to think seriously about finding a way to leave the church.

I couldn't get these thoughts out of my mind. Jim might be planning to take these people over to a type of concentration camp, where he would have full authority over them without having to worry about legal reprisals. I looked down at Candy sitting on my lap, and realized that I wouldn't be allowed to take her out of the church. I knew that Jim would force Ann to demand her return, or that Jim would find a way to kidnap her back again. I glanced up into the junior choir section of the balcony and saw the other children who lived with us and who called us Mom and Dad. Each of them was possibly facing a future that seemed insane. "At least if I stay in the church I can make sure they are safe." My thoughts were rambling incoherently.

At the next P.C. meeting Jim was waiting in the room as we

began to walk in. He wasn't smiling; in fact, he seemed to be upset about something. As soon as everyone sat down, his eyes narrowed and he removed his glasses and looked directly at Jack Beam. "I cannot trust a person who is unwilling to die for this Cause," he said. We all remembered the time that Jack had refused to go along with Jim's mass suicide idea two years before. "How can you be so enamored with life, when all it brings is pain?" he asked. His question was directed to Jack personally.

It didn't seem that death was imminent, so Jack agreed with him. Jim asked how the rest of the people in the room felt, and of course we all agreed that life was painful and boring and that we would all be willing to die for the Cause. The subject was dropped, and Jim discussed other issues for several hours. After a particularly intensive confrontation situation between a couple who were contemplating divorce, Jim asked Rose to bring in a "treat" for the counsellors. She brought out several bottles of wine. "Someone donated this wine to the church and I hated to see it go to waste, so I decided to share it with you," Jim said smilingly.

He poured the wine into paper cups and served it around the room himself. Most of the counsellors were happy for the opportunity to relax with a good drink of wine, but one counsellor, Carol Stahl, had never tasted an alcoholic beverage in her life. "I really don't want to drink, Father," she said apologizing as he tried to hand her the cup with wine in it.

"I said everyone in this room is to drink this wine, and that includes you. I have blessed this wine and it will be good for you." She didn't look at all happy about it, but she drank it. All the others in the room drank theirs, too. Jim made certain of this by giving it to a few people at a time while he stood and watched them drink. At the time, it crossed my mind that Jim might be giving us all poison, but I quickly dismissed the thought. "He isn't crazy enough to do something like that," I decided.

The meeting closed and everyone went home. I was relieved that there hadn't been any poison in the wine. Jim had simply given us a treat. Several of the other counsellors expressed surprise about this unexpected drink, and from the tone of their comments I was sure that they, too, had expected the worst.

The following day we went to visit Al's mother again, to tell her that we would be glad to accept her offer. "We appreciate what you are doing for us, Mom," Al said. "I don't know what we would have done without you."

"I'm glad you'll do it. I'd much rather have the rest home taken care of by someone I can trust than turn it over to strangers," she answered. Candy had come with us for the visit and Al's mother gave her a little outfit she had been making. Candy gave her a big hug and a kiss.

"You know, Mom, we have another problem. We have fourteen children living with us, and we'll have to find a place to live. Do you know where there might be a house we can rent?" I asked.

"Are you going to bring all fourteen children with you?" she asked in surprise.

"Yes," Al answered. "These are our children, and they'll all be living with us."

She promised to watch for a house, and we scanned the classifieds to see what was available.

The next weekend, in the church service, Jim had a "treat" for all the members. He brought in huge vats of homemade juice that had turned to wine. "I want to give you all a treat," he said magnanimously. "You can consider this as a giant communion service." Nearly a thousand members went up, one by one, as he gave each person a drink of the wine. It was delicious, and many of the children who had never been allowed to taste wine before agreed that it was good. Several of the children popped back into line more than once and went home that night giggly and tired. On the way home, Al and I discussed the time just two years before when almost a hundred people had lined up to be whipped for drinking wine.

Jim sent the message to all the P.C. members that there was going to be an extremely important meeting Monday night and that every P.C. person was to be there without fail. The meeting was to be held in the San Francisco temple, and any person who didn't attend would be subject to discipline.

As Al and I walked on to the stage area of the church where all the chairs had been set up for a meeting, we were delighted to see Larry Schacht. We hadn't see him for almost a year because he'd been at medical school in Mexico City. "This must really be an important meeting for Jim to have brought Larry here for it," Al said.

"I wonder what's so very important?" I asked. As we walked toward a couple of empty seats we got another surprise. Tim Stoen was in this meeting. He was excused from most of the services and most of the P.C. meetings because of his heavy work schedule as an assistant district attorney in San Francisco. He spent all extra time giving free legal advice to members of the three congregations. All Jim's staff workers were present, too, which was unusual. Most of the time one or two of them were out on a "secret mission" during the P.C. meetings.

We sat waiting to find out what had caused Jim to call all these busy people away from their duties for this meeting. We had only been seated a few minutes when Jim asked, "Are there any people in this room who still feel that they could enjoy a sexual relationship with a person of the opposite sex?"

Throughout the previous months, Jim had been gradually teaching the people in P.C. that we were all homosexuals or lesbians and that none of us were capable of giving or receiving satisfying heterosexual love. It had taken a long time to persuade every person in the room either to believe this or at least to make the public statement that we believed that Jim was the only person who was truly capable of sustaining a fulfilling sexual relationship with a member of the opposite sex.

Without the prior training that the rest of us had received, Larry Schacht and Tim Stoen both quickly raised their hands. I realized with dismay that these two men were about to learn a lesson well known to the rest of us.

"Larry, I'd like for you to stand up and tell us about your sex drive," Jim said kindly.

With no idea of the trap he was walking into, Larry naively answered, "Although I've been too busy in Mexico to have any relationships with women, I do have hopes for a good marriage in the future. I do fantasize about women. It helps me to pass the long hours down there, away from everyone I know and care about."

Jim smiled and asked Larry to be seated. He turned to Tim Stoen. "Would you like to share your feelings about sex with us, Tim?" he asked.

Tim stood up and answered, "It's true that my work keeps me too busy to enjoy a sexual relationship with any woman right now, Father, but I remember some experiences I've had in the past, and I enjoyed them. I love to touch a woman's body. Sex is one of the finest and most enjoyable sensations I know of." I braced myself for what I knew was coming.

He asked Larry to stand again and told Tim to remain standing until he was ready to talk to him. "Larry," he said sweetly, "you say that you have fantasies about women, but that you were too busy in Mexico to think about them. Well, then, would you like to tell us which women in this room you fantasize about?"

Larry looked around the room, while every woman in the room was praying that he wouldn't use her name. Smugly Larry began to point out the women that he either had or could have fantasized about. He was in trouble with the first name he chose. "Carolyn."

Jim nodded his head and gave a knowing "Go on, please."

Larry, encouraged by Jim's prompting, gazed down the rows, and began to name several of the women that he thought Jim would approve of. "Linda, Sandy, Meri, and Karen," and as an afterthought he added, "I even fantasize about Marcie some-times."

Jim had stood up and removed his glasses, something he only did when he wanted someone to receive the full impact of his angry stare. "Do you realize what you have just done Larry?" he asked sternly.

"Yes, Father," Larry answered innocently. "You asked me to name the women I fantasize about, and I did what you requested."

"You have named many of the women that you and others in this room know I have related to sexually. You even had the audacity to name my wife. Who in the hell do you think you are that you would dare to fantasize about my sexual companions? Do you think that any of the women you have named would want anything to do with you after they have made love with me?"

Larry looked crestfallen, and he shook his head in confusion. "Father, I didn't mean to offend you. I wasn't planning to ask any of these women to have sex with me. All I said was that I sometimes fantasize about them."

The more Larry said, the angrier Jim got. "How dare you choose women who have already stated several times in these meetings that they had never received sexual fulfillment from any man until they experienced lovemaking with me? It's bad enough that you openly defy my teachings that every man really longs for a male lover. You're almost a doctor, Larry. You know from your anatomy studies that the only glands a man can receive true sexual enjoyment from are in his rectum. I am deeply distressed that you haven't been here, week after week in this room, to learn the lessons I have been teaching the other P.C. members. I am disappointed to think that you, who are going to be this church's doctor, are still so hung up on your own male sexuality that you could dare to fantasize about women who can only be sexually satisfied by me. It shows that you believe you could take my place in their bedroom, but more than that, I believe you are fantasizing about taking my place as the leader of this group."

"Oh, no, Father," Larry's voice was filled with frustration. "You don't understand."

Once again Larry had used the wrong words, and now several of the women he had named stood up. Meri was the first to speak. "You're the one that doesn't understand, Larry. If you think I would ever consider having anything to do with you sexually you are sadly mistaken. After making love with Father, other men just make me sick. I had never received true sexual fulfillment until Father showed me his love. When he has sex with a woman he doesn't just ejaculate and then fall asleep. When Father makes love, he comes, and he comes, and he comes. His lovemaking is so powerful that no woman would ever want anyone else again."

Carolyn stood up next and sneered at Larry. "And if you think I'd ever want to have sex with you, you're crazy. You're nothing but a worm to me, Larry, and don't ever forget it." She sat down with a flounce, and Larry just stared at her in disbelief.

Jim nodded to Linda and she stood, walking over to Larry for emphasis. "I begged Father to have sex with me, and through his lovemaking I became a real woman. I'm sorry that he had to go through that to help me grow, but because of it I have learned that this Cause is the most important thing in the world. If you are fantasizing about me, Larry, you'd better quit, because you just make me sick."

Jim turned to Larry in disgust. "I hope you have learned tonight, Larry, that you are not capable of giving true love to a woman. It makes me almost nauseated that you would consider yourself worthy to fantasize about my wife, Marcie. She isn't here, so I'll speak for her. Marcie has often stated publicly that she doesn't want anything to do with any man but me. Because of the tremendous needs of this Cause, she has had to share me with other women, but that is a sacrifice she's willing to make. I do know that she would tell you that she does not want you to use her in your fantasies."

Larry was still standing, but he looked as if he had been beaten. His eyes were on the floor, his shoulders were drooping, and his fists had fallen open. Jim callously asked him, "Are there any other women you'd like to hear from in here?"

"No, Father," Larry answered humbly. "I just need some time to reevaluate my thoughts and my feelings. This is all so new to me. I don't understand a lot of what has happened here tonight, but that's probably because I've been away for so long. I apologize to the women I have named, and I promise that I won't ever use any of the women in this room to fantasize about again. I don't understand about homosexuality because I've never even considered it before. I guess I need to be in more meetings so I will be able to understand myself better. Please forgive me, Father, for being so ignorant."

"Of course, my son," Jim sounded loving again. "With that type of attitude I am certain that we can continue to work together. Several of the women in here will be talking with you in the next few days, before you return to Mexico, to help you understand my teachings about sexuality. I appreciate your humility." Jim had resumed his seat, put his glasses back on, and stopped to take a long drink of the orange juice beside him.

During Larry's long confrontation, Tim had remained standing as Jim had requested. He seemed to be uneasy as he realized that his turn was coming. Jim now turned to him and asked, "Tim, would you like to talk about your fantasies now?"

For some reason, Tim chose to be defiant, probably because he hadn't seen any of the brutal beatings in the public meetings; nor had he sat through the hundreds of hours of crazy sex confrontations that we had endured. Perhaps he was relying on the fact that Jim needed his legal knowledge and counsel. For whatever reasons, Tim refused to give in to Jim's degradation.

"Father, I've heard what all the women here said to Larry, but I still maintain that I have had sexual relations with women and enjoyed them. Sometimes, as I'm working long hours into the night, the only thought that keeps me going is my memories of holding my wife in my arms and making love with her. I know it felt good, and I'm not going to say now that it didn't."

Looks of disbelief and secret admiration were on the faces of the people in the room. Many of us felt the same emotions that Tim was voicing, but we had been too afraid to admit it in the hostile atmosphere of the P.C. council chambers. Even though we agreed with him, to have voiced our approval would have been considered high treason. Many of us were instructed to confront him.

Grace, of course, being his wife, was first. "Tim Stoen, you're always saying you're stoic. I don't know what you're thinking about now, but you're not stupid. You know what you're supposed to be saying here, so why don't you just say it?"

Tim stood, staring at his wife, but by now he was facing a matter of principle, and he decided he wasn't going to give in to Jim's demands, no matter what happened.

Several other members walked up to him, one by one, each person saying that they had admitted to their homosexuality or lesbianism, so why should he think he was special? "I don't know what you're trying to hold on to," Maria said angrily. "You've already said you don't have time for sex, anyway."

My turn came. I had been trying to think of another angle to use that would persuade Tim to stop being so stubborn and to say the words that we all knew would satisfy Jim. "Tim, I've often heard you say you are willing to die for this Cause. How could you be willing to die for it if you're not even willing to make a public statement that you're a homosexual for this Cause? Until you're able to say these words, you'd better never again say you'll die for the Cause."

Several more counsellors made their statements, but Tim remained unmoved. Finally, Jim realized that Tim was not going to give in, so he said, "Well, perhaps Tim needs time to think this over. We'll see how he feels about this some other time."

The following Monday night was to be our last P.C. meeting. As our attention focused on the front of the room, we were surprised to see a gun at Jim's side. He solemnly announced, "I have heard that someone in this room is contemplating quitting our church. I want you to know that I am disgusted with those among us who contemplate being traitors to a group that is doing so much good." My heart jumped into my throat, and for a moment I thought I might pass out. The gun at his side seemed to grow ten feet long.

Still, I reasoned, I hadn't actually told anyone that we were quitting. I had called in an excuse for every meeting we had missed. As Jim slowly pointed the gun toward the group of counsellors, everyone looked frightened. "Tonight I am going to make certain that there is no question in anyone's mind about what happens to traitors."

At this inopportune time, Carol Stahl had to use the bathroom. She stood up and asked for permission to leave. Jim pointed the gun directly at her. "Where do you think you are going?" he screamed.

"I'm sorry, Father, but I have to go to the bathroom and I can't wait!" She was trembling with fright, but Jim didn't seem to notice.

"I said no one is to leave this room tonight, and I mean it. If you must use the bathroom, you can do it right here."

"But Father, it's number two," Carol said pleading.

"I don't care, you're among friends." Larry brought out the large fruit can that Jim used to urinate in, and handed it to her.

"Can I have a blanket in front of me?" she asked quietly.

"No! If you really have to go, you should be able to do it in front of us here."

Carol contemplated for a moment and knew that she couldn't wait, so she pulled down her pants and sat on the can. The hundred people assembled in the room watched her while she had a bowel movement, and someone handed her a tissue to wipe with. Carol had turned crimson. Someone in the room made a weak attempt at humor and said, "Father must have scared the shit out of her," but a stern look from Jim made him realize that this was no time for humor.

"Tonight is a very serious night and I don't want anyone in this room to go to sleep." It was almost as if Jim were a hypnotist and he had commanded Grace to go to sleep. Immediately her head began to nod. "Grace, I don't want to have to shoot you. You'd better stay awake tonight."

Grace felt sleepy but she could hear the threat in Jim's voice, so she stood up and remained standing for the rest of the meeting. Jim continued to talk about the rumor he had heard about someone leaving the group. All of us, including me, assured Jim that we would never leave. As an object lesson he asked Valerie to stand up.

"You left this group once and returned. I want to be certain you are never going to leave again." Slowly, deliberately, he wiped the gun he had been holding, to get rid of his fingerprints. He handed it to Carolyn and asked her to wipe it clean again. When this was done he held the gun with a cloth as he handed it to Valerie. She took it and held the handle in a position as though she were going to fire it, at Jim's instruction. Then he took it back using a cloth, and placed it in a plastic bag.

"If you ever decide to leave this group again, I want you to always remember that I have this gun. Any time you should try to hurt our group we can place this gun, with your fingerprints on it, along with one of the incriminating confessions you have written, next to the scene of a crime. You will be convicted and spend the remainder of your life in jail. This is what any traitor deserves."

It felt like Jim was looking directly at me as he said the last sentence. I boldly met his eyes, trying to look innocent. I knew this was the last P.C. meeting I would ever attend.

The following Wednesday, Al and I went to our last church service together. We were trying to make it appear that we were still believers as we sang the songs and applauded the different testimonies. Jim's sermon was short, and before we knew it, it was discipline time again.

Chris Cordell was up for confrontation again, and once again it was for stealing. He had already been brutally beaten for this crime when Jim had sentenced him to 100 whacks. Now Jim had to think of a suitable punishment for this second offense. Chris's parents were both counsellors, and he remembered that they had become hostile after his last beating, so this time he declared, "Ten whacks with the board and then you will be sent to the Promised Land."

The children and adults in the audience looked up in shock. This was the first time that Jim had used the Promised Land as a punishment. He realized his mistake almost immediately and amended what he had said. "I don't mean he is going to our beautiful Promised Land. A few miles away from Jonestown there is a crocodile pit, where there are snakes and crocodiles. This is the section where Chris will be sent."

This was the first time Jim had ever admitted that there were crocodiles and snakes in the jungle, and again he had to amend his statement. "This crocodile pit is many miles from our land. When Chris goes there he will have to work from early morning until late at night."

Chris came up and took his ten whacks. He screamed in pain with each hit, but when it was finished, he did not faint as he had before. He was able to say "Thank you, Father," and return to his place in the choir.

Three more people were confronted and disciplined before a young black girl, Karen Carr, was called forward. "Karen, I have a note here that says you went into a department store and stole some sewing supplies. It says you got caught by a policeman. Is this true?"

"Yes, Father."

Jim flew into a rage. "You saw Chris get a hundred whacks for stealing, and yet you had the nerve to go into a store and steal! You will get a hundred whacks just like Chris did."

Al couldn't stand it. Karen was a frail girl, about thirteen years old, and the thought of her getting 100 whacks for such a minor offense made him angry. Chris had gotten 100 whacks for stealing a purse, and now he got ten whacks for stealing again. This didn't compare to the young girl's stealing a few little sewing supplies from a department store.

He wrote a note and handed it to Jim. "It may appear to some that this decision favors a white person over a black person. Karen has never been in trouble before, and she only stole a small item. Chris stole a purse, and on his second offense he is sent to the 'Promised Land,' which is something that all these young people feel is a privilege."

Jim glared at Al. "You don't understand," he said simply, and motioned for Ruby to begin the 100 whacks.

As Karen began to scream, Al walked out. I noticed him and followed him out to the parking lot. "Where are you going?" I asked him.

Al told me about his note and Jim's callous response to it. "I just can't stand it anymore," he said. "I'll go over to Mom's house on the bus, and you can pick me up there."

I told him that I'd have to go back in, that there was going to be a special P.C. meeting and that if we both missed it, Jim would have us up for discipline.

"I hate to leave you here, honey, but I'm going to tear this place apart if I have to watch another child being beaten. Just tell them that I'm not coming back."

Instead, though, I told them that Al had been angry about the beating, but that I was certain he would cool down. "That's up to you as a strong woman," Jim reminded me. "Al will do whatever you want him to." With Jim's instructions to shame Al into submission, I drove back with the children asleep in the van, to his mother's house. It was five in the morning so I just let them stay there until breakfast.

"I didn't tell Jim you were quitting because I know they'd take the kids away from us," I explained to Al the next morning.

He agreed that that was probably the best idea and that perhaps we could go every so often and keep Jim wondering about us. Now, with the rest-home work, we figured we'd be excused from a lot of the meetings anyway. Al didn't want to lose the children we loved so much, and yet he was repulsed by the thought of going to another service.

Our plans for moving were coming along nicely. Lillie and Linda were working at the rest home with us, and we'd found a big, old Victorian house in Oakland that was for sale. With our large, integrated family I thought this would be the perfect spot. There were five big bedrooms, a large yard, and a full basement with many extra rooms the children could play in. There was also a full attic that Al could eventually convert into a music room for the kids.

The house had been vandalized, so it was being sold for a reasonable price. We only needed a $3,000 down payment. I went back to Al's mother and asked her if she could loan us the money. Without hesitation she wrote out a check and told me to repay her whenever I could.

For six years, we'd all been told, "Your relatives won't help you if you need financial assistance" or "When you really need someone to stand by, only Father will be there." Yet Al's mother was more than willing to help us. I was beginning to realize the degree to which we'd been brainwashed.

At the following Monday's P.C. meeting I announced that our family would be moving to Oakland within days. "The house we're moving into has all the windows broken out and there's been a lot of vandalism inside, but it's big enough for all the children."

I went to Tish, who handed out the paychecks for the church workers, to pick up my final check for the previous month's work. "I've been instructed not to give you any more money," she said coldly.

"Why not?" I asked. "I've earned it. It's my pay for last month's work."

Tish answered, "Now you folks are going to have to support yourselves."

I wrote a hasty note to Jim, asking him to tell Tish to give me this check so we could pay our bills. "With this move, and our children all starting school again we need the money desperately. My mother-in-law has already given us a business, loaned us the down payment on our house, and given us some clothes for our children. We can't ask her to support them, too." I was trying to stay composed. "I'm sure that after a month we should have enough profit to support ourselves and the children, but we don't have money for this first month."

Jim said, "You said you would be able to support those children, and we aren't going to help you anymore."

"How will I pay bills and buy food?" I asked him, my voice icy.

"Return the children to me," he answered.

The subject was closed, and Jim started talking about other things. After a few hours passed, Jim announced that he was going to treat the counsellors again. Once more he passed some of the fermented grape juice he had served in the church. It was still a welcome treat after a long night of discussing problems. Most of the people drank their wine appreciatively, but a few decided against it.

"Who here did not drink their wine yet?" Jim asked. Three people raised their hands.

"Why not?"

Clarese said she was on a diet, Carol Stahl didn't like the taste of it, and Roz said she just didn't feel like it. "When I tell you to drink your wine, I mean just that." The angry tone in Jim's voice told the three that they'd better drink or else, and soon all three cups were emptied.

Jim's eyes slowly scanned the people seated in the room. He announced in a matter-of-fact voice, "Now that you have all finished your wine, I have something to say to you. The wine you just drank has a slow-acting poison in it. Within forty-five minutes each of you will begin to get very sick, and soon after that you will die. I have drunk the same wine and I will die with you."

I glanced around the room to see how the other counsellors were reacting. I was thankful that Al hadn't come to the meeting. At least the children would have a daddy. Jim had tried so many games in the past that I wasn't sure he had really poisoned us, but I had to accept the possibility that he might not be fooling this time. I glanced over at Carolyn Layton and noticed a faint smile on the corners of her lips. That smile could mean one of two things. Either Carolyn was happy to die, or she knew that he was just testing us again. I dismissed the possibility that she was happy to die. She was deeply devoted to her little son. So I decided that this was simply Jim's test. I sat back to watch the effects of what I had surmised would be another strategy move.

Jim McElvane was the first to react. He laid down on the floor near the rear of the counselling room, closed his eyes, and crossed his hands over his chest. "What are you doing, Jim?" Jim asked, standing up to see what was happening. "That poison can't be affecting you so quickly."

"No, Father," he answered, "it's just that I'm so glad that I am finally going to leave this painful life. I want to make myself comfortable and go quickly."

Patty Cartmell was the next to react. She started to run out the door, and the guards grabbed her. They brought her back to the front of the room.

"Where were you going, Patty?" Jim asked innocently.

"I'm sorry, Father, but I don't want to die. I know I've always told you I was willing to, but I don't want to die. I want to get out of here right now." Patty was fighting off the guards who were attempting to hold her. At a nod from Jim, another guard stepped forward with a rifle and shot her in the arm. She fell down and was quickly carried out of the room.

Suzy whispered under her breath, "That goddamned bitch, we never did trust her anyway." Suzy was one of Jim's close staff members, but sometimes she said more than she was supposed to. I knew I wasn't supposed to hear that comment.

"Are there any other traitors in here who want to try to get to a doctor?" Jim taunted.

No one moved. He had produced the desired effect. Fear was on every face. Jim had always said that people could be ruled by fear, and now he had proved it to himself. Forty-five minutes passed, and Jim finally announced that it had only been a test. Patty was returned to the room. The guard had shot her with a blank, so aside from the bruise on her arm she was all right.

"I have tested you all tonight. As you were reacting, I had my staff watching each of your faces to determine if you were indeed ready to die. I know now which of you can be trusted and which of you cannot. We will never mention this night to anyone. Patty, I hope you learned a lesson about yourself. You are still enamored with life, and until you are so tired of living that you want to die, you can never be trusted to do great things for this Cause."

Patty was silent, crestfallen. She had always been upheld by Jim as a woman who would do "anything" for the Cause, and now she had proved in front of everyone that she was a coward.

"I promise you, Father, that I will work much harder now to prove myself to you and to the group. I'm sorry for being such a coward tonight," she said sincerely.

As the meeting ended I walked over to Carolyn Layton. "You asked me once to tell you if I ever really needed help, and, Carolyn, I need it now. I don't want to have to give up my children. I love them."

Carolyn stared at me coldly. "Father has made a decision, and there is nothing I could do to change his mind."

I drove across the bridge toward our house, wondering how I was going to break the news to Al or the children. First I talked about it with Al.

"I'm not surprised," he said. "Jim must realize we're getting ready to quit the church and he wants those children back. We know we aren't going to be allowed to keep them after we get out, so we should probably begin to talk to them about moving."

We gathered our family together. "We just don't have enough money to support all of you," I told them sadly. "I asked Father to give us the money for this month, but he said we were going to have to send some of you back to the church instead." Candy started to cry.

Searcy, sensing the finality of what was happening, asked, "Please let me stay here with you. I don't want to live at the church."

I sadly told him that his mother wouldn't allow him or his brother or sister to continue to live with us, because we were leaving the church. We packed their clothes and possessions, and drove back across the bridge to the church. I let the children out in the parking lot where a counsellor was waiting for them, kissed them, and then drove away.

My last visit to the temple was a nightmare. Although we had decided to quit the church, I felt that I had to see our children once more. As I walked through the door, I realized that the guards had been warned about me. Usually I showed my "door pass" card and was allowed through. This time, they ignored the card and searched me thoroughly. When I went upstairs to sit in the audience, two counsellors came to sit directly behind me. This was unusual because most of the counsellors sat on the stage, and the two who were watching me were people Jim had assigned to watch traitors in the past.

As soon as little Candy saw me she came running from the balcony. "Mommy, mommy," she shouted as she jumped on my lap and showered me with kisses. "Mommy, please let me come home with you tonight," she begged, about to cry. One of the ushers came over with a frown on his face.

"Father said all the children have to sit upstairs with the junior choir. She can't sit here with you."

I was shocked. No usher had ever dared to speak to me that way before. "I've been working and haven't seen Candy for a week. I want to spend some time with her."

"I'm sorry, but my instructions are that no children can sit in this section," he said.

"Then where can I sit with her?" I persisted.

"I guess you can go sit in the junior choir section," he answered. As I started to move, one of the counsellors behind me said, "Never mind, I'm sure Father will let you stay here." Perhaps Jim wanted me where I could be watched carefully.

The song service started, and I sang the songs of praise to Jim with gusto. I clapped my hands and shouted hallelujah with the rest of the members. Instead of a sermon, Jim went directly into the discipline session. He called a woman who had once been a guard to the front. She had left the group a few weeks before and had returned to demand that she be given her children.

Jim first threatened her with "metaphysical destruction," but when he saw that she was unmoved, he resorted to threats of legal action. "You know, we have certain confessions that you have signed, and if we present these in court, you would most certainly be declared an unfit mother," he reminded her.

Several of the guards jumped forward and crossed their arms on their chests, signifying their stubborn strength. "You'd better leave if you want to get out of here alive," one of them yelled at her, and she fled down the back stairs.

I was horrified, and certain that Jim had confronted a mother as a lesson to me, too, that I would not be able to take Stephanie, Candy, Janet, Lillie, Beth, Searcy, Ollie, Najah, Joey, and Julie. I knew I had to get out of the building before he called my name, so I picked up Candy and headed for the restroom. Instead of stopping there, I continued down the back stairs and went to the back door. A guard met me and said, "No one is allowed to leave services."

I couldn't believe my ears. I was having to experience the regimentation that only ordinary members were subjected to, but as a P.C. member I had always before been given special treatment. I tried a last desperate attempt. "I'm a counsellor and this child is very sick. I have to take her to the doctor right away. Father gave me permission to go," I added in my most authoritative voice.

The guard backed off. "Father gave me permission" wasn't used lightly, because a person who lied about that usually got a beating. He hadn't been told yet that I was a traitor, so he let me leave with Candy.

I put my lovely baby on the seat beside me, and we drove around San Francisco for a while. I thought about Searcy, Ollie, and Najah—children I wouldn't be able to see again. Stephanie and Janet flashed through my mind. I knew that they'd miss Daphene and she would certainly miss them.

I drove to a coffee shop and Candy and I went inside.

I ordered two super-deluxe hot-fudge sundaes, and Candy and I enjoyed them down to the last spoonful of fudge at the bottom. We giggled and laughed. "I'm so glad you came back, Mommy. I thought you didn't want me anymore," she said as she gave me a big kiss. I thought my heart would break as I returned the kiss. Candy wouldn't again be allowed to have a hot-fudge sundae, and I was thankful that our last minutes together would be a pleasant memory. Once again Candy begged, "Mommy, you are going to take me home with you, aren't you?" I knew I couldn't take that risk. I was sure that my attempt to take her with me might cause Jim to make good the death threats he had repeatedly made against any traitors who tried to hurt the group.

We spent three wonderful hours together, and then I knew it had to be over. I took the child who had been mine since she was a young baby back to the church. The meeting was over. Searcy and Ollie saw me in the lobby and ran across the room to me. "We don't like it here, Mommy. Please let us move back with you." Ollie's pleading brown eyes had always made me give in to him, but now I knew I had no choice. Their natural mother was still very much a member and would never allow them to move out with a "traitor."

"I'm sorry, boys. Please believe me that I love you more than you'll ever know, but Father wants you to live with him here." I gave each of them a dollar to buy some food from the concession stand, kissed them good-bye, and left forever.

The trip home seemed to be a thousand miles long. All the way, I kept hearing the children saying, "Please, Mommy, we don't like it here. Please let us come back home with you."

Our house seemed empty with only five children. Our kids missed their little brothers and sisters. Our oldest daughter, Linda, had decided that she wasn't ready to leave the church, so she moved into the temple commune. Her fear of Jim's metaphysical gift was greater than her fear of the punishments. Since she was seventeen years old, we allowed her to make her own decision.

We consoled each other by saying, "Surely more church members will begin to realize how sadistic Jim has become and they will leave."

Daphene asked, "Then can we get Stephanie and Janet back?"

Eddie echoed, "And Searcy and Joey and Ollie."

Diana added, "And Candy and Najah can be our babies again?"

Nichol said, "I hope Linda and Beth and Lillie will want to live with us again, once they get away from there."

*

PART III

Those
Who Do Not Remember
the Past
Are Condemned
to Repeat It

*"I am preparing a Promised Land
for you in Jonestown. When you
get there all your tribulations will
be over. There will be no need for
discipline when you get away
from the capitalistic society of
America. There you will be able to
love and be loved. My black
seniors will finally have a place
where they will never again go
hungry or be forced to work."*
—Jim Jones

We had wanted the Human Freedom Center to help hundreds of people leave Jonestown and start a new life. Now there are only a few, and they are so confused that they don't know their enemies from their friends.

The first person who came to our center from Jonestown was Tommy Beikman, the son of Chuck Beikman who is accused of helping Linda Amos murder her three children. Tommy was the first person willing to testify at the local federal hearing and, as a result, was allowed to leave San Francisco. We gave him clothing that had been donated by a church in Santa Cruz, California. We gave him a place to stay and a lot of love and encouragement. Now Tommy has found a home with one of his relatives, who has promised him a new life.

Tommy told us something that made us very sad. Peter Wotherspoon had received another brutal beating in Jonestown— again for molesting a child. Now, Peter—with his wife and child—is dead.

Al and I looked through the list of dead in Jonestown and through the list of survivors. Entire families that I knew and loved had been wiped out.

A little girl named Stephanie Jones was in Georgetown, Guyana. But Tommy told us that it was a different Stephanie Jones. Our Stephanie had been murdered in Jonestown.

Julie, our feisty little Julie; she didn't want to die. We read the report of one of the guards who escaped that said they'd forced the poison into her mouth; she spit it out, again and again. Finally, they held her and forced her to swallow it. She's dead.

Searcy, Ollie, and Najah—murdered in Jonestown.

Lillie Victor—murdered in Jonestown.

Nita and her children, including Janet—all murdered in Jonestown.

Mike Rozynko—dead, also. We were with his sister when she tried to communicate with him over a ham radio, but his response to her questions was: "I'm very happy here. I don't ever want to come back to America."

Only one of the children that lived with us is alive: Joey had been sent back to Philadelphia to live with his mother. We don't know why, but we're glad Joey made it.

*   *   *

When we received word that Jim Jones's body had been positively identified, a flood of relief swept over me. He had always spoken about getting away, taking his favorites with him. Even when the P.C. first began, Jim would say, "Someday we will go away, and we will start life anew somewhere else."

Circumstances in Jonestown made me certain that Jones did not plan to die with his followers. A man who is planning to die doesn't give two trusted aides a suitcase filled with money and his own letter of introduction into another country unless he plans to leave with them.

The fact that so many letters and documents were still around indicated to me that he'd planned to "clean things up" before he left. All through the years, whenever Jim would think an investigation might be launched against him, he told us to "burn everything." In fact, before his followers went to Guyana, they had been told "burn everything in your house that relates to our church, so that no one will ever be able to use the documents against us."

I think that his insane desire to be remembered well in history would have caused him to destroy everything before he died, if he had indeed planned to die. The coincidence that most of his sons were in Georgetown during the massacre and that so many of his staff people survived is convincing evidence to me that Jim Jones had planned to begin his monster-ministry some place else. A man planning his demise doesn't store millions of dollars in foreign bank accounts.

Somehow, I assume, his plan went bad. Maybe one of the guards, carrying a weapon, saw his wife or baby convulsing in pain and foaming at the mouth, and did the world a great service by destroying the demon, Jones. And those he'd planned to take away with him are now left to face the questioning world alone, without the person who always gave them the answers.

The man who claimed to be the bravest man in the world first ran to Jonestown to hide, leaving his young members to face the 1977 press interrogation, and now, in an even greater tragedy, he has left them to answer all the unanswerable questions that they will be asked for years to come.

* * *

To Jim Jones, life was a bore. His only source of pleasure was observing his followers' total devotion to him. At first, he was content just to observe us loving and respecting him. When this ceased to satisfy him, he enjoyed watching us fear him. His need for pleasure became insatiable, and to derive enjoyment he wanted to watch us as we willingly suffered for him.

The only true sexual stimulation he received was as a voyeur, and he eventually took delight in humiliating us as he made us undress and perform deviant sex acts with one another.

Next, his pleasure came from pitting us against one another, in wrestling and boxing matches, and even in floggings.

Finally, his total pleasure came from watching as his members drank poison to die for him. He had created his ultimate spectator sport.

74